# The Complete Learning Spaces Book for Infants and Toddlers

## ACKNOWLEDGMENTS

We extend our special thanks to the Child Study Center: Infant and Toddler Program which is part of the Center of Excellence in Early Childhood Learning and Development located on the East Tennessee State University Campus. The director, associate director, teachers, and support staff have allowed us to work with them, take pictures, and assist with the process of making this book relate to the real world of infants and toddlers. The photographs in our book show infants and toddlers who are in this wonderful and developmentally appropriate environment where they are nurtured and inspired by caring professionals.

Many people have helped in the development of this book. Su Lorencen, Michael Talley, and Sarah Hackney took the marvelous photographs, which are such an important part of this book. Sarah also organized the pictures and permissions that assured that these visuals could be used effectively. April Lowrance was a great help in finalizing the details of the pictures and forms. The illustrations in the book were beautifully done by Stacy Larsen. As you can see in her drawings, Stacy is both an early childhood educator and artist. She sees the environment from the perspective of someone who has worked with this age group. Sheila P. Smith, our resident editor, worked diligently to make the manuscript perfect. Our special thanks to her for seeing the aspects that others would miss.

It is a great joy to work with Kathy Charner, our editor at Gryphon House. Her gentle and supportive manner brings out the best in writers. Since my first book with Gryphon House, *The Complete Book of Learning Centers,* Leah Curry-Rood and Larry Rood have nurtured my ideas. These three special people have helped make my creative efforts possible. The innovative books they have published with me would not have happened without their vision. Thank you.

## DEDICATION

This book is dedicated to:
The marvelous infant in our lives,
William Wells
and
The terrific toddler in our lives,
Caroline Grace

# Learning Spaces

## The Complete Book for Infants and Toddlers

**54 Integrated Areas with Play Experiences**

## Rebecca Isbell and Christy Isbell

**Illustrations by Stacy Larsen**

**Photographs by Sue Lorencen, Michael Tally, and Sarah Hackney**

*gryphon house, inc.*

**Lewisville, NC**

Reprinted June 2013

## LIBRARY OF CONGRESS CATALOGING-IN-PUBLICATION DATA

Library of Congress Cataloging-in-Publication Data

Isbell, Rebecca T.
   The complete learning spaces book for infants and
toddlers : 54 integrated areas with play experiences /
by Rebecca Isbell and Christy Isbell ; illustrations,
Stacy Larsen.
        p. cm.
Includes index.
   ISBN 978-0-87659-293-9
   1.  Nursery school facilities--Planning.  I. Isbell,
Christy. II.
Title.
   LB3325.N8I82 2003
   372.16--dc21

                              2003000134

# Table of Contents

# CHAPTER ONE

# Introduction

## Overview

*The Complete Learning Spaces Book for Infants and Toddlers* is designed for teachers and directors who want their classrooms to be wonderful learning places for very young children. It is for the teacher who understands that infants and toddlers learn best in an interactive environment; who realizes that infants and toddlers have preferences and need opportunities for participation that build on their individual interests; and who wants to plan areas that will expand learning opportunities for infants and toddlers, while building on what they know.

Infants and toddlers are unique. They have special ways of learning about the world and exploring their environment. Appropriate early experiences provide the base for knowing and understanding their world, as well as shape their early development. It is essential to design environments that match infants' and toddlers' way of learning and allow them to influence the process.

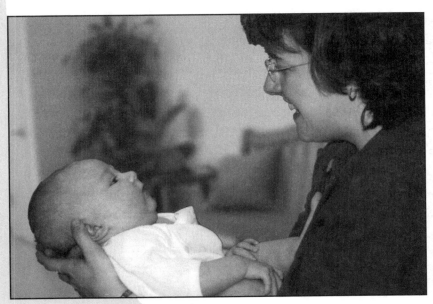
A responsive teacher interacting with a baby

## Very Important Person

The most important factor in a quality infant/toddler program is a caring and responsive teacher. This person interacts with infants or toddlers in a way that clearly communicates, "You are special and you are capable." The establishment of an emotionally supportive environment allows a child to explore his or her surroundings, while maintaining contact with this responsive person. This important teacher is a careful observer. She or he recognizes the cry of a specific baby and can identify the baby's favorite toy. She or he understands a toddler's creative words and recognizes food preferences. This observant teacher uses what she or he knows about the children in her or his care when selecting toys and materials, and when designing areas that interest and appropriately challenge infants and toddlers.

## Learning from Objects

Infants and toddlers want to know and learn. One of the ways infants and toddlers learn is by examining and manipulating objects. Non-mobile infants need objects close to them so they can see, touch, hear, and examine them. Toddlers, who are mobile, can have objects displayed in a manner that will invite them to move to an object and manipulate it. This exploration of objects makes important connections in the brain that will last a lifetime. Objects that are available to infants and toddlers in learning spaces must be determined as safe. Objects and materials must be non-toxic, washable, and non-flammable. Use a choking tube to assure that none of the objects are choking hazards. Finally, re-check objects periodically to see if they are still safe for infants and toddlers.

A young toddler manipulating a large peg

## Learning from Movement

For infants and toddlers, movement is a way of playing and learning. At first, infants discover their body parts and enjoy these discoveries. They put their hands in their mouth, grasp their feet, and blow "raspberries." With practice, they begin banging, pushing, pulling, and taking objects apart. This leads to grasping objects, while manipulating them with both hands. By experimenting with different ways to move themselves and manipulate objects, infants and toddlers begin to learn about their surroundings. When infants and toddlers use their bodies to accomplish tasks and influence their environment, they feel a sense of pride.

## Learning from Play

Play is an essential component of quality early childhood programs. During play, children learn and enjoy active participation. In playful activity, infants and toddlers find pleasure in repeating an action (practice play) or experimenting with a "novel" toy. Dramatic play allows toddlers to begin to take on a role, as they put on a firefighter's hat or place a cooking pot on the housekeeping stove. This dramatic play encourages toddlers to try out their world and establish relationships between the objects and people they know. Play influences their development in all areas: cognitive, language, social/emotional, and motor.

# Developmental Domains

*The Complete Learning Spaces Book for Infants and Toddlers* investigates five developmental domains: cognitive, language, social/emotional, sensory, and motor. It discusses ways infants and toddlers influence their development in these domains as they participate in the learning spaces. It is important to understand the five domains and how to effectively facilitate infants' and toddlers' development through the design, set up, use, and evaluation of learning spaces.

## Cognitive Development

Cognitive development is concerned with mental processes such as problem solving. Theorist Piaget (1963) developed a framework for understanding young children's cognitive development. Piaget believed that children interact with their environment to develop cognition. He noted that children have a desire to learn, which is encouraged **through** new events. He also viewed cognitive development as an active process wherein a young child constructs his or her own knowledge.

Piaget stated that infants and young toddlers (14 to 24 months old) are in the sensorimotor stage of cognitive development. In this stage of development, infants use their sensory and motor skills to learn about the environment. Older infants learn object permanence, the understanding that an object continues to exist even if they cannot see it. When this is accomplished, an infant will look for a toy after it is removed from his or her sight. Older toddlers (24 to 36 months old) may be moving into the preoperational stage of cognitive development, where they are using language functionally. Older toddlers in this stage are learning to draw pictures with crayons. They may also begin categorizing (sorting) objects by one characteristic, such as by color.

Observe an infant's and toddler's cognitive abilities at work during play. An infant or young toddler in the sensorimotor stage will participate in practice play, where banging, shaking, throwing, pushing, and pulling objects is predominate. Young toddlers begin using skills they have already learned to plan and construct their play with blocks, paper, washable markers, and glue. Older toddlers are beginning to participate in symbolic play, where they use pretend play. In this stage, they use traditional objects to pretend behaviors they have observed. For example, an older toddler will use a blanket to cover his or her baby doll when putting it to bed.

Vygotsky (1967) presented another theory of child development, which suggests that one of the ways young children learn is through interactions with adults and peers. Adults can scaffold infants' and toddlers' learning and development by helping and encouraging them to think on their own.

Using learning spaces for infants and toddlers is based on the principles of both Piaget and Vygotsky. Learning spaces are organized by the teacher to guide infants and toddlers in their own learning. Learning spaces work best for infants and toddlers when the teacher and other children are involved in their exploration and play.

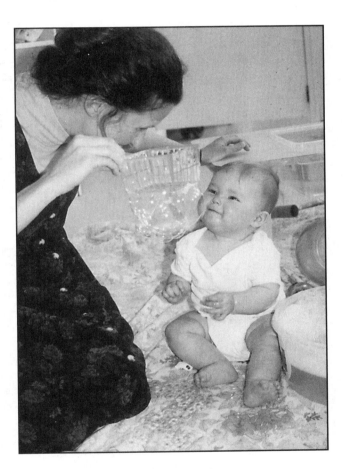

A teacher extending the experience of an infant

## Language Development

Language is typically thought of as spoken or written words. However, language is communication in many forms. For infants and toddlers, language can include gestures (waving goodbye), facial expressions (smiling), and body language (turning their head away from a loud sound). Young infants cry to indicate their needs. They also make sounds such as cooing and squealing. Around the first year of life, an infant will use the first word that stands for something (for example, "Mama" or "Dada"). Older infants and young toddlers will use more single words that are important to them, such as a person, pet, or a food. Toddlers will begin putting two words together. They often use telegraphic speech, saying only the most important words in a sentence and leaving out all the connecting words. A toddler might say, "More cookie" for "I want more cookies." Toddlers are also echolalic and often repeat words or phrases that they hear. They are creative language users, and if they do not have a word to describe something, they will make one up. Older toddlers will begin using simple sentences to make their needs known to others. Both infants and toddlers need an environment filled with written and spoken words and gestures so they can practice communicating in this critical stage of language development.

## Social/Emotional Development

For infants and toddlers, social and emotional development are very closely related and will be considered together in this text. Infants and toddlers learn how to relate to others through interactions with their parents, teachers, and other children. Each infant is born with his or her own temperament. Some are slow to warm up and others are eager to establish relationships. Young infants are unable to separate their own feelings from the feelings of others. Toddlers are beginning to understand that they have their own emotions, and they have the

very difficult task of learning how to manage these feelings appropriately. It is essential to recognize and respect each toddler's emotional level and to be responsive to his or her needs. A private space, for example, allows a toddler to regain his or her composure or reduce some of the stimulation in the classroom.

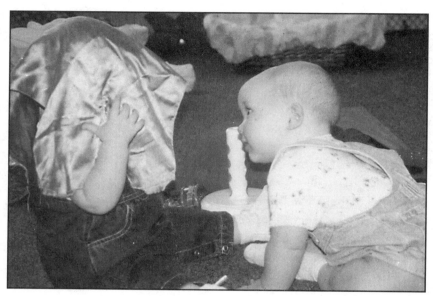

Where did the baby go?

Peekaboo, I see you!

Observing a young child in play reveals that child's social/emotional development. Young infants' play is primarily centered on their own bodies. As they grow older, infants participate in onlooker play, watching others playing, but not entering the play activity. Young toddlers will sometimes play with the same toys side-by-side (parallel play). However, young toddlers typically do not share or talk about their toys as they play. Older toddlers participate in associative play, playing common activities and occasionally exchanging toys or following the lead of another child.

## Sensory Development

There are five primary senses: vision, hearing, taste, smell, and touch. There are also two senses that tell us about our bodies and help coordinate our movement: vestibular and proprioceptive senses. The vestibular sense tells the body where it is in relation to the earth. It tells us if we are moving or standing still. The awareness of the body's position in space (for example, you know that your feet are on the floor) is the proprioceptive sense. Infants are capable of using the senses of smell and touch at a very young age. The senses of vision, hearing, taste, vestibular, and proprioception take time for young children to develop. All of the senses need to work together so that infants and toddlers can move, learn, and behave in a typical manner. The coordination of all seven senses allows infants and toddlers to learn about their world.

## Gross Motor (Large Motor) Development

There are two types of motor development. Gross motor development includes large motor activities in which children use their entire bodies, as in walking. Gross motor skills also include big arm and trunk movements that are used in activities like rolling, crawling, and throwing a ball. Children develop motor skills from head to foot. That is, they learn how to hold their heads up before they can sit up. After they can sit up, they can learn how to stand and then walk.

## Fine Motor (Small Motor) Development

Fine motor development includes use of the hands and fingers to complete activities. Infants learn how

to grasp an object first in the palm of their hands. Then, they grasp with their fingers. Finally they manipulate objects with their fingers. Young infants typically use one hand at a time to hold objects. Older infants hold an object in each hand and bring them to midline (the middle of the body) for play. Infants need easy-to-grasp toys such as rattles to hold in their hands. Toddlers develop the ability for one hand to do one thing, while the other hand does something different, as in stringing large beads. Older toddlers also learn to use tools such as washable markers and paintbrushes. They also manipulate objects in play, such as putting large pegs in a pegboard.

# Developmental Issues

All infants and toddlers develop at their own rate. The range of typical development is wide, and there are many genetic and environmental influences to consider. Some infants are born with very good muscle tone and lean bodies, which may help them develop gross motor skills at a faster rate. Other infants live in a language-rich environment and their verbal skills may be more advanced. In addition, infants typically focus on one or two areas of development at a time. For example, when an infant is learning to walk he or she is focusing on gross motor development. His or her fine motor and language development may slow down until he or she has conquered walking. Keep in mind that all developmental areas are closely related. For example, a toddler uses fine motor skills to carry out a cognitive task, such as placing shapes into a sorter.

## Developmental Age and Chronological Age

When planning learning spaces for the classroom, consider each infant's and toddler's chronological and developmental age. Chronological age is a child's actual age since birth. To determine a child's chronological age take the child's date of birth and subtract it from the current date. For example, if a child was born on 2-17-02 and today's date is

4-18-03, then the child's chronological age would be one year, two months, and one day.

A child's developmental age takes into account the child's skill level in all developmental domains. To determine a child's developmental age, observe the child's function in cognitive, language, social/emotional, and motor (gross and fine) areas. Use the developmental considerations listed at the beginning of each chapter in this book to assess children. It is natural for children to be more skilled in some areas of development than others. Therefore, consider the child's ability as a whole. When there is a wide discrepancy between a child's chronological age and developmental age, a suggestion that the child receive a thorough developmental assessment from a pediatrician or early interventionist may be necessary.

## Special Needs

The current trend is for more inclusive environments where children with special needs are integrated into classrooms with typically developing children. Infants and toddlers with special needs have unique strengths, and they are valuable assets in any classroom. Children with special needs may require more guidance or physical assistance to participate in learning spaces. No matter what the child's developmental age, it is of utmost importance to set up and use learning spaces that facilitate the learning process for all infants and toddlers. The open-ended nature of learning spaces makes them especially effective for all children.

Toddlers washing baby dolls in soapy water

## Safety Issues

Special safety considerations must be followed when designing learning spaces for infants and toddlers. Because they are learning motor skills and are unsteady on their feet when they start walking, their environment needs to be as safe as possible. There are state and federal regulations for child care facilities and safety standards imposed by toy and infant equipment manufacturers that should be followed. But, the largest responsibility for young children's safety is placed on those who set up and use the learning environment.

### HELPFUL HINTS FOR SAFETY

- *Toys and materials should be at least 1 ½" in diameter.*
- *Every infant and toddler classroom should have a choking (testing) tube readily available to check for choking hazards.*
- *Watch for small parts that might break off larger toys.*
- *Check teethers and rattles regularly, to assure that they are secure.*
- *Make sure that any strings, ropes, or cords are no longer than 12 inches.*
- *Stuffed toys should be lightweight, so as not to cause accidental suffocation.*
- *Materials used in infant or toddler classrooms should be washable, non-toxic, and nonflammable or flame retardant.*

# Carefully Designed Environments

An attractive space designed for infants

## Learning Spaces for Infants

When designing learning spaces for infants, organize items and materials together. These learning spaces can be set up in the classroom or they can be moved in and out of the classroom. This method of organization enables the teacher to develop a classroom environment that is both appropriate and interesting for infants. It also ensures that objects, movement, and experiences are included that positively affect all areas of development: cognitive, language, social/emotional, and motor. Carefully selected toys, materials, and props should be responsive to infants and encourage them to influence their environment. In these learning areas, they will be able to see items, play with them, and continue to use them as long as they are interested.

## Learning Spaces for Toddlers

Design and set up learning spaces for toddlers that group together equipment, materials, and props that encourage play, language, and discovery. These learning spaces enable children to be an active participant in their learning as they construct their understanding of their world. In learning spaces, they choose the materials and activities that interest them. *The Complete Learning Spaces Book for Infants and Toddlers* applies what is known about creating effective learning centers to the appropriate learning spaces for toddlers. This book uses the positive qualities of learning centers, but changes the layout and selection of materials to match the interests and developmental needs of toddlers.

The management of learning spaces is unique for toddlers. Some learning spaces remain set up throughout the year, while others are brought into the classroom for a specific period of time. Other adjustments allow the toddler more flexibility to move into and out of and use learning spaces at their own pace. These learning spaces are not designed to produce mini-preschools but rather are planned learning spaces where materials are grouped together to allow toddlers to influence their choices. These learning spaces are based on the understanding that toddlers have preferences and interests that can influence their environment. This interaction between the toddler and the environment respects each child's individuality.

Young toddlers experiencing bubbles together

## Benefits of Using Learning Spaces

The benefits of using planned learning spaces with infants and toddlers include the following:

- The materials infants and toddlers use match their interests.
- Infants and toddlers control the amount of time they interact with the object: a brief examination or a long investigation.
- Vocabulary is expanded, as new objects are introduced and concretely explored.
- Infants and toddlers stimulate their thinking by building on what they know.
- New experiences expand their thinking and language.
- Infants and toddlers experience cause and effect as they influence their environment.
- As infants and toddlers successfully participate in learning spaces, their experiences build their self-confidence.

# Matching the Environment to Infants
## What Are Infants Like?

From the beginning of life, infants are individuals with special abilities, temperaments, and interests. Although they are dependent, they are beginning the long journey to independence. They are developing attitudes about themselves, the people around them, and the world in which they live. Infants are striving to find answers to many questions, including: "How can I influence my environment?" "Will the teacher recognize my individual needs?" "Will my world support my desire to learn and explore?" "Can I move away when I'm tired of an activity?" and "Can I stay when I find something very interesting?"

First, she looks at the flower.

Each infant's unique characteristics should be respected. Just as some infants need to be fed every three hours and others much sooner or later, they also have different needs for experiences. A novel toy immediately intrigues some infants, while others may need a "warm up" period before they experience something new. Observant infant teachers will recognize these differences and support infants' special ways of learning.

Next, she smells the flower.

Finally, she feels the flower.

## Learning Spaces for Infants (Young Infants: Six Weeks to Eight Months and Mobile Infants: Six to 14 Months)

Learning spaces are carefully designed environments where materials and activities are grouped together. For example, a learning space can be filled with materials that infants can explore with their senses. With an adult's help, infants can feel the textures. Young infants can be placed in the learning space. Later, mobile infants will be able to move to the learning space on their own. In either stage, infants influence their environment.

# Matching the Environment to Toddlers
## What Are Toddlers Like?

This is a period of rapid development in all areas. Active toddlers are touching, manipulating, and moving. They are becoming more independent and capable of doing things for themselves. Their language acquisition is exploding, as they use gestures and meaningful words to communicate their feelings and ideas to other toddlers and to their teachers.

The classroom environment should reflect toddlers' developmental aspects, while creating a place for them to work and play. Toddlers need space to move and materials to manipulate. They should be able to make choices and participate in learning spaces that interest them. Each learning space should include many opportunities for language and literacy development.

Toddler attaching items to a sticky wall

## Learning Spaces for Toddlers (Young Toddlers: 14 to 24 Months and Older Toddlers: 24 to 36 Months)

Toddlers continue to explore their environment and the materials in it. They are sensory learners who observe and actively participate in their learning. They are also beginning to be involved in dramatic play. Learning spaces are an effective way to arrange an environment for toddlers. However, the management of these spaces should be developed to match the toddlers' way of exploring their world.

Several learning spaces, such as the Housekeeping and Motor Learning Spaces, should be available for toddlers throughout the year. Select other learning spaces to match the specific group of toddlers in the classroom, because they relate to the world of the toddlers or expand their experiences in appropriate ways. Toddlers will move in and out of learning spaces, rather than remaining for "Center Time" like preschoolers. Often, they carry items with them from one learning space to another. This is acceptable toddler play.

Early experiences with learning spaces should include learning about items in the space, clean-up time, and returning materials to a specific area. Toddlers need the teacher to model this learning and to support their beginning efforts. For example, the teacher can help toddlers who need assistance in taking clothing back to the Housekeeping Learning Space and blocks back to the Construction Learning Space. This helps toddlers learn where materials belong. Because learning spaces for toddlers are planned environments with related materials, they help toddlers organize their world, participate in selected activities, and make choices related to their individual preferences.

## Introducing Learning Spaces to Toddlers

Introduce learning spaces to toddlers by talking with them about how learning spaces are used. Visit each learning space with the children and let them manipulate the materials in the area. Model some of the play that is possible in the learning space or use some of the materials. Or, share an idea that toddlers can use in their play. As toddlers become more experienced, they will try out the ideas of

others and creatively use materials. This imitation and variation demonstrates the way toddlers learn. Later, they will use their problem-solving skills and individual way of doing things, as they become more confident in their growing abilities.

# Displaying and Valuing Learning

It is important to find effective ways to display the work of infants and toddlers. Valuing their work during these early years helps them understand that what they do and create is very important. Display some of their work at their eye level, so they can enjoy it as easily as the adults in their world. Documentation panels, introduced by the educators of Reggio Emilia, demonstrate the learning that is occurring as children participate in activities and projects. These panels include photographs of the young children as they explore and use materials. Examples of documentation panels, showing the work of infants and toddlers, are on page 308.

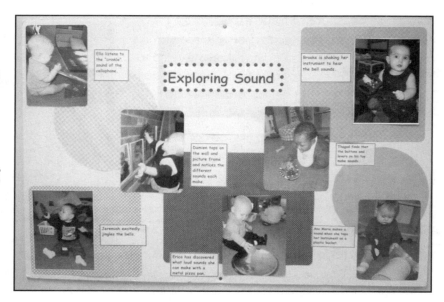
Documentation of infants learning about sound

# Book Organization: A Consistent Plan

*The Complete Learning Spaces Book for Infants and Toddlers* was designed to help busy teachers meet the challenge of creating an effective learning environment for infants and toddlers. It includes ideas for planning, using, and evaluating learning spaces for infants and toddlers that match their special way of learning.

Each of the following chapters focuses on a specific developmental period that occurs during the first three years of life:
- Chapter 2 focuses on the young infant: 6 weeks to 8 months of age
- Chapter 3 focuses on the mobile infant: 6 to 14 months of age
- Chapter 4 focuses on the young toddler: 14 to 24 months of age
- Chapter 5 focuses on the older toddler: 24 to 36 months of age

At the beginning of each chapter are developmental considerations that relate to each specific age group. These can be used to understand the learning that may occur during this time frame and how it influences environmental needs. Remember, these are only guidelines; each individual infant and toddler will progress at his or her own rate.

Each chapter includes learning spaces in the same basic format:
- Overview
- Learning Objectives
- Time Frame
- Letter to Parents
- Layout of the Learning Space, which is illustrated
- Vocabulary Enrichment
- Teacher- and Parent-Collected Props
- Activities
- The Essential Literacy Connection
- Adding a Spark
- Evaluation

The learning objectives provide a foundation for planning each learning space and indicate some of the learning that can occur. A letter to parents is included for each learning space. It explains what learning is occurring and often includes ideas for parents to do at home to support this learning. Sometimes the parents are asked to visit or participate in the classroom in a special way related to the topic. These communications are designed to help establish important connections with parents during these early years.

Each learning space includes an illustration that suggests an arrangement of equipment and materials. The Teacher- and Parent-Collected Props are other suggested items that may be included in the learning space.

During this critical period of language development, it is important to include many opportunities to enrich language. The vocabulary list identifies words related to the learning space that might be used with the infants or toddlers. This provides teachers with a focus for talking and interacting with the very young children.

The activities included in each learning space are designed to provide opportunities for infants and toddlers to learn in all domains: cognitive, social/emotional, language, and motor. In addition to the equipment and materials, use these activities to explore the learning space.

The Essential Literacy Connection recognizes that infants and toddlers need to be read to and have experiences with printed materials from the very beginning of their lives.

The questions at the end of each learning space help evaluate what the infants or toddlers are learning in the space. These will help to determine the effectiveness of the learning space and the individual learning that is occurring.

Webs are included at the beginning of the infant chapters and visually demonstrate how the learning spaces support integrated learning. In the toddler sections, the webs for each learning space show how holistic learning is occurring.

Throughout the book, there are photographs of infants and toddlers in developmentally appropriate environments. These visuals show infants and toddlers thriving in an environment that supports their developmental needs and is responsive to individual differences.

# Conclusion

Infants and toddlers are in a critical period of development. The classroom environment, where they spend a large amount of time, can have a tremendous influence on their development. The classroom should include a caring, responsive teacher who understands the unique capabilities and needs of infants and toddlers; who is observant and strives to understand the individuals in the classroom: each child's interests, temperament, and joys. A carefully designed environment responds to infants and toddlers and encourages their development in all domains: cognitive, social/emotional, language, and motor. Infant and toddler learning spaces can create an environment that supports learning and development for each child.

# CHAPTER TWO

# Young Infants
## Six Weeks to Eight Months

## Developmental Considerations

For the purpose of this book, young infants are considered to be between the ages of six weeks and eight months. Six weeks has been selected as a beginning point, since many childcare facilities begin accepting infants at this age. The primary consideration is that young infants are not mobile. Mobile is defined as creeping, crawling, or walking. Therefore, young infants are not capable of moving to get to an object of interest. A six- or seven-month-old infant who is crawling may be more accurately categorized as a mobile infant.

Within the young infant period, a wide range of developmental skills is achieved. Young infants are changing each day and learning new cognitive, language, social-emotional, sensory, and motor skills. Use the following information as a developmental guideline for young infants to assist in designing an appropriate environment for them. Keep in mind that each young infant is an individual and will develop at his or her own rate. The focus is not to push infants, but to encourage their development in all domains.

## Newborn

Newborns maintain a very flexed position with their arms and legs bent. Their hands are fisted most of the time. Newborns are barely able to lift their head up off a surface. They are able to see a human face, but only if that face is within a distance of three feet. Newborns will respond to sounds such as a bell, rattle, or voice. Many new sensations, people, and events are bombarding them as they try to organize their world.

## Three Months

By three months of age, infants are learning how to support themselves on their forearms when they are on their stomachs. Their head control is developing, and they can be held without their heads bobbing. They have a grasp reflex and, if a small object is placed in their palms, they will hold it for a brief period.

Three-month-old infants are visually attracted to lights, and can see their hands and large objects up to six feet away. They will attempt to localize sounds and will become quiet when they hear something they like. Infants this age will make cooing sounds and chuckle, and will smile at favorite people. They also will have different cries for different needs.

## Six Months

By six months of age, infants are becoming more social. Infants this age can play with a rattle, laugh, and smile socially. They can roll from their stomach to their back, and can sit with support. If given full support around their stomachs, they can stand and bounce. Six-month-olds can reach for toys, grasp a small object in the palm of their hands, and shake and bang a rattle. They can begin transferring toys from one hand to the other.

Six-month-old infants are able to see objects across the room, and are able to move their head and eyes in all directions to follow moving people or things. They listen to people as they talk. Six-month-olds begin babbling ("bababa") and may vocalize for pleasure or displeasure.

## Eight Months

Around the eighth month of life, infants learn how to sit independently for a short time. They are able to roll from their backs to stomachs, they can push up

Young infant enjoying a board book

on their hands while on their stomachs, and they may even get up onto all fours. Infants this age can use all of their fingers to grasp a small object, and they bring their feet to their mouths. They can bang two objects together at midline, and can hold a bottle or cup with two hands. They enjoy taking objects out of large containers.

Eight-month-olds begin to accidentally drop toys and then look for them. They can listen to familiar words and respond to their name, babble single sounds ("ba"), and may even "talk" to themselves. They begin cooperating in games like peek-a-boo and enjoy playing with noisy or musical toys.

# Responsive Teacher and Interactive Environment

Young infants develop an understanding of themselves through interactions with people in their world. Teachers working with infants should be consistently responsive to the needs of each child. Predictable behavior helps the infant understand that there are warm and caring people and an environment that understands and supports his or her emotional needs. Being responsive requires that the teacher be a careful observer and listen to infants.

Each infant has his or her own temperament and learning style. Recognizing these individual needs and determining how to interact with each infant is essential. A significant aspect of this responsiveness is arranging and using the classroom environment so it both matches and challenges developing infants. This includes both predictable daily routines and interesting interactions with teachers.

Caring words, personal time, and dependability support the emotional and intellectual development of infants. In this responsive, interactive environment, infants will be respected and their needs will be met. In turn, infants will learn trust and how to be in a loving relationship with others.

# Learning Spaces to Include in the Young Infant Classroom

The learning spaces in this chapter are recommended for the young infant classroom: *I Move, I See, I Touch, I Hear,* and *Language.* The term "learning space" is used to help teachers think about ways to organize their classrooms. In fact, several of these areas do not need their own space in the room. The *I See, I Touch,* and *I Hear* areas can be taken from infant to infant in a large, clear, plastic container. However, a bit more space is needed for the *I Move* and *Language* learning spaces to help meet the needs of infants and to keep materials available throughout the day.

All of the learning spaces on the following pages of this chapter are designed to remain available for the entire developmental period from six weeks to eight months. Young infants need stimulation in all these areas and opportunities for repetition. To keep infants' interest level high, rotate items in and out of the areas.

The web on page 31 shows how the learning spaces in this chapter support infants' integrated learning.

# I Move Learning Space

## Overview

Motor development is occurring at a very rapid rate during the first six weeks to eight months of life. During this time, young infants learn gross (large) motor skills such as how to hold up their head, push up on their arms, roll over, and sit up. Young infants also work on acquiring fine (small) motor skills such as reaching, grasping, and putting objects into their mouths.

It is important to encourage young infants' motor development, as well as diligently work on their language and cognitive skills. These three areas are very closely related in brain development. The *I Move Learning Space* will provide young infants with the space, opportunity, and activities necessary to learn and practice motor skills repeatedly.

## Learning Objectives

Young infants will:
1. Develop muscle strength in head, arms, and legs.
2. Gain experience with body movement.
3. View the world from a variety of positions.

## Vocabulary Enrichment

feet
hands
move
stomach
swing

## Letter to Parents

• • • • • • • • • • • • • • • • • • • • • • •

*Dear Parents,*
*Young infants are developing many important motor skills during the first eight months of life. They will learn how to hold up their head, reach for toys, roll over, and sit up. In our I Move Learning Space, we will be promoting these developmental motor milestones, while also encouraging language and cognitive development.*

*One of the important things we can do for young infants is allow them space to move. We will place brightly colored objects or musical toys on the floor to encourage the infants to move. You will also notice that we do not place your infant in a playpen, baby swing, or high chair for any length of time. These pieces of equipment restrict an infant's movement, so that they cannot practice their developing motor skills. It is also necessary for young infants to spend time on their stomachs when they are awake. This will help the infants develop the arm strength necessary for reaching, pulling up, and crawling. Come by and watch your infant "on the move!"*

# Layout of the I Move Learning Space

# Web of Integrated Learning for Young Infant Learning Spaces

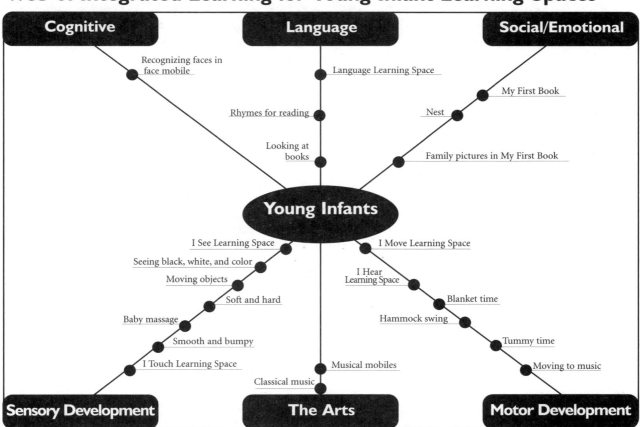

## Tips for Teaching Young Infants

1. Young infants need to spend many of their waking hours on the floor. Allow infants the freedom to move themselves. This is how they develop important motor skills they will use for the rest of their lives.
2. Young infants should not spend more than 30 minutes, two times a day (1 hour total), in restrictive equipment. This includes, but is not limited to, the following types of equipment: baby swings, strollers, high chairs, bouncy seats, and stationary play devices. Walkers are dangerous and should not be used with young infants.
3. Many young infants prefer playing while on their backs. However, all infants need to spend play time on their backs and on their stomachs. Infants develop head control and arm strength from time spent on their stomachs. They also learn how to push up on their arms and eventually crawl from lying on their stomachs.
4. Young infants should be encouraged to play with their hands and feet. Suspend toys above them to encourage batting, swinging, reaching, grasping, and kicking. Put brightly colored socks with rattles or bells on their feet or hands for play.
5. Young infants learn motor skills through repetition. Enjoy watching young infants practice a new skill over and over again, until they get it right!

## Teacher- and Parent-Collected Props

baby gyms
black and white toys
colorful toys that move
floor mats
foam wedge
horseshoe-shaped pillow
musical toys
play mats
soft balls
soft foam pillows covered with washable fabric
toys with wheels
washable blankets

## ACTIVITIES

# Hammock Swing

large blanket or sheet
two adults

- Place the young infant in the middle of the sheet.
- With another adult, grab the edges of the sheet securely and slightly lift the baby off the floor.
- Slowly and gently, swing the infant back and forth.
- Speak or sing softly to the infant as she moves. Use words such as *swinging, swaying,* and *rocking*. Keep your eyes focused on the infant.
  **Caution:** Do not lift the baby far off the floor, and only swing the baby ever so slightly.

# Tummy Time

hand towel or horseshoe-shaped pillow

- Place the young infant on his stomach with a hand towel rolled under his armpits or with his arm lying over a horseshoe-shaped pillow.
- Put brightly colored pictures, books, or toys on the floor in front of the infant.
- Infants love to be near their teachers, so lie down on your back on the floor (be comfortable).
- After a while, place the infant on your stomach, so that your tummies are touching.
- Sing or talk with the baby to encourage him to lift his head and look at you.
- You may sing or whisper the words, "I see you and you see me. Tra, la, la, la, la, la, la."

An observant teacher selects materials that are appropriate for infants.

# Nest

nest (see page 311 for directions)
various toys

• Place infant on her back inside the nest.
• Put an activity toy over her or hang objects above her.
• This position will make the baby feel safe and secure. It will also encourage her to bring her feet and hands together for play.

**ADDING SPARK TO THE I MOVE LEARNING SPACE**

*Place the young infant on a blanket close to a toy that will respond to random/reflexive movements. For example, use a musical ball or toy animal that will produce a sound when hit. Comment on the baby's activity with the toy, "You made the ball make music."*

## The Essential Literacy Connection
(* Available as a board book)

Boynton, Sandra. 2000. *Pajama Time!* New York: Workman Publishing Company. *A jump roping chicken, a pig on a swing, a Scottie in plaid pajamas, and an elephant in a fuzzy one-piece with feet all sing along in a barnyard dance.* *

Boynton, Sandra. 1982. *The Going to Bed Book.* New York: Simon & Schuster. *An assortment of animals on a boat take a bath, put on their pajamas, brush their teeth, and exercise before going to bed.**

Christelow, Eileen. 1998. *Five Little Monkeys Jumping on the Bed.* Boston: Houghton Mifflin Company. *As soon as they say goodnight to Mama, the five little monkeys start to jump on their bed. Trouble lies ahead as, one by one, they fall off and hurt themselves. After the doctor issues a stern order— "No more monkeys jumping on the bed!"—they finally fall asleep.**

Mayo, Margaret. 2002. *Wiggle Waggle Fun: Stories and Rhymes for the Very Very Young.* Illustrations by 24 different artists. New York: Alfred A. Knopf. *An illustrated collection of poems, songs, traditional verses, action rhymes, and stories that are appropriate for the young infant.*

Root, Phyllis. 2001. *One Duck Stuck.* Illustrations by Jane Chapman. Cambridge: Candlewick Press. *In this counting book, increasingly larger groups of animals try to help a duck that is stuck in the sleepy, slimy marsh.**

## Evaluation

1. Is the young infant able to move her arms and legs while on her stomach?
2. Is the young infant spending time on her stomach, back, and side?
3. Is the young infant attempting to move to get objects or in response to stimuli such as a sound?

# I See Learning Space

## Overview

Infants use their eyes to learn about the world around them. Newborns can see many things at birth, but it takes a few years before their vision is similar to that of an adult. Newborns can see movement and like to look at new things; they are especially interested in looking at faces. They also enjoy looking at geometric designs and pictures with a contrast of colors. They are particularly drawn to black, white, red, and yellow.

After young infants learn to hold up their heads, their vision begins to improve. Young infants focus on toys that are above, in front, and to the side of them. Later, they track (follow with eyes) objects as they move slowly from side to side. The *I See Learning Space* is designed to stimulate young infants' vision, so that they may function effectively in exploring their environment.

## Learning Objectives

Young infants will:
1. Focus on faces and objects.
2. Gain experience in watching moving objects.
3. Use vision to learn about the surroundings.

## Vocabulary Enrichment

eyes
face
look
mobile
see

## Letter to Parents

• • • • • • • • • • • • • • • • • • • • • • • • • • • • •

*Dear Parents,*

*We want to help your young infant develop all five basic senses. The* I See Learning Space *in our room is designed to help encourage your infant's vision. It takes time for a young infant to see well, but even newborn infants can see faces. Infants learn to identify their mothers' and fathers' faces very early on. Talk to your baby and make faces as you hold him or her in your arms.*

*After an infant can hold up his or her head, he or she can begin watching objects move. Brightly colored toys are fun and stimulating for young infants. Hold up objects and move them slowly, shaking them if necessary, to grab your infant's attention. Young infants like to watch mobiles that hang above their cribs. Soon your infant will begin moving his or her arms to reach for a toy he or she likes.*

## Layout of the I See Learning Space

## Tips for Teaching Young Infants

1. Give infants the opportunity to look at objects from different positions. Place them on their stomachs, backs, and sides.
2. When showing items to babies, begin by placing the objects on the baby's right side. Then place objects on her left side. Finally, place objects directly overhead.
3. Too many visual objects can over-stimulate infants. Do not clutter their environment. Spread out pictures and objects in the classroom. One mobile or a brightly colored toy is plenty for a crib. Also consider the designs on the sheets, blankets, and bumper pads. This may be more than enough visual stimulation for a very young infant.
4. Occasionally, mobiles should either be removed or replaced with different mobiles. An infant will become used to one mobile and will stop noticing it after it has been hanging over the crib for a long time.
5. Suspend mobiles in front or to the side of the infant's head, so that it may be easily viewed. But place the mobile high enough so that the infant cannot grasp it or pull it down.

6. Follow infants' cues. If they cry, turn their head away, or close their eyes, they probably need a break from the visual input. Try again later, when they become interested in the object.
7. At first, young infants will appear very serious and will not move as they look at new objects. Later, infants will move their arms and legs excitedly when they see something they like (such as Mom, Dad, or a favorite toy).

## Teacher- and Parent-Collected Props

baby gym
brightly colored play mat
brightly colored rattles and toys the infant can hold
mobiles
pictures or books of faces
pictures or objects that are brightly colored (particularly red and yellow)
pictures or objects with black and white geometric designs
sparkly paper or tinsel to hang from ceiling

Ribbons hung from an embroidery hoop respond to an infant's touch.

# Moving Objects

various brightly colored pictures or objects

- Young infants will focus first on your face.
- Move slowly around him, while talking, to encourage him to follow your face.
- Once an infant begins to look at moving objects, encourage him to track (follow with eyes) an object as you move it.
- Start by holding brightly colored pictures or objects approximately six inches above the infant's eyes.
- Then, slowly move the object right, back to center, and then to the left.
- Later, the infant can learn to follow objects from the center, up, and down.
- Be careful not to tire him with this activity.

# Black and White or Color?

various designs in color and black and white
rattles, mobiles, simple picture books, magazine
    cutouts, and other yellow and red playthings

- Young infants are attracted to black and white and brightly colored objects.
- They particularly like faces and objects that move.
- Simple black and white geometric designs and bull's eye designs catch their attention.
- Colorful designs with yellow and red are also interesting to them.

# Face Mobile

family photographs or magazine pictures
glue or laminate
index cards
clothes hanger or mobile base
string or yarn

- Make a face mobile for the young infant's crib.
- Glue family photos or magazine pictures to an index card (or laminate them).
- Then, string the photos (face down) to a clothing hanger or mobile base.
  **Caution:** Make sure that the pictures and mobile are secure and that the infants cannot reach them and pull them down.

## More Ideas for Mobiles

various objects, such as teddy bears, brightly colored toys, CDs, and so on
materials to make a mobile

- Common classroom or household objects make great mobiles for young infants.
- Use your imagination and follow the interest of the infants.
- Hang the objects facing down so the infants can see them.
- Remember to change or remove the mobiles occasionally so the infants do not become tired of them.

**ADDING SPARK TO THE I SEE LEARNING SPACE**

*The following fingerplay, "Beehive," provides a hand to look at and the bee sound to anticipate.*

**Beehive**
*Here is the beehive,*
*Where are the bees?*
*Hidden away where nobody sees.*
*Watch, and you see them come out of the hive.*
*Buzzzzzzzzzz.* (Use fingers to tickle the baby, while making the bee sound.)

## The Essential Literacy Connection
**(* Available as a board book)**

Boynton, Sandra. 1982. *Moo, Baa, La La La!* New York: Simon & Schuster Children's. *This whimsical book, featuring nontraditional text and animal characters, is sure to entertain. The language pattern is intriguing for the listening infant.**

Brown, Margaret Wise. 2001. *Goodnight Moon: Lap Edition.* Illustrations by Clement Hurd. New York: HarperCollins Children's Books. *A little rabbit bids goodnight to each familiar thing in his room. This classic story is told with gently lulling words.**

Carle, Eric. 1996. *Brown Bear, Brown Bear, What Do You See?* New York: Henry Holt. *Infants hear about a new creature on each page, as they enjoy this repetitive, predictable picture book.**

Hindley, Judy. 2002. *Eyes, Nose, Fingers, and Toes: A First Book All About You.* Illustrations by Brita Granstrom. Cambridge: Candlewick Press. *A group of toddlers demonstrate all the fun things that they can do with their eyes, mouth, hands, legs, and feet.*

Seuss, Dr. Theodor. 1998. *My Many Colored Days Board Book.* Illustrations by Steve Johnson and Lou Fancher. New York: Alfred A. Knopf. *This rhyming verse associates colors with emotions. "Red days are for kicking up one's heels and blue ones for flapping one's wings. Purple days are sad, pink are happy…" The sounds of words and patterns interest the listening infant.**

## Evaluation

1. Does the young infant appear to focus on your face?
2. Does the young infant show interest in black and white or brightly colored objects?
3. Does the young infant attempt to track (follow with eyes) slow-moving objects?

# I Touch Learning Space

## Overview

Young infants use their sense of touch to discover and learn about their bodies and the world around them. Infants also need to be touched and held. Touch demonstrates love and nurturing to an infant. Firm touch such as hugging or massage is calming to an infant. Young infants who receive adequate physical contact with their mothers or teachers thrive, while infants who are not held or touched may have long-term emotional problems.

Most infants demonstrate a preference for certain types of touch. Some prefer to be firmly patted on the back, while others like to be cuddled in your arms. Stimulating infants' touch sensation helps them refine this sense. The I Touch Learning Space is designed to give appropriate touch to young infants in a manner that will not over-stimulate them.

## Learning Objectives

Young infants will:
1. Experience the world through touch.
2. Demonstrate a preference or dislike for certain types of touch.
3. Seek out touch input with their bodies.

## Vocabulary Enrichment

cuddle
hands
hold
soft
touch

The I Touch Learning Space may be a large, clear, plastic container filled with a variety of textures. You may carry the container around the room to be used with young infants.

## Letter to Parents

• • • • • • • • • • • • • • • • • • • • • • • • • • • • •

*Dear Parents,*
*Touch is one of the most important senses to stimulate in young infants. Just like their need for food and water, infants have to be touched to grow and develop. Touching your infant shows that you love and care for him or her. Some infants prefer to be cuddled in your arms. Some infants like to be firmly patted on the back, while other infants prefer to be rubbed. What does your baby like? Let us know, so that we can use that touch method to help calm and nurture your young infant.*

*In our I Touch Learning Space, we will provide many loving touches such as snuggling and massage. We will also help your young infant develop his or her sense of touch. We will provide a variety of fun experiences with new textures such as fur and velvet.*

## Tips for Teaching Young Infants

1. Help young infants touch objects by placing them on or near a texture or by rubbing a texture on their body.
2. Observe a young infant's response to materials and follow her signals. It may be a small response, such as closing her eyes or turning her head. Or it could be a larger response, like a smile or cooing sound. For example, if she cries when you rub taffeta on her hands, stop and take note. You can try this texture again, after she has matured a little.
3. Use a firm, but gentle touch to apply textures to a young infant's skin.
4. When helping a young infant touch a texture, begin with her hands (where sensation is best). Then move to her arms, legs, feet, and stomach.
5. Be especially careful when rubbing material on a young infant's face. Some infants are particularly sensitive to touch on their face. They may like feeling a texture on their hands or body but not on their face.
6. Use one texture at a time. For instance, do not rub satin on an infant's stomach and fur on her back at the same time.
7. Give infants time to think about one texture, before moving on to the next. For example, rub a cotton ball on a young infant's hands and feet, wait for a few minutes to see how she reacts, and then apply a different material to her hands and feet.

## Teacher- and Parent-Collected Props

bumpy ball
carpet samples
colorful toys
cotton balls
hypo-allergenic baby lotion
large, clear, plastic container with lid
paper to crumple
rattles
stuffed animals
washable blankets
washable fabrics such as satin, corduroy, fur, and velvet

## ACTIVITIES

Baby lying on tummy and painting.

## Soft and Hard

various soft items
various hard items

- Softly rub the infant's favorite stuffed animal or blanket on his hands and feet.
- Tell the baby "soft" and watch his reaction.
- Wait a minute.
- Gently rub a hard toy (such as a rattle) on his hands and feet.
- Say "hard" to him and watch his reaction.
- Then, allow the young infant to experience the items in his own way.

## Smooth and Bumpy

various textures

- Rub a smooth texture, such as satin or silk, on the baby's body and say "smooth."
- Wait a minute.

- Rub a bumpy texture, such as corduroy, on her body and say "bumpy."
- Then let the infant explore the textures by herself.

## Blanket Time

large pieces (at least 2' x 2') of soft material, such as sheepskin, fur, satin, shag carpet, bath mat, and so on

- Place a large piece of soft scrap material on the floor.
- Remove the baby's clothing, except for his diaper, and place him on the material to play.

## Baby Massage

baby lotion, optional

- Firm touch, like a massage, is very calming for young infants.
- Cup your hand with your fingers together.
- Slowly and firmly stroke down an infant's body (always stroke down towards their feet).
- Begin with the back, then move to the arms, and finally the legs and feet.
- Do not massage an infant's face, head, or stomach, as these are very sensitive areas of the body and the infant may not enjoy having them touched.
- If desired, use baby lotion during the massage. Ask the infant's parents which lotion they prefer you to use.

**ADDING SPARK TO THE I TOUCH LEARNING SPACE**

*When changing or playing with the baby, let her touch your clothing, hair, and face. Talk about what the infant is feeling.*

## The Essential Literacy Connection
**(* Available as a board book)**

Hathon, Elizabeth. 1999. *Oh Baby!: A Touch-and-Feel Book*. New York: Penguin Putnam Books for Young Readers. *This is a photographic book for babies. They can feel the teddy bear's soft and furry tummy, peek at themselves in the Mylar mirror, sniff the flower scent patch, and more!**

Katz, Karen. 2000. *Where is Baby's Belly Button?* New York: Simon & Schuster Children's. *In this multicultural peek-a-boo book, babies can lift a flap to find out the answers to questions such as "Where are baby's eyes?"**

Kunhardt, Dorothy. 1990. *Pat the Bunny*. New York: Golden Books. *Pat the Bunny has been a classic since 1940. With texture, peek-a-boo, mirrors, and more, this timeless book encourages babies to gurgle with glee.**

## Evaluation

1. Does the young infant demonstrate a particular like or dislike of certain textures?
2. Does the young infant move his body to feel objects or materials?
3. Is the young infant showing a particular preference for a loving touch (hug, firm patting, massage, or rubbing)?

# I Hear Learning Space

## Overview

Newborns have a well-developed sense of hearing when they are born, yet they do not know how to process what they hear. It takes time for their brains to learn how to organize all the sounds they hear. They prefer quiet sounds such as your voice. So, talk and sing quietly to them (they don't care if you can't carry a tune). Young infants do not like loud noises, and they often cry in response to other infants crying. However, loud noises do help babies learn how to locate sounds. Eventually, young infants learn to turn their heads toward the sounds. They will also learn how to identify familiar voices. In the *I Hear Learning Space*, young infants will experience a variety of sounds.

## Learning Objectives

Young infants will:

1. Experience a variety of sounds.
2. Develop the sense of hearing.
3. Hear spoken language.

## Vocabulary Enrichment

ears
listen
music
sound
voice

The *I Hear Learning Space* may be a large, clear, plastic container filled with items that make a variety of noises. The container may be carried around the room, to be used with young infants.

## Letter to Parents

• • • • • • • • • • • • • • • • • •

Dear Parents,

Young infants tend to like soft sounds and high-pitched, soothing voices. Infants also enjoy listening to music with a steady beat, such as classical music. Even if you cannot carry a tune, infants love for you to sing to them. So, sing to your baby throughout the day, even during routine tasks such as diaper changing.

We will be promoting your infant's sense of hearing in the I Hear Learning Space of our room. In the I Hear Learning Space, we will help young infants experience music through movement. We will make rattles that provide unusual sounds, we will play with your infants using toys that make sounds and encourage movement, and we will sing and talk with them, of course!

## Layout of the I Hear Learning Space

## Tips for Teaching Young Infants

1. Observe how different infants react to sound and musical experiences.
2. Positive signs indicating that infants are responding to sounds in the room include opening their eyes wide, turning their heads to the sound, smiling, babbling, or cooing.
3. Negative signs that indicate that infants are not enjoying the sounds they hear include closing their eyes, crying, or turning away from the sound.
4. Be careful not to over-stimulate young infants with too many sounds or sights at one time. For example, it may be too much to play music while you are reading a baby a book and giving her a bottle, while other babies are crying in the room.

## Teacher- and Parent-Collected Props

paper to rattle
rattles
recordings (tapes and CDs) of different types of rhythmic music such as classical, country, and pop
tape or CD player
toys that make music and sounds

**ACTIVITIES**

Infant uses homemade shakers to make music.

## Classical Music

various recordings of classical music
tape or CD player

- Some experts believe that there is a relationship between infants listening to classical music, such as by Mozart or Bach, and future skills in math, science, and the performing arts.
- Infants will enjoy the variation of sound, rhythm, pitch, and pattern found in classical music.
- Find opportunities to allow even the youngest infants to listen to classical music, such as during meal times, naptime, and quiet play times.

## Voices and Singing

various naptime songs, such as "Rock-a-Bye Baby," "Baby Mine," "Hush Little Baby," and "Kumbaya"

- During feeding or preparation for naptime, hold and cuddle young infants.
- Look at them and sing songs softly.
- A soft voice will get their attention and help them learn about sounds and words.

## Homemade Rattles

empty medicine bottles or small plastic juice bottles
aluminum cans
dry cereal, uncooked rice, and dried beans
duct tape
hot glue gun (adult only)

- Create rattles that vary in the sound they produce.
- Place a variety of materials into small bottles. (Tamper-resistant clear medicine bottles or small plastic juice bottles fit nicely into an infant's hand.)
- Hot glue the lids to bottles or cover aluminum can openings with duct tape.
  **Caution:** Hot-glue guns are used by adults only, and not while children are around.
- Give the rattles to young infants to hold and shake.
- If desired, play music and help the infants shake their rattles to the beat.

# Moving to the Music

various recordings of music
tape or CD player

- Play different types of music from your collection.
- Hold an infant in your arms and dance to the music.
- Make sure you support his head.
- Try different movements, to match the beat of the music, including swaying up and down, marching, swaying slowly, swishing from side to side, and bouncing gently.
- Say appropriate words to go with the activity, such as *bouncing, marching, swaying, up, down, slow,* or *fast.*

### ADDING SPARK TO THE I HEAR LEARNING SPACE

*Sing "Clap, clap, clap your hands. Clap your hands together." Move the infant's hands together as you sing. Observe and follow her interest in continuing this musical activity.*

## The Essential Literacy Connection
(* Available as a board book)

Boelts, Maribeth. 1995. *Lullaby Babies.* Illustrations by Don Sullivan. Morton Grove, IL: Albert Whitman & Company. *A series of poems, which present various mother animals singing to their babies, ending with a human mother and child.*

Boynton, Sandra. 1997. *Snoozers: Seven Short Short Bedtime Stories for Lively Little Kids.* New York: Simon & Schuster Children's. *These seven short stories bring chuckles before bedtime. The table of contents has colorful picture tabs that allow children to choose the story they want to hear.**

Seuss, Dr. Theodor. 1996. *Mr. Brown Can Moo! Can You?: Dr. Seuss's Book of Wonderful Noises.* New York: Random House. *Mr. Brown is an expert at imitating all sorts of noises in this introduction for babies to the wonderful mishmash world of sounds. Listen to the cow's MOO, the frying eggs' SIZZLE, and the thunder's BOOM BOOM BOOM. There are plenty of noises for everyone!**

Seuss, Dr. Theodor. 1996. *There's a Wocket in My Pocket!" Dr. Seuss's Book of Ridiculous Rhymes.* New York: Random House. *A host of inventive creatures and rhymes exposes babies to many common household words: the nupboard in the cupboard, ghairs beneath the stairs, and the bofa on the sofa!**

## Evaluation

1. Does the young infant demonstrate a like or dislike for particular sounds or music?
2. Is the young infant turning his head toward loud sounds?
3. Does the young infant focus on your face when you are talking or singing to him?

# Language Learning Space

## Overview

From the beginning of life, young infants should be exposed to the world of oral language, books, print, and literature. These early experiences can help children develop an interest in and an ability to communicate, read books, and enjoy the printed word. The goal of the *Language Learning Space* is to make appropriate materials easily accessible to teachers during the daily routine and when young infants are alert.

## Learning Objectives

Young infants will:

1. Listen to and respond to the oral language of the teacher.
2. Have the opportunity to see and touch books that interest them.
3. Listen to books, poems, and literature.
4. Experience the enjoyment of literature.

## Vocabulary Enrichment

book
picture
read
smile
talk

## Letter to Parents

• • • • • • • • • • • • • • • • • • • • • • • • • • •

*Dear Parents,*

*Even the youngest infants show interest in the sounds of language. They especially enjoy being cuddled and held as they are talked to and read to. It is very important that infants have positive experiences with books and literature during the first year of life. They should be read to and talked to very often. These early experiences stimulate an interest in language and books.*

*Our* Language Learning Space, *which is located in the young infant space, contains materials that are appropriate for your baby. We will read and tell stories, rhymes, and poems to your infant. He or she will be able to hold and look at books with pictures of people and objects that are interesting to him or her. The* Language Learning Space *contains board books that infants can explore with their mouths and hands.*

# Layout of the Language Learning Space

## Tips for Teaching Young Infants

1. Put a low and stable storage bookcase in this area. Turn books face out so the covers are visible.

2. Display book covers and the illustrations in books to visually stimulate infants. Place enlarged pictures from books or illustrations on the floor or low on the wall for young infants to enjoy. It is helpful if you laminate the pictures or place them behind a Plexiglas frame (see page 311 for instructions). Photos of the infants and readers in the classroom will add a personal touch to the space.

3. Place board books in this space. Board books are sturdy enough for infants to explore using their mouths and hands.

4. Put a soft rug on the floor with large soft pillows for sitting comfortably. Add soft toys, blankets, and pillows on the floor. These items add softness and comfort, encouraging both young infants and teachers to come into the area.

5. Observe an infant's response to books, rhymes, and stories. Does she open her eyes wide? Does she smile? Does she shake her arms or kick her legs? Does she snuggle into the reader? Does she make sounds? Can you tell if there is a particular book that she enjoys? Reread favorites for her to enjoy.

## Teacher- and Parent-Collected Props

board books

foam pillows that are covered with a variety of textured, washable materials

old stuffed toys and blankets that can be washed and sterilized

washable rugs for the floor area

**ACTIVITIES**

# Rhymes for Reading

various rhymes with patterns

- Select rhymes that include interesting patterns of words and phrases.
- About once a week, introduce each infant to a rhyme. During the week, repeat the same rhyme to each infant.
- Notice if the infant is interested in the rhyme and seems to enjoy the pattern of the language. Observe whether an infant is intrigued by a specific rhyme or poem.
- Over the next month, continue to use the poem that captured her interest as others are introduced.

# My First Book

several photographs of familiar things, such as parents, siblings, grandparents, the teacher, a pet, or a bottle
glue
poster board
clear contact paper or laminating materials
scissors
duct tape

- Select photographs of people, pets, or items that are familiar to the infants.
- Glue each photo onto poster board and cut out, leaving a poster board edge around the picture.
- Laminate or cover the photographs with clear contact paper.
- Attach several pages together with duct tape to form a book.
- Young infants will explore this book over and over because it contains recognizable and important things.

# Textured Books

various soft textured materials, such as corduroy, fur, velvet, or satin
tape
old board book

- Select materials that can be safely mouthed.
- Tape pieces of fabric onto the cover of an old board book.
  **Note:** Young infants are more inclined to handle and mouth books with interesting covers to touch.
- These textured book covers also protect and help hold together the board books.

Infant explores the texture of bark in a book.

**ADDING SPARK TO THE LANGUAGE LEARNING SPACE**

*Create a language game with the baby by saying, "Where is (child's name)'s leg?" Gently touch and move the baby's leg and say, "Here is (child's name)'s leg!" Continue with arms, tummy, and feet, as long as the infant demonstrates interest in participating.*

# The Essential Literacy Connection
(* Available as a board book)

Boynton, Sandra. 1982. *But Not the Hippopotamus.* New York: Simon & Schuster Children's. *These quirky humorous pictures make a pleasant change for adults, while the lulling text is just what babies want to hear.*\*

Chorao, Kay. 1991. *The Baby's Lap Book.* New York: Penguin USA. *Designed for little listeners to snuggle on a reader's lap, this collection of perennially popular stories is perfect for babies.*

Martin, Bill Jr., & Archambault, John. 2000. *Chicka Chicka Boom Boom.* Illustrations by Lois Ehlert. New York: Aladdin Paperbacks. *A rollicking rhyme that relates what happens when the whole group tries to race each other to the top of a coconut tree.*

Opie, Iona Archibald. 1996. *My Very First Mother Goose.* Illustrations by Rosemary Wells. Cambridge: Candlewick Press. *A collection of more than sixty nursery rhymes, arranged in the loose framework of a day's activities, from morning until night.*

Prelutsky, Jack. 1986. *Read-Aloud Rhymes for the Very Young.* Illustrations by Tolon Brown and Mark Chaffin. New York: Alfred A. Knopf. *This collection of more than 200 short poems by American and English authors will delight infants.*

Silberg, Jackie, & Schiller, Pam. 2002. *The Complete Book of Rhymes, Songs, Poems, Fingerplays, and Chants, Vol. 1.* Illustrations by Deborah C. Wright. Beltsville, MD: Gryphon House Publishers. *This is a collection of more than 700 selections for young children. Words, phrases, and sounds captivate the infant's interest.*

## Evaluation
1. Is the young infant focusing on the sounds of language in books and poems?
2. Is the young infant demonstrating anticipation of reading a book with increased body movements or by making sounds?
3. Can you identify the infant's favorite book or poem?

# CHAPTER THREE

# Mobile Infants
## 6 to 14 Months

## Developmental Considerations

Mobile infants are considered to be between 6 and 14 months. The hallmark of this age period is independent movement from one place to the next. Mobile infants are up and going. They may creep, crawl, cruise, walk, or even run to get an object that they want. Their language is progressing from vowel sounds (cooing) to simple meaningful words such as "Dada" and "Mama." They like to bang, push, and pull objects while playing by themselves (solitary play). Mobile infants begin playing simple games such as "peek-a-boo" and "pat-a-cake." They learn simple self-care skills, such as finger feeding and drinking from a cup. As mobile infants become more capable of using their bodies, they want more independence and will naturally progress to "toddler-hood."

The following developmental areas are provided as a guideline for observing mobile infants. They are listed on the page in order of typical acquisition. Keep in mind that most 6- to 14-month-old infants will not follow this developmental progression exactly. Each infant will have his or her own interests and natural abilities, which will influence his or her developmental rate. An individual infant's development and interest will impact the design of the environment.

## Cognitive
- Works to get toy that is out of reach
- Bangs and shakes toys (practice play)
- Interested in sounds of objects
- Responds to a simple request with a gesture
- Drops objects on purpose
- Takes rings off stacking toy
- Responds to simple verbal request
- Demonstrates how to drink from cup
- Gives toy to adult upon request
- Looks for toy that is removed (object permanence)

## Social/Emotional
- Responds playfully at mirror
- Cooperates in games directed by adult
- Likes to be in constant sight or hearing of adult
- Resists adult control
- Shows toy preferences
- Plays alone (solitary play)

## Gross Motor
- Sits independently
- Rolls from back to stomach
- Crawls
- Stands, holding on with both hands
- Walks along furniture (cruising)
- Stands independently
- Walks a few steps independently

## Language
- Coos (uses vowel sounds like "aah" or "ee")
- Babbles single consonant ("ba")
- Shows understanding of words by appropriate behavior
- Uses exclamatory expressions ("oh-oh")
- Says "no" meaningfully
- Names one or two familiar objects

## Sensory
- Looks for dropped toy
- Distinguishes between objects that are near and far
- Uses two eyes together to focus on an object (binocular vision)
- Listens to familiar words

## Fine Motor
- Reaches for object with one hand
- Transfers object from one hand to other
- Bangs two cubes held in hands
- Releases object on purpose
- Turns wrist for object manipulation
- Puts objects into container
- Brings spoon to mouth
- Points with index finger
- Turns over small container to obtain tiny objects inside

A responsive teacher interacts with two mobile infants.

The learning spaces in this chapter are designed to encourage mobile infants' development in all these domains. These planned learning spaces provide opportunities for mobile infants to influence their own environment. They also allow infants to set their own pace, as they select materials and activities to guide their learning.

The web on page 55 shows how the learning spaces in this chapter support infants' integrated learning.

# Motor Learning Space

## Overview

Infants will learn more motor skills during their first year than at any other time in their lives. They will learn how to hold their heads up, sit, stand, crawl, and walk. Babies learn each motor skill through repetition, which is often referred to as practice play. They will practice sitting up without support hundreds of times before they accomplish this skill. Because young infants are not mobile, they are capable of exploring only their immediate surroundings. As older infants begin to crawl or walk, they become more independent in their explorations and their world expands. Mobile infants can move to objects that interest them, even if those objects are across the room.

Motor skills are typically separated into fine (small) motor and gross (large) motor skills. Fine motor skills involve use of the hands (for example, grasping). Gross motor skills involve the whole body (for example, walking). The *Motor Learning Space* will give infants the appropriate space and objects to encourage their motor development in meaningful ways.

## Learning Objectives

Mobile infants will:
1. Develop gross motor coordination.
2. Enhance body strength and coordination.
3. Increase exploration of the environment through movement and interactions.

## Time Frame

This indoor learning space should be available to infants throughout the year. New materials may be added to provide continued interest in the activities and learning space.

## Letter to Parents

• • • • • • • • • • • • • • • • • • •

*Dear Parents,*

*Infants learn more motor skills during the first year of life than at any other time. It is so exciting to watch them roll over, sit up, or walk for the first time. The Motor Learning Space will give your infant many experiences with motor movement. It is very important that infants spend time on the floor where they can move around and use their motor skills. Therefore, our Motor Learning Space will have plenty of space, different floor heights, mirrors, and toys to encourage the infants to move around and learn about their environment. Come and visit this learning space so you can enjoy seeing your infant moving and learning.*

# Layout of the Motor Learning Space

# Web of Integrated Learning for Mobile Infant Learning Spaces

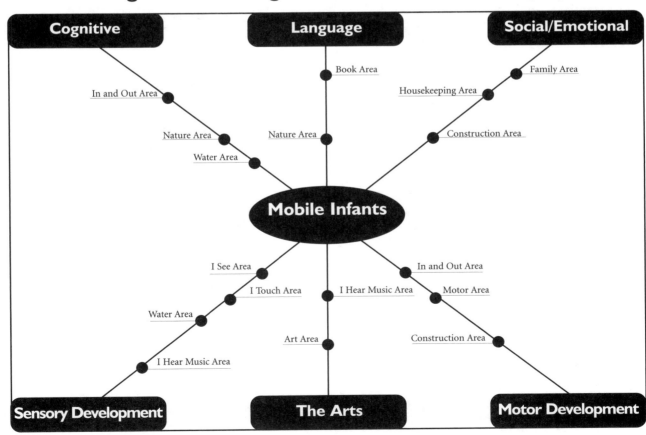

**Cognitive**

**Language**

**Social/Emotional**

Book Area

In and Out Area

Family Area

Housekeeping Area

Nature Area

Nature Area

Construction Area

Water Area

**Mobile Infants**

I See Area

In and Out Area

I Touch Area

I Hear Music Area

Motor Area

Water Area

Art Area

Construction Area

I Hear Music Area

**Sensory Development**

**The Arts**

**Motor Development**

This learning space requires enough floor space so that several infants and an adult can move around in the area at one time. Gross motor activities encourage infants to be interactive, so it is best if this learning space is placed away from cribs. A carpeted area of the room will be more comfortable and will encourage infants' movement.

## Vocabulary Enrichment

climb
find
go
pull
push
roll
sit
stand
walk

## Teacher- and Parent-Collected Props

activity gyms
balls of all sizes
blankets
carpet or floor mats
furniture for climbing, sliding, and stepping up/down
	(e.g., plastic playground equipment)
large cardboard boxes
musical toys that move
non-breakable mirrors
pillows
push toys
riding toys
tunnels

## ACTIVITIES

**SPECIAL NOTE:**
Mobile infants are able to sit up independently and are beginning to move around their environment. They need the opportunity to practice new motor skills over and over. Provide plenty of floor space for them to move around in and safe objects for them to manipulate so they can pull, push, climb, stand, cruise, and walk. Mobile babies should spend very little time in playpens, bouncy seats, highchairs, or swings. This type of equipment restricts infants' ability to move and limits their motor development.

## Carpeted Risers

carpeted riser (see Chapter 6 for directions)

- Place at least one carpeted riser on the floor.
- Put toys on top of the riser to encourage mobile infants to pull up and stand beside it.
- If desired, place objects on the riser on the opposite side from the infant, to promote crawling up and down to reach the objects.

## Bouncing Babies

children's songs suitable for bouncing activities

- Gently bounce babies on your knees while singing songs such as "Ride a Cock Horse."

### Ride a Cock Horse

*Ride a cock horse to Banbury Cross,*
*To see a fine lady upon a white horse;*
*Rings on her fingers and bells on her toes,*
*And so she makes noise wherever she goes.*

- This helps develop the infant's balance and coordination.
- Begin with easy, rhythmical bouncing and when the infants are ready, work towards larger, more exciting bounces.

Bouncing babies enjoy watching each other.

## Ball Play

large rubber or plastic lightweight balls

- Sit on the floor a few feet away from an infant.
- Roll the ball to her.
- Ask her to roll the ball back to you.
- At first, the ball may stick to her hands or accidentally slip out, but encourage her to keep trying.
- Sing or describe as you play: "You roll the ball to me, and I roll the ball to you."

- If the ball rolls away, help the baby roll, crawl, or walk to get it. This is good practice, too!
- After retrieving the ball, resume this game.

## Light in a Box

medium-size box
scissors
iridescent contact paper
flashlight

- Cut off one side of a medium-size box.
- Cover the inside of the box with iridescent contact paper.
- Show an infant how a flashlight turns off and on.
- Place the flashlight inside the box.
- The mobile infant may move up to or inside the box, experiment with turning the light on and off, or watch how the light beam responds to his movement.

## Move Outside

items from the Motor Learning Space
blankets

- Take items outside for a new experience.
- Push toys, balls, and cardboard boxes are easy to carry.
- Place blankets outside on a grassy area.
- Ask one or two infants to sit or lie down on the blanket.
- Pull one or two infants around on the blanket and talk about the grass, trees, birds, or sunshine.
- Allow the mobile infants to explore the outside through movement.

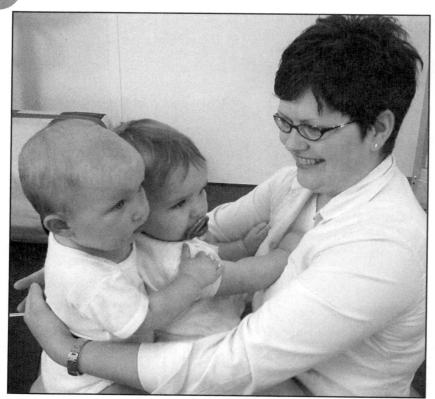

Infants moving with their teacher on a gymnastic ball

## Give the "Just-Right Challenge"

Place toys slightly out of the reach of mobile infants. This will encourage them to move to get the object. For example, if an infant is beginning to pull to stand, place objects on low tables or risers. Carefully observe the infant as she tries to get the object to provide the "just-right challenge" for that particular infant. If you put the toy too far away, she will give up. If you place the toy too close, she will become bored with the task. If the challenge is just right, she will want to repeat the task of getting the toy again and again. Follow the infant's lead and when she tires of the activity, move on to something else.

### ADDING SPARK TO THE MOTOR LEARNING SPACE

*Movement and music go together, so add music to the learning space. Infants enjoy moving to music from the very beginning of their lives. Play music and dance together or help younger infants move to the beat. Imitate the movements that the infants make. Mobile infants will enjoy imitating the movements to songs such as "Ring Around the Rosie," "Row, Row, Row Your Boat," and "If You're Happy and You Know It."*

## The Essential Literacy Connection
(* Available as a board book)

Oxenbury, Helen. 1987. *All Fall Down*. New York: Simon and Schuster. *Sing, run, dance, and drop are part of a day's fun. The children's activities are illustrated in this picture book.**

Wardlaw, Lee. 1999. *First Steps*. New York: HarperCollins. *Enjoy the thrill of watching a young child move from his toy to Mom.**

Williams, Sue. 1996. *I Went Walking*. New York: Harcourt. *Watch the lively parade of a child and his animal friends.**

## Evaluation

1. Is the infant moving to get objects that are out of reach?
2. Is the infant moving independently in the learning space?
3. Is the infant exploring objects through movement in/around the environment?

# I See Learning Space

## Overview

Infants are not born with the ability to understand the world through their eyes. They must learn to use and refine their sense of vision. While a baby's vision is better than was once believed, he still lacks experience using his eyes. Opportunities for infants to learn how to focus on and discriminate between objects will refine their sense of vision. As infants develop head control, their ability to use their vision improves. Mobile babies begin to compare what they are seeing with past experiences. They also seek out and look at things as a method of learning about their environment and the things in it.

Infants in the *I See Learning Space* should be in a quiet and alert state. This learning space works best when placed in a part of the room where distraction is minimal.

## Learning Objectives

Mobile infants will:
1. Use their eyes to learn about the world around them.
2. Explore new objects through vision.
3. Develop eye-hand skills through meaningful activity.

## Time Frame

This learning space should be available to mobile infants throughout the year.

### Letter to Parents

*Dear Parents,*

*During the early years of life, young children learn how to use their eyes. Their eyes allow them to understand their surroundings. We have designed an I See Learning Space to help your baby develop his or her sense of vision. This learning space will include pictures of faces, mobiles, black and white designs, and brightly colored toys for your baby to explore.*

*Babies find faces very interesting. Please bring in a recent picture(s) of your baby and his or her family members. Label the back of each picture with the name you would like your baby to use for each family member. You may also write stories or information on the back of the pictures or on a piece of paper. These pictures will be used to make your baby his or her own photo album.*

## Layout of the I See Learning Space

The *I See Learning Space* should be incorporated into a part of the room that has few distractions (such as a corner or a crib area). Consider your lighting options. Combining natural light with lights that may be turned on or off works well within this learning space.

Use unbreakable mirrors of various sizes in the learning space. Adhere large mirrors to the wall so that babies can see their entire bodies. Give older infants unbreakable hand-held mirrors to look at themselves.

## Vocabulary Enrichment

dark
eyes
face
light
look
see
watch

## Teacher- and Parent-Collected Props

beach ball
blankets
brightly colored sheer material or scarves
brightly colored toys
bull's eye and geometric designs (black and white or
        bright color contrasts)
clear contact paper or laminating machine
construction paper
large mirrors
pictures of faces, family members, and infants in the
        group
rattles
shiny wrapping paper
simple picture books
tinsel
yarn or string

**ACTIVITIES**

# My First Family Album

photographs of the infant and family members
inexpensive photo albums or construction paper,
    glue, and clear contact paper

- Ask parents to bring in labeled photos of their child and the child's family members (see Letter to Parents).
- Make a family photo album with these photographs.
- Use a small, inexpensive photo album or plastic bags. Or, make an album by gluing the pictures to construction paper.
- It is best to place only one photo on each page.
- Label each photograph.
- Laminate each page, or cover each page with clear contact paper.
- Turn the pages slowly for the infant and name each family member.
- This family album often becomes the baby's first and favorite book.

# Hanging Objects

objects suitable for hanging from the ceiling
string, yarn, or elastic

- Attach objects such as beach balls, soft books, and stuffed animals from the ceiling of the room with string, yarn, or elastic.
- Suspend objects close enough to the floor so that infants can touch, pull, hit, and shake them.
- Make sure the toys are slightly higher than the infants' heads so that they do not pose a safety hazard. Objects should be securely fastened to the ceiling and checked periodically for safety.
- Remember that things look different when they are overhead instead of on the floor.
- Be creative with your object selection. Some items to consider include:
  - beach balls

- blankets
- brightly colored soft toys
- scarves or sheer fabrics
- tinsel

A hanging beach ball invites the infant to create movement.

# Who's That?

large photographs of each infant in the room
laminate or clear contact paper

- Attach large (approximately 8" x 10") photos of all the infants in your classroom on a wall, placing the photos as close to the floor as possible.
- Leave an inch or so between each photo.
- Label each photograph with the infant's first name.
- Talk to the infant as you identify the babies in the photos.
- Encourage them to "see" the baby and use the baby's name.
- Mobile infants will identify their friends before they recognize themselves.

- Mobile infants may wish to touch or manipulate the photograph as you talk about the baby. Therefore, before putting the photographs on the wall, you may want to laminate or cover them with clear contact paper.

## Rolling Photos

large oatmeal container with lid
contact paper
photographs of each infant in the classroom and
     family members
pictures of people from magazines

- Cover a large oatmeal container, including the lid, with contact paper.
- Using one container for each infant, securely tape photos of the infant, her family members, or magazine pictures of people to the container.
- This activity will encourage older infants to move to get to the pictures as they roll away.

An infant sees pictures of herself and friends as she rolls the tube.

## Colorful Bottle Shakers

several small, clean, plastic drink bottles with lids
clear syrup
food coloring
hot glue gun (adult only)

- Wash and dry several plastic drink bottles. Small bottles work best because they are easy for infants to hold.
- Fill each bottle approximately one-third full with clear syrup.
- Add several drops of food coloring and mix.
- Glue the lids to the bottles using a hot glue gun. **Note:** Use a hot glue gun when the children are not around.
- Mobile infants will love shaking and turning the bottles.
- Other materials can be added to the bottles to create different visual interest, for example, glitter, small colorful balls, tinsel, and so on. **Note:** Periodically check the bottles to be sure that the lids are securely fastened.

**Bubble Recipe**
*2 cups liquid detergent*
*6 cups water*
*¾ cup sugar*

*Mix the ingredients and let sit for 4 hours.*

**Hardy Bubble Recipe**
*1 gallon water*
*1 cup of liquid detergent*
     *(Joy or Dawn works best)*
*¼ cup glycerin (to add*
     *strength)*
*1 teaspoon mineral oil (adds*
     *rainbow color)*

*Mix the ingredients and let sit for one day.*

# Bubbles, Bubbles, Bubbles

bubble mixture (see page 62)
plastic tub
plastic tablecloth or shower curtain
clothes hanger
berry plastic mesh baskets

- Make a bubble mixture (see page 62).
- Pour the mixture into a plastic tub.
- Cover the floor with plastic and place the tub on the floor.
- Interested infants can sit around the tub, watch the bubbles being produced, and touch the bubbles.
- Make a large wand out of a clothes hanger and use it to create enormous bubbles.
- Infants can use berry baskets or plastic containers to create their own bubbles.
- This activity may be slippery, so mobile infants will need careful supervision.

# Peek-a-Boo

several scraps of fabric large enough to cover an infant's head or eyes

- Older infants will enjoy playing peek-a-boo with a friend.
- Using transparent fabric, netting, or other translucent fabric will be very interesting for them because they will still be able to see the other people in the learning space.
- When this activity is used on the changing table, the infant will imitate the teacher's actions.

## ADDING SPARK TO THE I SEE LEARNING SPACE

*Turn off the lights in the room and shine a flashlight on objects in the room. Let the infants help you direct the flashlight at objects of their choosing. Name the objects as you go.*

## The Essential Literacy Connection
**(\* Available as a board book)**

Christian, Cheryl. 1996. *Where's Baby?*. New York: Star Bright. *This lift-the-flap photography book will have infants eager to discover hidden surprises.*\*

Hoban, Tana. 1993. *Black on White*. New York: Greenwillow. *Infants will enjoy the contrast of white and black, as they begin to associate labels with the pictures in this wordless book.*\*

Hoban, Tana. 1996. *Of Colors and Things*. New York: Mulberry. *Color photographs illustrate various items infants may see in their world. The photographs are easier to see than artist drawings.*

Isadora, Rachel. 1985. *I See*. New York: Greenwillow. *This book goes through the day of a child, illustrating what she sees. It includes objects young readers can recognize, name, and repeat.*\*

## Evaluation

1. Is the infant indicating interest in objects by smiling or maintaining visual attention?
2. Is the infant attempting to reach, grasp, and move towards objects?
3. Is the infant demonstrating a preference for certain faces or objects?
4. Does the infant recognize familiar pictures of people and/or objects in the learning space?

# I Touch Learning Space

## Overview

Infants use all their senses to help them learn about and understand their surroundings. From birth, infants use their sense of touch. Most babies show an obvious preference for warm and soft environments; therefore, we swaddle infants in blankets and hold them close to comfort them. As infants become mobile, they use their sense of touch to help them decide whether they want to reach or grasp an object.

Introducing mobile infants to a variety of textures and materials is important to their cognitive and motor development. The *I Touch Learning Space* will give infants in this stage of development the opportunity to learn about and explore their environment.

## Learning Objectives

Mobile infants will:
1. Develop the sense of touch.
2. Explore a variety of textures.
3. Discover preferences for certain textures.
4. Develop fine motor skills through manipulation of textures.

## Time Frame

This learning space should be available to infants throughout the year. Rotate materials to maintain mobile infants' interests.

## Letter to Parents

• • • • • • • • • • • • • • • • • • • •

*Dear Parents,*

*The I Touch Learning Space in our classroom helps infants learn about their world through their sense of touch. It gives our infants experiences with a variety of textures such as soft, firm, fuzzy, bumpy, and smooth. It is amazing to watch infants, as they feel materials such as corduroy, fur, or paper for the first time. The different feel of objects will encourage infants to use their hands to reach, grasp, and manipulate. The I Touch Learning Space will allow our infants to develop the sense of touch, which they will use throughout their lives.*

# Layout of the I Touch Learning Space

Place the *I Touch Learning Space* in a part of the room where children are free to explore the materials. You may want to do some of the activities in a tiled area or outside where cleanup is easier. Textured materials, such as carpet squares, may be attached to walls or floors. You can also hang them from the ceiling with string or elastic, low enough to the floor so they can be touched and pulled. Materials such as cornstarch or oatmeal can be placed in a plastic baby pool or a large cardboard box. If possible, cover the floor, walls, and ceiling with a variety of textures. Make sure that each texture is at least 6" x 6" so that the babies can fully explore the texture. Leave space between each texture and do not overlap them.

## Vocabulary Enrichment

| | |
|---|---|
| cold | hot |
| dry | soft |
| feel | touch |
| hard | wet |

## Teacher- and Parent-Collected Props

carpet squares
clear plastic containers (to store or organize props)
cotton balls
dog toys with texture (make sure they are clean before using)
foil
ice cube trays
large bowls and spoons
plastic baby pool
plastic sheets or shower curtains
ribbon
sandpaper (several different grains)
scrap fabric such as satin, lace, fur, cotton, polyester, taffeta, silk, denim, burlap, spandex, and netting
stuffed animals
wax paper
wrapping paper
yarn

**ACTIVITIES**

# Warm and Cold

table or plastic floor cover
ice cubes
bowls
warm water
washcloths

- Sit infants at a table or on a plastic-covered floor.
- Give each infant an ice cube.
- Encourage the infants to explore the cold feel of the ice on their hands and mouth.
- Watch the ice melt. As the ice cubes melt, they may pose a choking hazard, so closely supervise the activity.
- Talk about the "cold, wet" feeling.
- Give each infant a bowl of warm water and a washcloth.
- Encourage them to experience the difference in how the warm water feels on their hands and faces.
- Talk about the "warm, wet" water.

# Pool Fun

2 sheets
small baby pool
dry oatmeal or cornmeal
cups and funnels

- Place a small baby pool on top of a large sheet on the floor.
- Cover the inside of the pool with a sheet and add a texture. Edible textures such as dry oatmeal or cornmeal are great.
- Remove the infants' clothing. (Leave their shirts on, if desired.)
- First, sit the babies outside the pool.
- If they choose, you may help them sit inside the pool to play and explore.
- Add cups and funnels to the baby pool to encourage new experiences.

Infants sitting in a plastic tub and feeling cornstarch

# Goopy

1 box cornstarch
4 to 5 cups water
plastic bowls
plastic table cover

- Make a mixture of water and cornstarch. Combine until the Goopy is a runny consistency.
- Make the mixture immediately before presenting it to the infants.
- Place plastic bowls with the mixture on a plastic-covered table.
- Demonstrate how the mixture flows and runs when held in the hands.
- Some infants will immediately want to put their hands in the Goopy and others will watch before they are willing to try.
- Respect the temperament of the individual infant and support his beginning participation.
- **Note:** This mixture is non-toxic, but do your best to discourage the children from putting it in their mouths.

# Sticky Wall

large cardboard box

contact paper

items to stick to the wall, such as metal juice tops, plastic lids, cardboard pieces, small plastic disposable cups or glasses, plastic flowers, and so on

- Select a large cardboard box that is the appropriate height for mobile infants.
- Cover the outside of the box with contact paper.
- Securely attach contact paper, sticky side out, to the outside of the box.
- Collect a variety of items for the infant to stick to the wall.

  **Note:** Be sure all items are safe for infants and do not pose a choking hazard.

A mobile infant attaching juice tops to a sticky wall

## ADDING SPARK TO THE I TOUCH LEARNING SPACE

*Collect several pieces of fabric with various textures. Soak the fabric pieces in water and freeze. Soak pieces of the same textured fabric in warm water. Place both the frozen pieces of fabric and warm, wet fabric pieces in a plastic tub. Infants can explore the various textures and feel the temperature differences.*

## The Essential Literacy Connection
(* Available as a board book)

Hills, Tad. 2001. *My Fuzzy Farm Babies: A Book to Touch and Feel.* New York: Little Simon. *This book includes farm animals with durable, large pieces of various textures for children to feel.*

Isadora, Rachel. 1985. *I Touch.* New York: Greenwillow. *This book walks through the day of a child and illustrates what she feels, using objects young readers can recognize, name, and repeat.**

Kunhardt, Dorothy. 1990. *Pat the Bunny.* New York: Golden Books. *Play peek-a-boo, smell the flowers, and pat the bunny with Paul and Judy, in this classic, interactive, touch-and-feel book.**

Oxenbury, Helen. 1987. *Tickle, Tickle.* New York: Little Simon. *This multicultural book with clever illustrations and text tells about children playing in the mud, taking a bath, and getting ready to sleep.**

## Evaluation

1. Is the infant attempting to manipulate materials with her hands?
2. Is the infant improving fine motor coordination as she reaches, grasps, or manipulates materials?
3. Is the infant attempting to move toward materials through rolling, crawling, or walking?

# Housekeeping Learning Space

## Overview

The *Housekeeping Learning Space* is an important component of the infants' area. Some of the first dramatic play occurs in this setting because infants have experience with the home and related props. Mobile infants are beginning to know what happens in housekeeping and are making important connections with materials and people. During this stage of play, the props should be real items that clearly communicate their use. Mobile infants will visit this familiar learning space frequently. Some infants will be able to carry *Housekeeping Learning Space* props to other parts of the room for additional play.

## Learning Objectives

Mobile infants will:

1. Expand listening and expressive vocabulary while participating in play.
2. Dramatize roles and happenings that relate to the family and home.
3. Use props to represent items in the home environment.

## Time Frame

This learning space should be available during the entire year. Periodically, change some of the props to help maintain the children's interest in the learning space and the play that is occurring. This learning space works well with infants at a variety of developmental levels. Each can participate at her own level, while learning from the others in the learning space. Infants will often repeat an action or play sequence they observe, making it their own. After repeating observed behaviors, infants will venture into creating their own play.

## Letter to Parents

Dear Parents,
The Housekeeping Learning Space *is an essential part of your child's classroom. This traditional learning space enables mobile infants to pretend they are mommies, daddies, babies, brothers, or sisters. They begin to dramatize roles that occur in the home: cooking, eating, and cleaning. In the early years of a child's life, play is one of the major ways he or she learns. This familiar home environment, with items they recognize, provides the perfect place to begin this creative process.*

*We are always looking for "new" items to add to the* Housekeeping Learning Space. *Some very popular props in this learning space include hats, baby clothes, fancy dress-up clothes, small rocking chairs, and real pots or pans. If you have any of these items let us know, and we can add them to our* Housekeeping Learning Space.

# Layout of the Housekeeping Learning Space

The *Housekeeping Learning Space* should include a baby bed, stove, refrigerator, and a low table. Hooks or knobs on the wall can serve to display dress-up materials. A small rocking chair and some cleaning items, such as a broom or sweeper, can add realism to the learning space. Real plastic dishes, pots, and pans are also appropriate for this age.

## Vocabulary Enrichment

babies
cleanup
cook
dinner
dress up
family
kitchen
refrigerator
stove
telephone
vacuum cleaner

## Teacher- and Parent-Collected Props

full-length unbreakable mirror (essential)
baby bed or cradle
variety of empty food containers (such as milk, cereal, cookies, crackers, and other items that mobile infants have experienced)
dress-up clothes that are easy to put on and take off (include both male and female items)
hats
home appliances (these can be made from cardboard boxes)
items that children may be familiar with and have seen at home
play stove, refrigerator, and sink
small table with chairs
telephone (table style and cordless)

**ACTIVITIES**

## Fabric for Creations

large scraps or remnants of fabric
camera

- Encourage the children to use the fabric pieces creatively to drape, wrap, and tie the fabric around them.
- Help mobile infants see their creations in the mirror and share them with others.
- Take pictures of the infants in their creations and display the photos.

## Phone Book

pictures of children, teachers, aides, custodians, and
    directors
notebook
pen or marker

A telephone inspires a mobile infant in the Housekeeping Learning Space.

- Make a "phone book" filled with pictures of the mobile infants.
- The infants can use the picture phone books when they are playing with the phone.

## Seasonal Clothes Collection: Winter

clothing items that are worn in cold weather, such as
    caps, gloves, scarves, heavy coats, earmuffs,
    vests, sweaters, or boots

- Add these clothing items to the learning space when the weather becomes cool.

## Tools

variety of combs and brushes
spoons

- Give the infants a variety of combs and brushes.
- Add spoons to the learning space to encourage new self-feeding skills.
- Mobile infants are beginning to imitate simple behaviors, such as brushing their hair and using the spoon.
- Help them brush the hair of stuffed animals and dolls.

Problem solving: Which broom should I use to clean up?

## Cleanup

items that could be used by mobile infants to clean a
house, such as a push floor cleaner, dust mop,
broom, dustpan, dust cloths, bucket, mop,
sponges, and empty spray bottles

• Mobile infants enjoy cleaning up the room.
• These props encourage participation and imitation
of actions.

## Multicultural Play

multicultural baby dolls
clothing from cultures of children in the classroom
empty packages of different foods

• Add these materials to the learning space to
provide the opportunity for multicultural play.

## ADDING SPARK TO THE HOUSEKEEPING LEARNING SPACE

*Place a collection of different
types, sizes, and textures of
sponges in a bucket. A spray
bottle with a small amount of
clear water will also add interest.
The sponges and water will inspire
related play in the Housekeeping
Learning Space.*

## The Essential Literacy Connection
### (* Available as a board book)

Buck, Nola. 1998. *How a Baby Grows*. New York:
HarperCollins. *Easily recognizable illustrations help
infants begin to identify the objects in their world.* *

Oxenbury, Helen. 1981. *Dressing*. New York: Simon
and Schuster. *This simple, one-word picture book
guides mobile infants through the steps of dressing.* *

Tuxworth, Nicola. 1997. *Let's Look at My Home*.
New York: Lorenz. *Labeled photographs of items
around the home categorized by the areas around
the house.*

## Other Printed Materials

phone books
magazines
newspapers
cookbooks

## Evaluation

1. Is the infant using props to pretend in play?
2. Is the infant using words or gestures in the
*Housekeeping Learning Space?*
3. Is the infant returning to the *Housekeeping
Learning Space* frequently?
4. Is the infant interacting with other infants or
teachers in the *Housekeeping Learning Space?*

# Book Learning Space

## Overview

From the beginning of life, infants should be exposed to the world of books, print, and literature. Positive early experiences can build a foundation for interest in books and enjoyment of the printed word. The goal of this learning space is to make appropriate materials easily accessible so the teacher and infant can use these items during the daily routine. Mobile infants will be able to select, touch, and manipulate the interesting literacy materials grouped in this space. They will demonstrate their enjoyment of particular books and stories as they revisit favorites in this learning space.

## Learning Objectives

Mobile infants will:

1. Hold and manipulate books, including those they can recognize.
2. Anticipate the sharing of a book and a positive interaction with the teacher.
3. Develop listening skills by participating in familiar stories and fingerplays.

## Time Frame

This learning space should be set up for the entire year. Change the books and materials throughout the year, but favorite books should remain to be revisited. New items will capture the focus of mobile infants, and familiar materials will inspire their participation. Observe each infant's interest in specific books and select these to remain in the *Book Learning Space*. Rereading books and hearing repeated phrases leads to recognition of the sounds of language and the desire to echo these patterns as language develops.

## Letter to Parents

• • • • • • • • • • • • • • • • • • • • • • • • • • • • • •

*Dear Parents,*

*Infants are interested in language and the sounds of literature. They enjoy being read to and experiencing the interaction with a responsive reader. We know how important the first year of life is for beginning a positive experience with books and literature. Our Book Learning Space contains materials that are appropriate for your child, and we will be reading stories, poems, and rhymes to him or her. In this space, he or she will be able to hold and turn the pages of a personal book that includes pictures of people and items that are important to him or her.*

*The Book Learning Space contains many board books. Infants who use their senses to learn about everything can explore these tough and "mouthable" books. We also have collections of nursery rhymes, poems, and other literature that infants enjoy hearing. This variety of materials is selected to nurture an interest in language and books.*

*It is important for you to read and talk with your mobile infant during this first year. Remember, your infant is storing this information in his or her amazing brain and making language connections that will last a lifetime.*

# Layout of the Book Learning Space

The *Book Learning Space* should have a low and stable storage bookcase. Arrange books with the cover facing out so they are visible to infants. Include a soft rug on the floor with large, soft pillows for sitting comfortably. Soft toys and blankets can add softness to an inviting book learning space. This coziness adds to the pleasure of literacy experiences. Display pictures or illustrations on the floor and/or low on the wall. This makes them visible for the sitting or crawling infant. It is helpful to laminate pictures or place them behind a Plexiglas frame (see page 311 for directions). Photos of mobile infants "reading" a book independently or with a teacher will add personal interest to the *Book Learning Space*.

## Vocabulary Enrichment

books
enjoy
favorite
listen
pictures
poem
rhyme
story

## Teacher- and Parent-Collected Props

board books
foam pillows covered with a variety of textures and washable materials
old stuffed toys and blankets that can be washed and sterilized
rocking chair or low soft chair
washable rugs for floor area

**ACTIVITIES**

## Rhymes for Reading

collection of rhymes with interesting patterns of
words and phrases, such as:

### To Market, To Market
*To market, to market, to buy a fat pig.*
*Home again, home again, jiggity jig.*
*To market, to market, to buy a fat hog.*
*Home again, home again, jiggity jog.*

### Hush Little Baby
*Hush little baby, don't say a word.*
*Papa's gonna buy you a mockingbird.*
*If that mockingbird won't sing,*
*Papa's gonna buy you a diamond ring.*

- During the week, repeat the same rhyme for
  infants to enjoy.
- Observe if the infants are interested in the rhyme
  and seem to enjoy the pattern of the language.
- Note a specific rhyme or poem that intrigues an
  infant. Over the next month or so, continue to
  use the poem that captures the infant's interest as
  others are introduced.

## Pointing and Identifying

book with pictures or photographs
of familiar items

- Books with pictures that are
  uncluttered and clearly visible
  work best for this activity.
- Ask the infant to point to or
  touch the picture of a familiar
  item. For example, "Show me
  the ball," or "Touch the ball."
- This labeling and/or indicating
  of familiar items is an early step
  in literacy development.

## Personal Book

photographs of parents, grandparents, teacher,
relative, dog, and so on
zipper-closure plastic bags
glue
cardboard
stapler
tape

- Make a personal book for each infant using
  pictures of important people, pets, and items that
  the infant has experienced.
- Glue each picture on a separate piece of
  cardboard and place it in a plastic bag. Close it
  securely with staples or glue. Cover this edge
  with tape.
- Staple together several pages to form the pages of
  a book.
- This personal book is a wonderful introduction to
  books, because it contains recognizable items and
  things that are important to the infant. Infants will
  examine this book repeatedly. Later, they will
  share their book with others.

A big board book is appealing to two mobile infants.

# A Big Book with Doors

large piece of heavy cardboard
magazines or old catalogues
scissors (adult only)
glue or tape

- Use a large piece of heavy cardboard to create a wall-mounted big book for the infants.
- Cut out pictures from magazines or old catalogues of people and things the infant has experienced.
- Cut doors that a mobile infant can open in the piece of cardboard. Behind each door, glue or tape a picture that the infant can identify.
- Refer to the board as a "big book."
- Demonstrate how the door opens and "presto," a picture appears.
- Encourage infants to open other doors to see what is behind them.
- Follow the infants' lead and let them choose the doors they want to open. They may open a few or several—let them decide.
- Keep the big book in the *Book Learning Space* as long as the infants are interested in the process. Remove the book when they are no longer interested.
- Reintroduce this big book later with different pictures behind the doors.

### ADDING SPARK TO THE BOOK LEARNING SPACE

*Include a book that has a soft animal or fuzzy character to support the story. Examples include* Pat the Bunny *by* Dorothy Kunhardt, Animal Kisses *by* Barney Saltzberg, Night-Night, Baby *by Elizabeth Hathon, and others. Talk about the prop and then identify it in the book's text and illustrations.*

A big "book" with doors invites an infant to open and look inside.

## The Essential Literacy Connection
**(\* Available as a board book)**

Brown, Margaret Wise. 1991. *Goodnight Moon*. New York: HarperCollins. *Alternating black and white and color pictures illustrate the little bunny's goodnight wishes.*\*

Carle, Eric. 1996. *Brown Bear, Brown Bear, What Do You See?* New York: Henry Holt. *Children meet a new creature on each page, as they enjoy this repetitive, predictable picture book.*\*

dePaolo, Tomie. 1997. *Tomie's Little Mother Goose*. New York: G. P. Putnam's Son. *Classic nursery rhymes with dePaolo's colorful illustrations.*

Wright, Blanche Fisher. 1998. *The Real Mother Goose*. New York: Scholastic. *Bright colors and simple illustrations introduce infants to many classic nursery rhymes.*\*

## Evaluation

1. Is the infant focusing on sounds of the language of books or poems?
2. Is the infant demonstrating anticipation of the reading of a book? For example, does she increase body motions and/or make sounds when she sees the book being selected?
3. Can you identify a favorite book or poem for each infant? Is this information recorded for future reference?

# Construction Learning Space

## Overview

Mobile infants are learning about how objects look, feel, and work. They are exploring individual items and beginning to combine them with other objects. Providing opportunities for infants to manipulate, combine, and build with objects enriches their understanding of objects and provides experiences to develop motor abilities.

## Learning Objectives

Mobile infants will:

1. See and touch a variety of building materials selected for use.
2. Combine several materials to learn the properties of each object separately and together.
3. Learn vocabulary labels for construction materials in the *Construction Learning Space*.

## Time Frame

This learning space can be set up in the classroom throughout the year. It can be removed when infants lose interest in this type of play and reintroduced when interest and/or manipulative skills are more developed.

## Letter to Parents

• • • • • • • • • • • • • • • • • • • • • • • • • • • • •

*Dear Parents,*

*Next week, we are introducing a new learning space and collection of building materials. For many years, experts in early childhood education have supported the value of blocks and building materials for young children. Blocks are viewed as an essential element in preschool programs because of the important learning that occurs when children use these materials. Mobile infants can also learn from this type of learning space, when adapted to their special needs and developmental level.*

*You will notice that our Construction Learning Space contains soft blocks, small cardboard boxes, and other materials that can be manipulated by mobile infants. These beginning experiences provide opportunities for infants to build and discover how materials can be combined. This is one of the first steps in developing symbolic understanding and learning language related to building activities. You will see that some of the materials are also in the outdoor area to provide additional opportunities for your infant to explore.*

# Layout of the Construction Learning Space

This is a noisy learning space where lots of activity occurs. It should be placed where it does not disturb the quiet areas of the classroom. Storage of blocks and building materials should be designed so mobile infants can see what is available. Smooth area rugs absorb some sound and provide a level surface for mobile infants to use for construction.

## Vocabulary Enrichment

blocks
box
build
fall
feel
stack
tower

## Teacher- and Parent-Collected Props

brown grocery bags
items for building, such as coffee cans, juice containers, plastic cups, plastic containers, paper rolls, egg cartons, milk cartons, plastic mixing bowls, metal tins, shoeboxes, individual pizza boxes, empty tin cans (with top edge taped), wood scraps, phone books, gift boxes, and plastic plumbing pieces
old newspapers (for stuffing)
small- and medium-size cardboard boxes

**ACTIVITIES**

# Making Box Blocks

variety of sizes of cardboard boxes
tape
contact paper or fabric

- Collect a variety of cardboard boxes in sizes that can be manipulated by a mobile infant. Tape openings closed with tape.
- Cover the boxes with contact paper, fabric, or keep them natural. (Infants can watch the construction of the blocks and/or participate in the process.)
- Place the blocks on the floor for infants to explore and manipulate.
- If necessary, demonstrate how blocks can be stacked or rearranged. When an infant is interested, she can copy this stacking or try another way of arranging the blocks.

# Throw-Away Plastic Containers

various sizes and shapes of
    transparent plastic containers with lids
glue
assortment of objects to place
    inside containers

- Make a collection of plastic containers that mobile infants can explore and combine.
- Put an object inside some of the containers to interest the infants as they move, stack, and combine the building materials.
- Securely glue the lids to the containers so that they can be stacked in different ways.

# Scrap Wood

wood blocks in sizes ranging from 1 ½" to 6"
**Note:** sometimes wood can be obtained free from
    carpenters or home building stores
sandpaper

- If necessary, sand the edges of these blocks before placing them in the *Construction Learning Space*. Be sure to include unusual shapes and sizes, since these novel items will capture the infants' interest. Unique blocks add interest to building.

# Raised Platform

wooden pallet (from a home supply store or one
    used in an industrial setting)
plywood and/or linoleum
construction glue

- A platform that is about 6" off the floor provides a special building place for the mobile infant.
- Use glue to cover the top and two sides of this simple platform with plywood and/or linoleum to produce a smooth building surface.
- Mobile infants will be able to reach, stack, and combine building materials on the platform.

A collection of plastic cups can be used for construction.

# Textured Blocks

scrap foam
a variety of textured materials

- Use pieces of scrap foam to create texture blocks.
- If desired, cover the foam with uniquely textured materials, such as vinyl, coarse upholstering fabric, washable fuzzy material, or felt.
- Textured blocks will connect with the mobile infant's sensory capacity.

# Individual-Size Cereal Boxes

8 to 10 individual-size cereal boxes
materials to cover boxes, such as wrapping paper and tape, contact paper, spray paint, and so on

An infant stacks cardboard boxes.

- Cover the individual-size cereal boxes or leave them natural. You can wrap them in gift paper, cover them with contact paper, spray paint them, and so on.
- Place a collection of cereal boxes in a low

container that allows the mobile infants to select the ones they will use, take them out of the container, and return them when finished.
- These small boxes are a great size for little hands.

# Book of Construction

photographs of infants with blocks and/or things they have used in building
materials to make a scrapbook

- Take pictures of infants participating in the *Construction Learning Space.*
- Label these with the infants' names and dates.
- Display the scrapbook, "Our Construction Learning Space," so it can be used to inspire additional building.

**ADDING SPARK TO THE CONSTRUCTION LEARNING SPACE**

*A medium-size box can be covered with mirror-finish contact paper. This new block will look different, and infants can combine it with other building materials in a unique way. It can also be used as a reflective surface for building.*

## The Essential Literacy Connection
**(* Available as a board book)**

Barton, Byron. 1997. *Machines at Work*. New York: HarperCollins. *The machines that demolish and rebuild at the construction site illustrated in this book will inspire infants.**

Hoban, Tana. 1992. *Dig, Drill, Dump, Fill*. New York: Mulberry. *This wordless picture book allows infants to imagine what each machine is doing and to create their own stories.**

Imershein, Betsy. 2000. *Trucks*. New York: Little Simon. *A colorful picture book of construction equipment including a bulldozer and concrete mixer.**

## Evaluation

1. Have you observed the mobile infant touching and combining building materials?
2. Does the mobile infant enjoy building with the materials?
3. Does the mobile infant use gestures and/or language while building in the *Construction Learning Space?*

# Art Learning Space

## Overview
The arts are an important part of the "whole" development of mobile infants. The *Art Learning Space* introduces materials that are a part of this creative process. In the *Art Learning Space*, mobile infants can observe, enjoy, and participate in artistic activities that are developmentally appropriate. This introduction to art will encourage their interest in color, design, and composition.

## Learning Objectives
Mobile infants will:
1. Observe beautiful designs and colors presented in photos, paintings, or posters.
2. Experiment with art materials that are interesting and appropriate.
3. Develop language that relates to art and the creative process.

## Time Frame
This learning space should be available during the year with materials added or removed to maintain interest and encourage continued use.

## Letter to Parents

● ● ● ● ● ● ● ● ● ● ● ● ● ● ● ● ● ●

*Dear Parents,*
*Did you know that babies enjoy art? In the infant area, we are including an Art Learning Space that is appropriate for the mobile infant. Art is very important when we think of the total development of the child. Our Art Learning Space allows the infant to experiment with media such as paint, paper, and clay. Of course, all items included are non-toxic and safe for infants to taste. Although these art materials are safe, they do not taste great—so one try is usually all that is needed.*

*We are taking photographs of the infants while they are painting, so you can see your artist at work. These early masterpieces are only the beginning of the many art experiences they will have this year. We will share these with you as they are created, and we will display many of them on the documentation panels in our classroom.*

## Layout of the Art Learning Space

MURAL COMPLETED 7/17/02

Materials for the *Art Learning Space* should be easily accessible for the teacher to use throughout the day and year. A low surface to work on should be included in this learning space. Display art materials and tools so the mobile infant can see the choices and possibilities. Cover prints of artwork with laminate or clear contact paper and display them at a low level, so mobile infants can enjoy the colors and designs.

## Vocabulary Enrichment

beautiful
brush
clay
colors: red, blue, green, black, and white
painting
paper
picture

## Teacher- and Parent-Collected Props

big brushes
big pieces of scrap linoleum
edible clay
foam soap
large sheets of manila and colored paper
newspapers
non-toxic paints
paint rollers
posters of art
roll of clear plastic to cover floor
roll of white paper
sponges
tape: masking, electrical, duct, and so on
washable fingerpaint (thicker consistency)

## ACTIVITIES

**Special Note:** Remember that using language to accompany activities is a wonderful way for infants to make connections between what they are doing and words. "Maria is using red paint. Jerome is feeling the clay."

Fingerpaints encourage an infant to mix colors.

## Finger/Hand Painting

large mat
butcher or construction paper
tape
several colors of washable fingerpaint

- Cover a large mat with butcher or construction paper.
- Tape the paper securely to the mat, so the infants can sit on the paper.
- Place interested infants on the paper.
- Place spoonfuls of washable fingerpaint on the paper within the reach of mobile infants.
- Infants will feel the paint and rub it on their hands.
- After this experimentation and some modeling by you, mobile infants will spread the paint across the paper using their hands.
- Observe their interest and participation. When interest sags, add a spoonful of another color of paint.

  **Variation:** Cover the mat with foil or an old sheet. Different canvases will make the painting respond in unique ways.

## Foaming Bath Soap

soap foam
clear plastic

Painting with foam on bubble wrap is an exciting experience for an infant.

- Bath soap for babies is available in foam. This soap foam may be colored and scented.
- Cover a low table or riser with clear plastic.
- Squirt the foam on the table for the infant to touch, mash, and push around.
- Allow time for exploration because this is the major focus of infants using this medium. Don't rush the process.
- Only add more foam when the baby indicates that he has used up the current amount or wants more.
- If soap foam gets in the infant's eyes, rinse with clear water.

## Salt Clay

1 cup all-purpose flour (not self-rising)
½ cup of salt
1 teaspoon powdered alum
⅓ to ½ cup of water
water
bowl and mixing spoon
food coloring

- Combine flour, salt, and alum in a bowl. Add a little water at a time and stir until it is the consistency of pie dough. Knead until dough is thoroughly mixed.
  **Note:** This clay has an interesting texture that infants will enjoy. It will also dry well if you want to keep their creation. If the clay is to be reused, store in an airtight container.
- Start with white clay and provide lots of time for experimentation. Later, add food coloring to provide new interest in the clay.

## Printing with Familiar Items

familiar items/tools with interesting designs that produce a unique print such as sponges, potato masher, small cars with wheels, flowers, combs, paper cups, and so on
plastic storage dish

tempera paint
1 tablespoon dry laundry detergent
low baking dish or aluminum pan
butcher paper or white paper

- Group a number of familiar items together in a plastic storage dish. Select tools that have an interesting design and produce a unique print.
- Make a thick tempera paint mixture and add a tablespoon of dry laundry detergent (to make the paint washable).
- Place the paint in a low baking dish or aluminum pan.
- Cover an entire low table with butcher or white paper.
- Encourage the mobile infants to select the tool to use for their print.
- They can dip the tool in the paint and make a print on the paper.
- This paper print can be used for several days. Each day the infant can add tools and colors to enrich the growing art project.

## Crumpling Paper

colorful magazines
scissors (adult only)
cardboard or poster board
white glue

- Cut out pages from the magazine and place them in the *Art Learning Space*.
- Cut a large piece of cardboard or poster board to the size that will work for a group picture.
- Place the cardboard on the floor for the infants to use as the base for their crumpled picture.
- Encourage the infants to select magazine pages from the stack to crumple. They will enjoy the crunching sounds and the feel.
- After they have explored the properties of the paper, let the mobile infants dip the paper into white glue and attach it to the cardboard base.

# Bumpy Paint

bubble wrap
tape
tempera paint
large brushes

- Tape bubble wrap to a low table.
- Mix tempera paint until it has a thick consistency.
- The infants paint the bubble wrap with large brushes.
  **Note:** Painting on the bubble paper makes their work have greater dimension. In addition, the color will have interesting properties when painted on the plastic. Varying the surface used for painting can produce interesting results and enrich the creative process.

## ADDING SPARK TO THE ART LEARNING SPACE

*House-painting brushes and rollers are easy for older mobile infants to manipulate. The infants enjoy the action of moving the brush and using water. Go outdoors and find a wall that can be "painted." Take several buckets to hold the water used during painting. Help older infants dip the brushes and rollers into the water and then "paint" the wall. Later, bring the brushes and rollers back into the Art Learning Space so they can be used with paint on large sheets of paper.*

## The Essential Literacy Connection
### (* Available as a board book)

Eho, Jerome. 2002. *Colors*. Hauppauge, NY: Barron's Educational Series. *This sturdy book, held together with a rattle, illustrates pictures in both primary and secondary colors.\**

Hubbell, Patricia. 1998. *Wrapping Paper Romp*. New York: HarperCollins. *This delightful poem allows infants to watch a young child crumple through the papers and ribbons that came with her present. (Board book is available.)*

Shaw, Charles. 1993. *It Looked Like Spilt Milk*. New York: HarperCollins. *White shapes on a blue background will spark the infant's imagination on each page. \**

Walsh, Ellen Stoll. 1989. *Mouse Paint*. San Diego: Harcourt Brace. *Three white mice discover what happens when primary colors are mixed.\**

## Evaluation

1. Is the infant experimenting with art materials?
2. Is the infant using the paint and/or clay?
3. Is the infant showing an interest in a specific material?

# I Hear Music Learning Space

## Overview

From the first day of life, infants are stimulated by the sounds of music. Mobile infants will attend to musical sounds and move in response to the rhythm. This early interest in music provides an avenue for experiencing the world in a very special way. This music learning space focuses on introducing sounds, rhythms, and musical instruments in an appropriate way to infants. The collection of materials in the designated learning space allows the musical environment to respond to mobile infants' special interests and individual paces. Infants can move to the learning space and choose items that capture their interest. They can interact with materials and then move on when they tire of the musical item. The observant teacher can determine the developing musical interest of mobile infants and adjust the environment to meet these needs.

## Learning Objectives

Mobile infants will:
1. Develop their sense of hearing.
2. Experience a variety of types of music, instruments, and voices.
3. Become familiar with classic children's songs and fingerplays.
4. Recognize familiar songs and enjoy their repetition.

## Time Frame

This is a very interesting learning space for infants, as their auditory abilities and musical intelligence are developing. Because of space restrictions in most infant spaces, this learning space can be portable and move in and out of the classroom on a regular basis. The *I Hear Music Learning Space* provides opportunities for grouping the materials, instruments, and recordings so that they are easily accessible and used frequently. It is important that infants are exposed to a variety of music including lullabies, classical music, singers, bands, children's recordings, and music from different cultures.

## Letter to Parents

Dear Parents,

*In recent years, there have been a number of articles in newspapers and magazines that stress the importance of using music during the early years of children's development. Some experts have found that music encourages intellectual development and makes important connections in the developing brain. Others say that music should be enjoyed for its own sake and for the beauty that it can bring to children's lives. For all of these reasons, we are including music in our infant room.*

*Throughout the year, you will notice a music learning space in the infant space. This I Hear Music Learning Space will provide your infant with many musical experiences. Here, they can listen, move, and participate with music. We will include a variety of recordings, musical instruments, and other items that produce musical sounds. If you have recordings or CDs that your family enjoys, we would like you to share them with us. These special musical recordings will be enjoyed by all of us in the I Hear Music Learning Space. We would also like to invite you to come sing, play, or participate in our music program.*

*Sing with your infant whenever you can. It doesn't matter to your baby whether you can carry a tune or not. Your baby will enjoy this very special experience, and it will strengthen the bond between you and your baby.*

## Layout of the I Hear Music Learning Space

Choose a quiet area of the classroom to display and use musical materials. It is helpful to have soft materials in the learning space to absorb sound and contain the music in the space. Fabric, pillows, or a covered twin mattress will help with sound absorption. Use plastic storage tubs to collect and store the musical instruments and sound-makers. Put a boom box that produces high-quality sound in this space, as well as a collection of tapes and CDs in a storage unit.

## Vocabulary Enrichment

| | |
|---|---|
| bells | shakers |
| boom box | singer |
| drum | song |
| music | sounds |
| musician | tambourine |
| recordings | tape player |
| rhythm | |

## Teacher- and Parent-Collected Props

recordings and CDs including a variety of music, such as classical, pop, country, bluegrass, rock, rhythm and blues, Latin American, and jazz (many good recordings can be purchased inexpensively from used record stores)

simple rhythm instruments, such as drums, bells on elastic, rhythm sticks, or shakers

soft couch or chair

toys that produce musical sounds, such as balls that chime

washable rugs and pillows

# Listening to Music

tape or CD player
a variety of musical recordings, such as lullabies, jazz,
    children's recordings, folk, and so on

- Each day share a musical recording in the learning
  space. Vary the kind of music that you play.
- Expose the infants to different types of music, so
  they can experience the wide range of
  opportunities for listening enjoyment.
- Many infants will begin to demonstrate their
  musical preferences by increased movement,
  laughing, or making sounds.

# Music for the Time of Day

boom box
a variety of "mood" music

- At different times during the day, use the boom
  box to play music to support the mood or activity
  occurring. This helps infants connect this as the
  place where music is made.
- For example, during rest time select quiet and
  relaxing music, such as harp music or soft singing.
  During a busy time, select upbeat and spirited
  music such as a march by John Phillip Sousa.
- This matching of mood and activity helps the
  infant begin to connect the music to their life
  experiences.

# Toys That Make Music

toys that produce sounds such as a ball with a bell
    inside, a pull- or push-toy that makes a musical
    sound, xylophone, or a jack-in-the-box

- Include the toys in the *I Hear Music Learning
  Space.*
- Sometimes you will need to demonstrate the
  action required to set the sound into motion.
- Involve the infant in activating the toy and
  comment on the musical sound that is being
  produced.
- Infants will repeat the action needed to produce
  musical sounds many times.

# Clothesline Music

heavy yarn or clothesline
string or fishing line
several items that produce sounds, such as metal
    lids, pie pans, measuring spoons, empty tin cans,
    metal pipes, clay flowerpots, and so on

- Run a heavy piece of yarn or a clothesline
  between two points in the classroom.
- Make sure the line is low enough for mobile
  infants to hit the items attached to the line.
- Use string or yarn to hang items that produce
  sounds on the line.
- Mobile infants can move to the learning space and
  hit the items they choose. They can produce
  different sounds and discover patterns of rhythm.

## Musical Chants

a variety of chants

- Chants that are not sung, but simply spoken in a rhythm, are very interesting to the infant who is beginning to talk.
- They enjoy listening to and echoing the repetitive phrases. For example:

> *Peas porridge hot,*
> *Peas porridge cold,*
> *Peas porridge in the pot,*
> *nine days old.*

Several infants enjoying music as they participate with their teacher

## Musical Name

drum

- Use a drum to tap out the name of the infants in the *I Hear Music Learning Space*.
- The pattern corresponds to the syllables in the name. For example: Beverly—clap, clap, clap.
- Say the infant's name and clap the rhythm. (Encourage the infants to join in the clapping.)

## Sound Makers

Playing a drum together in the I Hear Music Learning Space

pie pans, containers, and so on
variety of sound-makers, such as large wooden
     beads or plastic blocks
sheet or blanket

- Place mobile infants on a sheet or blanket.
- Give each infant a pie pan they can fill with items to produce sounds.

- Demonstrate filling and shaking the pans.
- Some objects may fall out of the tin onto the sheet. Infants may enjoy placing the objects back into the tin because it makes a sound.
- Vary the materials that are used to make the sound makers.

# Sounds Outside

blank cassette tape
tape recorder

- Make a recording of sounds an infant might hear outside. Examples of outdoor sounds include a car, train, car horn, dog, cat, wind chimes, door slamming, ambulance, construction sounds, or truck.
- Leave a few seconds of blank tape between each sound.
- Play the tape for the infants and identify the sounds as you hear them.
- Ask the infants, "Do you hear the dog barking?"
- This will encourage auditory discrimination, as the infant listens to environmental sounds.

**ADDING SPARK TO THE I HEAR MUSIC LEARNING SPACE**

*Bring a guitar or ukulele into the I Hear Music Learning Space. Pluck the strings or strum a chord. This new kind of sound will be intriguing. High pitches are especially interesting to infants; they often attend to this sound. Allow mobile infants to strum, pluck, and enjoy the sounds of a stringed instrument.*

## The Essential Literacy Connection
(**\* Available as a board book**)

Brown, Marc. 1999. *Favorite Hand Rhymes.* New York: Dutton. *A beautifully illustrated collection of rhymes and fingerplays.*\*

Manning, Jane. 1998. *My First Songs.* New York: HarperCollins. *An illustrated book of favorite children's songs including many classics and the traditional words.*

Rosen, Michael. 2002. *Going on a Bear Hunt.* Illustrations by Helen Oxenbury. Cambridge: Candlewick. *A lively tale of a family's outdoor adventures through various landscapes.*\*

Trapani, Iza. 1998. *The Itsy, Bitsy Spider.* Watertown, MA: Charlesbridge. *Six illustrated verses of this favorite song. Infants enjoy the fingerplay that can be used in conjunction with this book.*\*

## Other Printed Materials
pictures of bands, orchestra, dancers, and singers

## Evaluation
1. Does the infant move to the different musical rhythms?
2. Can the infant activate musical toys and/or make music with simple instruments?
3. Does the infant enjoy listening to the music?

# Water Learning Space

## Overview

Water mesmerizes young children. Natural materials, such as water, encourage mobile infants to explore and experiment as they learn about their world. As mobile infants interact with water, they develop their coordination and find approaches for using tools. The responsiveness of water encourages them to experience and understand cause and effect. Because water is such a high-interest substance, the *Water Learning Space* also has the potential to build their attention span, while involving them in meaningful activities.

## Learning Objectives

Mobile infants will:
1. Learn about a natural element in their environment.
2. Develop fine motor coordination as they manipulate the material and tools.
3. Experiment with a material that is responsive to their actions (cause and effect).
4. Use problem-solving skills as they determine ways to move and pour water.

## Time Frame

This learning space focuses on water, but other materials could be substituted in the learning space at a later time (for example, snow or soapy water). Because of the versatility of the *Water Learning Space*, it is possible to use it and the tools at many times during the year. By changing the natural material, play and learning are expanded. Use of the *Water Learning Space* can also be extended.

## Letter to Parents

Dear Parents,
Many infants are curious about the water in their environment. They are interested in a puddle of water after the rain, the water fountain, and the dog's bowl of water. We are adding a Water Learning Space that will build on this interest. In the learning space, they will pour, measure, and experiment with the properties of water. They will use different tools such as cups, funnels, and tubes as they develop their fine motor coordination. It is amazing how long young children will concentrate on using water in their play.

The Water Learning Space provides interesting materials that encourage your child to learn and experiment. It is a great learning space because it combines enjoyment and learning. If you have any interesting items that could be used in water play, bring them in and watch as the children explore them.

# Layout of the Water Learning Space

Group the *Water Learning Space* around a low table with two plastic tubs containing water. Cover the floor and table with plastic. This learning space may become slippery, so close supervision is needed. Place the containers of tools for the *Water Learning Space* so the children can select what they would like to use and return the items when they finish experimenting.

## Vocabulary Enrichment

dump

fill

pour

tools: cup, funnel, spoon, and bucket

water

## Teacher- and Parent-Collected Props

clear, plastic storage containers (to store and organize tools)

funnels

kitchen tools, such as large spoons (with and without draining holes), manual eggbeater, large plastic saltshakers, strainers, and so on

large plastic turkey-basting syringe

plastic bottles (in a variety of sizes), cups, eggs, tubing, and tubs

plastic sheeting or shower curtain liners (to place under the tubs and on the floor)

small buckets

rubber animals

sponges

**ACTIVITIES**

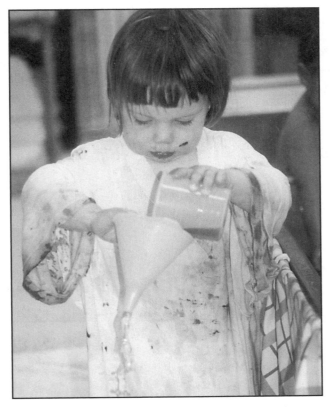

Eye-hand coordination is necessary to pour water into a funnel.

# Experimenting and Playing

variety of tools, such as cups, large spoons, and
    plastic bottles
container of water

- When the *Water Learning Space* is first introduced,
  the focus should be on the children playing and
  experimenting with the water. Very few tools are
  needed for this exploration—just a few cups of
  various sizes for pouring, large spoons for dipping,
  and plastic soda bottles. The focus is on
  understanding water and how it moves.
- Don't rush the experimentation. Infants need time
  to use the water in many different ways.
- When interest wanes, add a container that
  includes some new tools.
- Let the infant select the next item to be used in
  the water play.

# Building a Float

materials that will float, such as Styrofoam trays or
    pieces, wood scraps, sponges, corks, leaves,
    small balls, and so on
storage container
container of water

- Collect materials that can be used to construct
  something that will float.
- Place the items in a container near the water.
- Demonstrate how the materials float.
- The infants can determine when they want to add
  other floating things.

# Soapy Water

mild liquid dish detergent or baby shampoo
container of water
several washable items, such as plastic dishes, doll
    clothes, baby dolls, and eating utensils

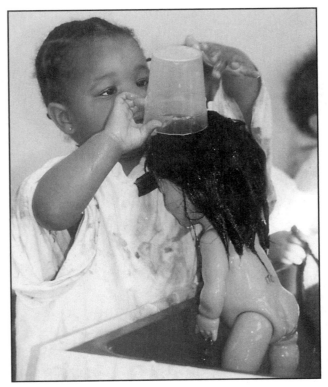

Washing a baby doll with water

- Add mild liquid dish detergent or baby shampoo to one of the water containers.
- Encourage experimentation to determine the "new" properties of the water. How does it feel? How does it pour? How does it smell?
- Pose questions and provide sufficient time for the infants to experiment.
- When interest in experimentation wanes, add items that can be washed in soapy water.
- Provide a place to dry washed items.
- If a mobile infant gets soap in her eyes, rinse them with clear water.

## Dropping and Splashing

storage container
several waterproof/washable items, such as a small tree branch, several sizes of rocks, comb or brush, eating utensils, and other interesting items
container of water

- Mobile infants are curious about what happens when things are dropped in the water.
- The *Water Learning Space* is the perfect place for mobile infants to experiment.
- Fill a plastic container with items that the children can use to determine, "What happens when this is dropped into water?"

## Ice Water

various containers, such as ice cube trays, small plastic containers, plastic glasses and cups, plastic flower pots, plastic drink bottles, and so on
water table
food coloring

- Freeze water in different sizes and shapes of containers.
- Place the ice shapes into the empty water table.
- Children can experience the cold feel and discover how the items thaw.

- To change the visual appearance of the ice and add new interest, fill some of the containers with colored water.

### ADDING SPARK TO THE WATER LEARNING SPACE

*What happens when water is a different color? Add blue food coloring to change the visual appearance of the water. The infants can experiment to determine if the blue water responds to their actions in the same manner as clear water.*

## The Essential Literacy Connection
(* Available as a board book)

Jonas, Ann. 1997. *Splash!* New York: Greenwillow. *A young girl and a variety of different animals play and splash around a pond.*

Miller, Dorothy. 1997. *Water Play.* New York: Simon & Schuster. *This book shows children different doing a variety of activities with water.**

Smee, Nicola. 2002. *Splash! Splash!* Hauppauge, NY: Barron's Educational Series. *This book has fun pictures, a rhyming text, and ends with a touch-and-feel page.**

## Evaluation

1. Is the mobile infant interested in experimenting with the water?
2. Can he use a variety of tools to explore the properties of water?
3. Is the mobile infant beginning to pour, fill, and empty containers?
4. Is the infant using language as she experiments with water in her play?

# In and Out Learning Space

## Overview

The *In and Out Learning Space* provides mobile infants with opportunities to develop their grasp and release of objects. After infants have learned to grasp a variety of objects, they become interested in removing items from containers. Remember that holding onto an object is easier than letting go. Therefore, infants learn how to take things out of containers before they learn how to put them in. At first, they will release a rattle or toy by accident. After a lot of practice and exploration, mobile infants discover they can control their hands to drop an object. Some one-year-olds can even drop one shape into a shape-sorter. Notice the variations of each infant's grasp and release and vary materials accordingly.

## Learning Objectives

Mobile infants will:

1. Have experiences to develop fine motor skills.
2. Develop grasp and release of objects.
3. Use vocabulary that accompanies in and out activities.

## Time Frame

This learning space will be interesting to mobile infants for approximately two weeks. You can bring the learning space back at a later time when you feel infants may be interested again in the materials and activities.

## Letter to Parents

Dear Parents,

During the end of the first year of life, infants become very interested in grasping toys and objects of all different sizes. They use their hands to take things out of containers. Later, they begin to put things back into containers. One of their favorite games to play becomes dumping toys out of a box, putting toys into a box, and dumping them out again. Our In and Out Learning Space will help mobile infants discover how to remove and replace objects from a variety of containers. This activity will also assist your infant in learning how to finger feed him/herself, which is a very important personal skill.

## Layout of the In and Out Learning Space

IN AND OUT

Collect *In and Out Learning Space* props in a large plastic container. This helps in retrieving the items and in storing them for easy access. The container can be carried into the *In and Out Learning Space*. Spread materials on the floor so mobile infants can select and manipulate the items that interest them.

## Vocabulary Enrichment

fingers
hand
hold
in
let go
out
touch

## Teacher- and Parent-Collected Props

blocks
large and medium pegboards and pegs
large crayons
large plastic storage containers with lids
plastic bowls and cups
snap beads
sewing spools
shape-sorters
small- and medium-size clear plastic containers
washable markers

## ACTIVITIES

**Special Note:** Mobile infants will learn to remove objects before they can put them back into a container. Give the infant plenty of time to explore and practice taking objects out of containers. If the mobile infant needs assistance, you may demonstrate how to remove and replace the object. However, be sure to allow time for them to "figure it out by themselves." Step in if you observe them becoming frustrated with the process.

Infants are fascinated by putting objects inside a box.

# Hand-Made Pegboards

thick crayons
washable markers
empty thread spools (decorate, if desired)

small plastic hair rollers
scissors (adult only)
shoebox
playdough
wet sand
Styrofoam

- Use crayons, washable markers, spools, and hair rollers as pegs.
- Use scissors to punch holes in the lid of a shoebox to make a pegboard (adult only).
- Push the "pegs" down through the holes in the shoebox lid into playdough, wet sand, or Styrofoam.
- Let the infants pull the items out of the Styrofoam and then try to put them back.

# Slot Box

medium-size cardboard box or plastic container
scissors (adult only)
variety of items to drop through slots, such as metal juice lids, blocks, pieces of sponge, balls, beads, old CDs, and so on

Juice lids go inside the clear plastic jar.

- Cut openings into the side of the box or container at different heights and widths.
- Turn the box so the infant can see inside or reach inside to retrieve items.
- Mobile infants can drop an item through the slot and see it inside the box.

## Straws

straws
carry-out cups with lid

- Collect a variety of cups with lids.
- Demonstrate how to remove the straws or let infants determine how to do this on their own.
- Let the infants take out the straws and try to put them back inside.

## Container Play

small cardboard boxes
plastic butter tubs
pie pans
buckets
coffee cans
pots and pans
metal mixing bowls
clear plastic containers
small toys

- Begin with shallow containers, because they are easier for small hands to reach inside and pull out objects.
- Bring out deeper containers as infants' skills progress.
- Infants love to make noise. The sound of a toy dropping into a container makes them want to practice this task repeatedly.

## Finger Foods

a variety of finger foods

- One of the best activities to encourage grasp and release is finger feeding.
- Begin by spreading large crackers on a plate.
- After the child has accomplished the challenge of picking up the crackers, progress to dry cereal, such as Cheerios, or small pieces of cooked vegetables on a plate.
- Finally, give mobile infants individual raisin boxes, small plastic bowls with dry cereal, and plastic snack containers with oyster crackers.
- Allow the infants time to play and practice self-feeding.
- For an infant, getting the food into his mouth is the best reward!

A jewelry box provides an opportunity to place a toy inside a container.

**ADDING SPARK TO THE IN AND OUT LEARNING
SPACE**

*Collect a clean, one-gallon plastic
bucket with a handle (ice cream
buckets are perfect). Use fishing
line to suspend the bucket by its
handle from the ceiling. Make
sure to hang the bucket slightly
above the infant's head. Mobile
infants will enjoy putting items in
and out of the hanging bucket.*

## The Essential Literacy Connection
**(\* Available as a board book)**

Carter, David. 1993. *In and Out*. New York: Little
Simon. *This colorful, pop-up book demonstrates
directions to infants.*

Filipowich, Bob. 2000. *In and Out*. Norwalk, CT:
Innovative Kids. *Infants will enjoy taking the
animals of this foam book in and out of boats, trains,
and cars.*

Godon, Ingrid. 2000. *In, Out and Other Places*.
Hauppauge, NY: Barrons Juveniles. *Nelly mouse
and Caesar frog demonstrate comparisons to infants
through their play.\**

Hill, Eric. 2000. *Where's Spot?* New York: G. P.
Putnam's Sons. *This lift-the-flap book follows a
mother dog around the house while she searches for
her puppy.*

## Evaluation

1. Is the infant attempting to remove objects from
containers?
2. Is the infant trying to drop objects back into large,
open containers?
3. Is the infant interested in finger feeding?

# Family Learning Space

## Overview

An infant's family is very important to her during her early years of development. Each family unit has a tremendous impact on the infant's development and personal security. It is very important for the teacher and family to establish a cooperative relationship and work together for the child's benefit. This learning space will clearly demonstrate how family members are valued in the infant classroom and in the program.

## Learning Objectives

Mobile infants will:

1. Learn that the center and their teacher value their family.
2. Identify the pictures of family members that are on display in the *Family Learning Space*.

Mobile infants' families will:

1. Discover that the infant teachers value them and their knowledge of their children.
2. Identify the important people and pets in the lives of their mobile infant.
3. Communicate interest and concerns with the teacher to support their developing infant.

## Time Frame

This learning space can be set up when a "new" baby is entering the program. It can be displayed throughout the year with new pictures added as changes occur.

## Letter to Family

Dear family of (child's name),

We are happy that your infant is a member of our community. It has often been said, "Parents are the first teachers." This is a belief we share. You are the most important people in the life of your young child. We share your desire to have the best program for your mobile infant. It is important that we work together to meet that goal.

The transition from home to a new environment— the infant classroom—is a challenging one. This learning space will include new people and new infants to see and learn about. During this time, we want to make a strong connection with the family and incorporate personal items into the infant space. As a part of this process, we are setting up a Family Learning Space in the classroom that focuses on each infant's family.

You can help us by collecting pictures of the important people in your infant's life, which we will display in the Family Learning Space. Suggestions for pictures include parents, grandparents, brothers, sisters, aunts or uncles, and family friends. Pets are also important members of some families. Please place the pictures in a plastic bag and label them to indicate the name of the person and their relationship to the infant. We want to be sure that we use the correct name for family members so the infant will store these names for future use.

Again, welcome to our center. We look forward to a long and happy relationship with you and your mobile infant. Visit our Family Learning Space often to learn about the other infants in our program and their families.

## Layout of the Family Learning Space

On a low display board, set up pictures of the infants' family members. Take a picture of the infant and place it in the center of the display with the infant's family pictures around it. Include homemade books that have photographs of family members (see page 102). Music and recordings about families add a special sound to the learning space. Include items that are home-like and soft, such as blankets, rugs, pillows, and soft furniture. Translucent fabric, such as gauze or netting, can be draped from the ceiling to make the *Family Learning Space* more inviting.

## Vocabulary Enrichment
(these names should match those used by the family)
brother
family
Father (or preferred name)
friend
grandparents
home
Mother (or preferred name)
pet
pictures
sister

## Teacher- and Parent-Collected Props
baby dolls
blankets and other soft items
music about families
pictures of family members
recordings of family members talking, reading, or
    singing
wallpaper sample books
zipper-closure plastic bags

**ACTIVITIES**

# Family Wallpaper Book

a discontinued wallpaper sample book
photographs of each infant's family members
glue

- Use a discontinued wallpaper sample book to form the base for your book about families.
- Identify a page or two that will contain the pictures of a specific infant's family.
- On one of the pages, place a picture of the baby and make copies of the pictures of family members to include on the page.
- Include the baby's name, family members, and specific names of people. Be sure to use the names preferred by the family.
- Place this book in the Family Learning Space, where pictures of the family members are displayed.
- If family members do not have or bring pictures, have your camera ready to take photos when delivery or pick-up is occurring. Every infant needs to have pictures of some family members to enjoy.

A homemade book about his family captures this mobile infant's attention.

# Musical Family

- Use the names for family members that relate to the culture of the infant.
- Sing and do the following fingerplay (tune: "Where Is Thumbkin?"):

> *Where is Mama?*
> *Where is Mama?*
> *Here I am, here I am.*
> *How are you today, Mama?*
> *Very well, I thank you.*
> *Run away, run away.*

Repeat the same pattern and finger movements with the names of other family members.

> *Where is Father?*
> *Where is Brother?*
> *Where is Sister?*
> *Where is Baby?*

Last verse:

> *Where is my family?*
> *Where is my family?*
> *Here they are, here they are.*
> *How are you today, sirs?*
> *Very well, I thank you.*
> *Run away, run away.*

- Infants will enjoy hearing this fingerplay over and over again.
- As it becomes familiar, they will participate in the motions and join in on the familiar words.

# Sounds of Home

blank cassette tape
tape recorder

- Make a recording of some of the sounds that the mobile infant might hear at their home.

- Some possible sounds include a door closing, toilet flushing, phone ringing, television or radio playing, pots and pans banging, family voices, dog barking, cat meowing, timer ticking, or water running.
- Play the tape and identify some of the sounds as the infant hears them.
- Allow time between each sound, so the infants can process what they are hearing.

# Featured Family

photographs of family members
construction paper or glittery wrapping paper
glue or tape

- Feature one infant's family for a one-week period.
- Invite the infant's family members to come into the *Family Learning Space* during lunch or snack time.
- Display pictures and interests of the family on a panel in the learning space.

The featured family of an infant

- Family members could bring in the infant's favorite foods or snacks.
- Take pictures of the family members visiting the classroom.

# A Family Mobile

pictures of family members
copy machine
dowel rod
fishing line
assorted materials to decorate the mobile

- Use the photographs you took during the Featured Family activity above.
- Make copies of pictures of family members. Use these copies to create a mobile.
- Use a dowel rod as the base of the mobile and fishing line to attach the pictures.
- Add ribbons and streamers for visual interest.
- Hang the mobile over the changing table, so the infants can see and identify family members while their diapers are changed. Rotate as different families are featured.

# Family Photographs

disposable camera or old camera
    with film
carrying bag
directions for taking pictures of
    the infant and family

- Send home a note similar to the following:

*Dear Parents,*
*Would you take some pictures at home with your infant and family members? Include pictures of where the infant eats, sleeps, and plays.*
*These will be included in a book about "My Family and Where I Live." When you finish, send the camera and film back to the center. We will develop and display these photos in the* Family Learning Space *of our classroom.*

- Place the note into a carrying bag, along with a camera and film, and send it home with the infant's parent or caregiver. Rotate the bag until every family has had a chance to take it home.
- When all of the families have finished, develop the photos and make a book entitled "My Family and Where I Live." Make one for each infant.

Teacher and family make important connections

### ADDING SPARK TO THE FAMILY LEARNING SPACE

*When a "new" baby enters the classroom or a family expands, share that in the Family Learning Space. When the new family is added, revisit the families that are already displayed in the learning space.*

## The Essential Literacy Connection
**(\* Available as a board book)**

Blackstone, Stella. 2000. *Bear's Busy Family.* Cambridge, MA: Barefoot Books. *Bright and colorful illustrations show Bear's relatives in various roles.\**

Curtis, Marci. 2002. *Big Sister, Little Sister.* New York: Puffin. *Photographs show sisters involved in activities throughout the year.*

Frasier, Debra. 2002. *On the Day You Were Born.* New York: Harcourt. *Celebrate life with this boldly colored, rhythmical book.*

Morris, Ann. 1996. *The Daddy Book.* Photographs by Ken Heyman. Parsippany, NJ: Silver. *A multicultural photo book of how children interact with their fathers.*

Oxenbury, Helen. 1981. *Family.* New York: Little Simon. *Simple pictures and one-word labels are included in the pictures of a family.\**

Spinelli, Eileen. 2001. *When Mama Comes Home Tonight.* New York: Simon & Schuster. *An infant enjoys a peaceful evening with his/her mother, after she comes home from work.\**

Williams, Vera. 1997. *More More More, Said the Baby.* New York: HarperCollins. *Enjoy the affection three little children receive from their loved ones in this delightful book.\**

Ziefert, Harriet. 2001. *Brothers Are for Making Mudpies and Sisters Are for Making Sand Castles.* New York: Puffin. *Children will see that sisters and brothers are special with these stories about how loving siblings spend their time together.\**

## Evaluation

1. Is the mobile infant focusing on pictures of family members and responding in an observable manner?
2. Can the mobile infant point to pictures of family members?
3. Does the mobile infant choose to move to the *Family Learning Space?*

# Nature Learning Space

## Overview
Mobile infants are budding young scientists. They are interested in exploring everything in the world around them. The items they have already experienced in nature particularly intrigue them, such as grass, water, and plants. Encourage their curiosity in both the infant classroom and outdoors. The *Nature Learning Space* will provide a place and items that the mobile infant can explore freely to build on their interests.

## Learning Objectives
Mobile infants will:
1. Explore the nature items in their environment.
2. Observe changes in growing things.
3. Learn about the world around them, both indoors and outdoors.
4. Recognize words and labels that relate to nature.

## Time Frame
During the year, there are times when more nature items are available to be studied by mobile infants. For example, in the fall, there are many things to be explored, compared, and touched such as leaves and cones. In the spring, there are flowers, buds, and grass to be enjoyed and examined. The scientific interests of mobile infants can be nurtured by setting up a *Nature Learning Space* in the classroom that encourages them to observe, explore, and learn about nature during these seasons.

## Letter to Parents

● ● ● ● ● ● ● ● ● ● ● ● ● ● ● ● ● ●

*Dear Parents,*
*As the spring season begins, your infant will begin to notice flowers blooming or grass on the lawn. We are building on the infants' interests by setting up a Nature Learning Space in our classroom. In this learning space, mobile infants will be able to explore flowers, grass, and leaves. They will see some of the beautiful things that appear in our environment during spring.*

*When you take a stroll with your infant, draw attention to the changes that are occurring. Help your child notice the beautiful things around you. As the old saying goes, "take time to smell the flowers."*

## Layout of the Nature Learning Space

On a low table, set up seasonal items that can be examined by mobile infants. Around the table, hang pictures of natural items that are in the environment. Place several of the same items, such as leaves, pine needles, and so on in a low container. Cover the floor with plastic, so crunching and touching can occur. Make the learning space inviting and attractive, so mobile infants will want to explore the materials.

## Vocabulary Enrichment

beautiful
bud
flower
fruit
grass
grow
pretty
seasons: fall, winter, spring, summer
smell
touch
tree

## Teacher- and Parent-Collected Props

broom and dustpan
pictures of natural items in the environment
plastic bags (for collecting natural items)
seasonal nature items
small hand-held vacuum cleaner
small plastic tubs (for grouping collections)

**ACTIVITIES**

# A Nature Book

various items collected outside
zipper-closure plastic bags
stapler
masking tape or packing tape

- Collect items on the playground and during walks to use to make a book.
- Place the collected items into zipper-closure plastic bags.
- Staple several bags together to resemble a book. Cover the staples with tape to secure the book.
- Keep the book in the *Nature Learning Space*.

- Place rocks in an aluminum pan so infants can examine and manipulate them.
- Infants will enjoy putting rocks in the pan and hearing the sounds the rocks make when they hit the container.

# Painting with Nature Items

green and brown tempera paint
pie pans
various items from outside, such as a pine tree
    branch, cat tail, dried flower, and so on
large sheet of butcher or construction paper

- Pour tempera paint into pie pans.
- Let the infants select and dip nature items into the tempera paint.

Big rocks in metal pans invite exploration.

# Rock Collection

stones and rocks in a variety of shapes and colors
aluminum pan

- Make sure rocks are an appropriate size for mobile infants to manipulate and they pass the choke tube test.

Exploring and removing the silk from an ear of corn is fascinating to this mobile infant.

- Help them use the nature items to paint on the paper.
- After the mobile infants finish painting, attach the nature item to the picture.
- Display the art in the *Nature Learning Space*.

**ADDING SPARK TO THE NATURE LEARNING SPACE**

*Bring in a colorful blooming plant that can be admired and touched. Display it in the Nature Learning Space for mobile infants to experience in their special way.*

## The Essential Literacy Connection
**(* Available as a board book)**

Cousins, Lucy. 1992. *Flower in the Garden.* Cambridge: Candlewick. *This durable, cloth book has simple pictures and labels that will introduce the names of objects in nature to mobile infants.*

Crossley, David. 2001. *Look Out Ladybug.* Hauppauge, NY: Barron's Educational Series. *A tiny edged-out track moves across each page of this book, allowing infants to follow the path of a ladybug as it moves through the world.**

Pledger, Maurice. 1998. *In the Forest.* San Diego, CA: Solver Dolphin. *This interactive, touch-and-feel book illustrates the various textures found around the forest.*

## Evaluation

1. Which nature items are the most interesting to each infant?
2. Is the mobile infant choosing to move to the *Nature Learning Space* for exploration?
3. Is the mobile infant manipulating nature items?

# CHAPTER FOUR

# Young Toddlers
## 14 to 24 Months

## Developmental Considerations

For this book, young toddlers are considered to be between the ages of 14 and 24 months. Young toddlers are continuing in their acquisition of new developmental skills. They are able to move around the room independently, either by crawling or walking, but there are lots of bumps and falls as they go. Young toddlers are developing a strong sense of self. They want to try to accomplish things by themselves, practicing over and over until they can do it (practice play). They typically do not "play together" but may interact as they play alongside each other (parallel play). Young toddlers desire to control others, and there may be a lot of pushing and pulling going on in the classroom. However, young toddlers are also beginning to demonstrate love and affection for others. They want to be with their teachers, and they are beginning to imitate simple adult activities. Therefore, it is important that their teachers go into the learning spaces and play alongside them.

Teachers should model appropriate behaviors and play possibilities for the young toddlers while in the learning spaces.

Use the following information to select appropriate materials and activities to use in learning spaces. There is a wide variation in the abilities of young toddlers in each classroom. For example, some can use two-word sentences, while others can only say "Dada." Consider both the needs of the individual toddler and the needs of the group as a whole when setting up learning spaces. Observe their play and change the materials within the learning spaces to make them match the young toddlers' skills while providing a challenge.

## Cognitive
- Looks at books
- Exhibits practice play
- Puts things into containers
- Points to or names 4 body parts
- Follows 2-step requests (Get the shoe and bring it here.)
- Removes socks
- Shows interest in toileting
- Points to objects outside

## Language
- Indicates wants by grunting and pointing
- Says at least 2-3 words
- Makes animal sounds
- Uses 6 or more words
- Hums or sings
- "No" and "mine" are favorite words
- Imitates two-word phrases

## Social/Emotional
- Hugs and loves doll or toy
- Listens to stories and rhymes
- Shows a variety of emotions (fear, anger, guilt, anxiety, and joy)
- Names familiar people in pictures
- Wants teacher within sight (or hearing)
- Exhibits parallel play (beside another child)

## Sensory
- Has depth perception (can see heights and depths of objects)
- Can screen out sounds that are not useful

## Gross Motor
- Walks a few steps
- Walks independently
- Runs stiffly
- Squats in play
- Climbs on furniture
- Walks with legs closer together
- Climbs stairs holding rail with one hand

## Fine Motor
- Turns pages of book one at a time
- Points at objects
- Puts small object in bottle
- Scoops with spoon
- Scribbles with marker spontaneously
- Stacks tower of 3 to 4 blocks
- Fills and dumps containers
- Takes rings off stand

Individual toddlers will progress through these skills at different rates.

The learning spaces in this chapter are recommended for use with young toddlers. They have been designed to use young toddlers' sense of independence as a helpful tool in the learning process. The learning spaces focus on typical toddlers' interests and developmental skills, but can be adjusted to meet an individual toddler's needs. Toddlers can select their personal favorite objects and materials from the ones that you have chosen, based on your knowledge of young toddlers' developmental needs. By selecting their favorites, toddlers are able to influence their environment.

# Motor Learning Space

## Overview

During the second year of life, young toddlers are continuing to develop the motor skills that they will use throughout the rest of their lives. These include both gross (large) and fine (small) motor skills. There may be great differences in the skill level of each toddler in the classroom. Many young toddlers are just learning to walk (12-17 months), while others will be learning to run (18-24 months). Some young toddlers will just be learning how to scribble with a crayon (12-15 months), while other toddlers will be able to imitate a circle (20-24 months). At first, young toddlers' movements will look uncoordinated and they may have many bumps and bruises. As with some developmental areas, repetition is the key, and, with practice, their movements will become smooth and fluid.

Motor skills are closely tied to social and emotional development and cognitive development. Children need fine motor skills to help them learn about shapes, sizes, and even math. Children who have poor motor skills tend to have lower self-esteem. Teachers need to provide young toddlers with both outdoor and indoor spaces for practicing their motor skills. This *Motor Learning Space* is an indoor learning space that requires adequate space and materials for young toddlers to work on refining their gross and fine motor skills every day.

## Learning Objectives

Young toddlers will:
1. Move around independently in the room.
2. Learn new gross and fine motor skills.
3. Become more coordinated in gross and fine motor skills.
4. Participate with other toddlers in meaningful activities.

## Time Frame

This learning space can remain available for the entire year. Periodically remove old items and replace with new ones to help children maintain interest.

## Letter to Parents

• • • • • • • • • • • • • • • • • • • •

*Dear Parents,*

*Young toddlers seem to learn something new every day. During the second year of life, toddlers learn many important gross motor skills such as walking, running, climbing stairs with one hand held, and throwing a ball. They will also learn fine motor skills such as scribbling with a crayon, pointing, and putting objects into a container.*

*The Motor Learning Space will be inside our classroom and will give young toddlers the appropriate space and toys to learn new motor skills. They will be playing games such as "Ring Around the Rosie" and "The Hokey Pokey," to help them become more coordinated and balanced in their movements.*

## Layout of the Motor Learning Space

## Web of Integrated Learning

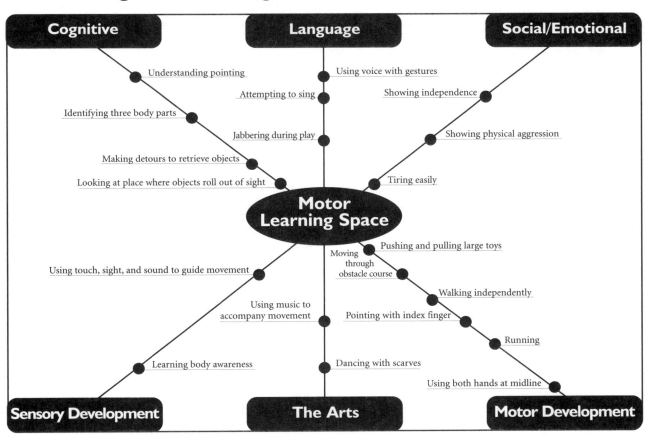

**Cognitive**

Understanding pointing

Identifying three body parts

Making detours to retrieve objects

Looking at place where objects roll out of sight

**Language**

Using voice with gestures

Attempting to sing

Jabbering during play

**Social/Emotional**

Showing independence

Showing physical aggression

Tiring easily

**Motor Learning Space**

Using touch, sight, and sound to guide movement

Using music to accompany movement

Learning body awareness

Moving through obstacle course

Pushing and pulling large toys

Walking independently

Pointing with index finger

Running

Dancing with scarves

Using both hands at midline

**Sensory Development**

**The Arts**

**Motor Development**

An important aspect of the *Motor Learning Space* is floor space. The learning space should be in an area of the room (preferably carpeted) where young toddlers can practice walking, climbing, hopping, and jumping. You may set up an obstacle course in this learning space to provide appropriate motor activities. The obstacle course might include carpet squares to step across, a mat to roll on, and a small indoor slide to go down.

## Vocabulary Enrichment

arms
clap
feet
hands
head
legs
run
walk

## Teacher- and Parent-Collected Props

carpet squares
carpeted cylinders (see page 307 for directions)
foam wedges (see page 309 for directions)
large balls (gymnastic balls)
large mirrors attached to the wall
mats
pull and push toys, such as a corn popper, vacuum cleaner, or lawn mower
riding toys
riser (see page 312 for directions)
rocking boat or teeter-totter
small indoor slide
small soft balls

## ACTIVITIES

# Obstacle Course

assorted props, such as a large container, carpet squares, slide, large balls, and so on

A gymnastic ball is a new piece of equipment for the toddler.

- Design a simple obstacle course using two or three different props.
- Introduce the obstacle course to the toddlers and demonstrate how to complete the course. You may need to help the toddlers through the obstacle course the first few times. Then, they can practice alone or with a little assistance.
- Change props when you see that the toddlers are losing interest.
- Select two or three stations in the obstacle course that match the developmental needs of toddlers in the classroom. Examples of stations include the following:
  - Throw small balls into a large container
  - Climb over foam wedges or cylinders
  - Step from one carpet square to the next
  - Go down the slide
  - Ride a riding toy
  - Push a large ball
  - Crawl across the floor

# Get Moving

several simple songs or rhymes with movements

- Select two or three simple, repetitive songs with movements to share with the toddlers.
- Toddlers will want to sing and move to their favorite songs over and over.
- Allow them the opportunity to select their favorite songs to act out.
- Some simple songs or rhymes for young toddlers include the following:
  - "Pat-a-Cake"
  - "The Beehive" (see paged 37)
  - "The Wheels on the Bus"
  - "Ring Around the Rosie"
  - "If You're Happy and You Know It!"

# Scarf Play

several scarves of different colors, sizes, and fabrics
container to hold the scarves
music to accompany movement

- Choose scarves of many different colors and sizes for movement play. Long, transparent scarves are particularly interesting to young toddlers.
- Let each toddler select one or two scarves from your container.
- Turn on some music and demonstrate different ways to move a scarf. Describe your movements as you go. For example, "The scarf is on my head" and "Wave the scarf in the air with your arm."
- After experimenting with the scarves, change the type of music to encourage different movements. Classical music may encourage slow, flowing movements while pop music may promote fast movements, such as twirling in circles while holding the scarf.

Scarves move with dancing toddlers.

**ADDING SPARK TO THE MOTOR LEARNING SPACE**

*Add a Sit-n-Spin or beanbag chair to the learning space.*

# The Essential Literacy Connection

**(* Available as a board book)**

Boynton, Sandra. (1993). *Barnyard Dance*. New York: Workman Publishers. *Familiar farm animals are involved in dancing and moving.*

Hoban, Tana. (1973). *Over, Under and Through and Other Spatial Concepts*. New York: Simon & Schuster. *This wordless, black and white picture book introduces the vocabulary for various spatial concepts.*

Litzinger, Rosanne. (1998). *You Can't Catch Me*. New York: HarperCollins. *A child runs and hides from her pursuer until she is caught in a hug from her Mommy.** 

Oxenbury, Helen. (1987). *Clap Hands*. New York: Simon and Schuster. *A multicultural baby book that illustrates a busy day in an early childhood program.** 

Raffi. (1990). *Shake My Sillies Out*. Illustrations by Allen and David Allender. Bancyfelin, Carmarthen, UK: Crown. *Toddlers will giggle as they watch fidgety forest animals shake their "sillies" out before going to bed.*

# Evaluation

1. Is the young toddler walking or running to move around?
2. Is the young toddler pushing and pulling toys while walking?
3. Is the young toddler pointing with his index finger?
4. Is the young toddler playing alongside other toddlers?

# I See Learning Space

## Overview

By one year of age, an infant's vision skills have become much more effective. However, their visual acuity is not yet 20/20. They must hold or stand closer to objects than adults. Young toddlers can look for and find hidden toys. They study themselves in the mirror, and they can begin to point to familiar objects in a picture book. Toddlers are also developing their visual perceptual skills, which is the ability to make sense out of what one sees by associating it with things one has seen before. For example, a toddler can identify her favorite teddy bear from a pile of many stuffed animals.

The *I See Learning Space* should be an area where young toddlers further develop their visual acuity and visual memory through playful activities. The *I See Learning Space* will also provide toddlers with new experiences and materials that will encourage their visual perceptual skills.

## Learning Objectives

Young toddlers will:

1. Understand their world through their sense of vision.
2. Begin to see differences in objects.
3. Begin to associate words with what is seen.
4. Develop eye-hand coordination.

## Time Frame

Make the *I See Learning Space* available to young toddlers throughout the year. It may include planned fine motor activities (for example, shape sorters) for children who would like to participate.

## Letter to Parents

• • • • • • • • • • • • • • • • • •

Dear Parents,

In the I See Learning Space, *young toddlers will increase their understanding of the environment using their vision. Toddlers in this area will have the opportunity to experience new and exciting materials such as sponges and fingerpaint. They will also begin to use their eyes to recognize differences and similarities between objects.*

*Young toddlers are learning to find hidden objects using their eyes. Enjoy playing "Hide and Seek" with your toddler at home. Try hiding your child's favorite stuffed animal under a table and ask him or her to find it.*

## Layout of the I See Learning Space

## Web of Integrated Learning

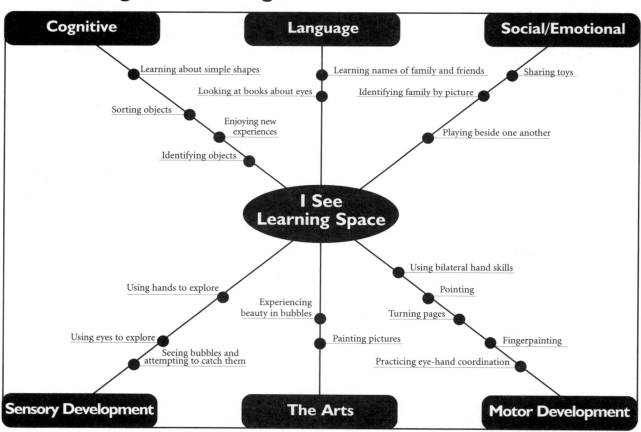

**Cognitive**

Learning about simple shapes

Sorting objects

Enjoying new experiences

Identifying objects

**Language**

Learning names of family and friends

Looking at books about eyes

**Social/Emotional**

Sharing toys

Identifying family by picture

Playing beside one another

**I See Learning Space**

Using bilateral hand skills

Pointing

Experiencing beauty in bubbles

Using hands to explore

Turning pages

Painting pictures

Fingerpainting

Using eyes to explore

Seeing bubbles and attempting to catch them

Practicing eye-hand coordination

**Sensory Development**

**The Arts**

**Motor Development**

The *I See Learning Space* should be located in an area of the room where toddlers can manipulate objects and complete planned art projects. It would be useful to have this learning space in a part of the room where there is natural light. Also, consider that you may need to turn out the lights in this area of the room for some activities.

## Vocabulary Enrichment

blue
bubbles
green
in
look
out
paint
red
see
watch
yellow

## Teacher- and Parent-Collected Props

bubble wands and bubbles
clear plastic containers
coffee cans and lids
color beads
color blocks
fingerpaint
flashlights
paper
rings and ring stand
shape sorters
simple picture books
single-piece puzzles
sponges
sunglasses
washable markers

# Catch the Bubbles

liquid detergent
water
glycerin
assorted sizes of bubble wands

* This is a great outdoor activity.
* Make bubbles by mixing liquid detergent with water. Add a few drops of glycerin to the mix to make the bubbles stronger.
* Blow bubbles and ask toddlers to catch the bubbles with their hands.
* Use different sizes of bubble wands. Large bubbles move slower and are easier to catch than small bubbles. This encourages visual tracking and eye-hand coordination.
* If a toddler gets soap in his eyes, rinse with clear water.

# Sponge Shape Sorting

large coffee cans with lids
contact paper
sponges
scissors (adult only)

* Wash and dry the large coffee cans.
* Cover the cans with contact paper.
* Cut sponges into circles, squares, and triangles.
* Cut shapes in the plastic lids to fit each sponge shape.
* Replace the lids on cans.
* Toddlers love putting objects into containers and then taking them out.

# Put Your Finger on the

## _____!

- This is a good game for beginning object identification.
- Ask the toddlers to put their fingers on objects in the learning space. For example, say, "Put your finger on the floor."
- Start with simple objects such as a chair, table, book, or crib, and then move to more difficult objects, such as a doll bed, pot, or spoon.

This young toddler sees herself in the mirror and responds to her moves.

# Photo Book

small photo album
several pictures of each child's family
paper
marker

- Place one picture on each page of a small photo album.
- Write a sentence about that family member and place it at the bottom of each photo.
- Label the front of the book with the child's name and picture.
- Read the book to the child, helping her point to pictures of each family member.
- Let the young toddler have access to this book throughout the day.

# Fingerpainting

fingerpaint
surface on which to paint, such as paper, plastic, tabletop, and so on

- Begin by encouraging the toddlers to explore fingerpaints using their touch and vision.
- Gently encourage the toddlers to use their index fingers to paint.
- As they become more skilled, suggest that they imitate you as you draw horizontal lines, vertical lines, and circular motions with your fingers.
- Remember that it is the process, not the product that is important.

You look different when I wear sunglasses.

**ADDING SPARK TO THE I SEE LEARNING SPACE**

*Provide a collection of plastic sunglasses for young toddlers to wear. Include sunglasses with different color lenses, sizes, and shapes.*

## The Essential Literacy Connection
**(* Available as a board book)**

Christian, Cheryl. (1996). *Where's the Baby?* New York: Star Bright. *This lift-the-flap photography book will have toddlers eager to discover hidden surprises.**

Hoban, Tana. (1993). *Black on White.* New York: Greenwillow. *Young toddlers will enjoy the contrast as they begin to associate labels with the pictures in this wordless book.**

Hoban, Tana. (1996). *Of Colors and Things.* New York: Mulberry. *Color photographs illustrate various items toddlers may see in their world. The photographs are easier to see than artist drawings.*

Isadora, Rachel. (1985). *I See.* New York: Greenwillow. *This book goes through the day of a child. It illustrates what she sees. It includes objects young readers can recognize, name, and repeat.**

## Evaluation
1. Is the toddler able to place rings on a ring stand (in no particular order)?
2. Is the toddler able to locate familiar objects in the room?
3. Is the toddler attempting to scribble on paper?
4. Is the toddler able to place one shape into a simple shape-sorter?

# I Touch Learning Space

## Overview

One way that young toddlers learn about the world is through their sense of touch. This learning space allows toddlers to explore and experiment with a variety of objects and materials. It is important to let toddlers think of new and different ways to interact with the materials. Toddlers may use their hands and feet, as well as tools, to learn about new substances and textures. This encourages their creativity and their fine motor skills.

Toddlers in the *I Touch Learning Space* will be active. You will need to closely supervise them in this learning space, because you will be using materials that they may want to explore with their mouths.

## Learning Objectives

Young toddlers will:

1. Begin to understand the world through the sense of touch.
2. Learn about different textures.
3. Build creativity, as they participate in sensory activities.
4. Develop independence in manipulating materials.

## Time Frame

Keep the *I Touch Learning Space* set up for at least two or three weeks. Observe children in the learning space to determine when they stop exploring. Then, close the learning space and bring it back at a later time. Keep the *I Touch Learning Space* in operation for a longer period if the toddlers' interest remains high.

## Letter to Parents

• • • • • • • • • • • • • • • • • • • • • •

*Dear Parents,*

*Our I Touch Learning Space gives toddlers the opportunity to learn about the world through their sense of touch. In this area, toddlers will explore a variety of textures such as smooth, hard, soft, rough, bumpy, slippery, and squishy. Toddlers also will be able to use tools such as funnels, sifters, and paintbrushes. As you can tell, this learning space will be fun and educational for your toddler as he or she develops knowledge about his or her environment.*

*Please bring in any scraps of fabric or material that you may have at home. This will help us create an exciting I Touch Learning Space for your young toddler.*

## Layout of the I Touch Learning Space

## Web of Integrated Learning

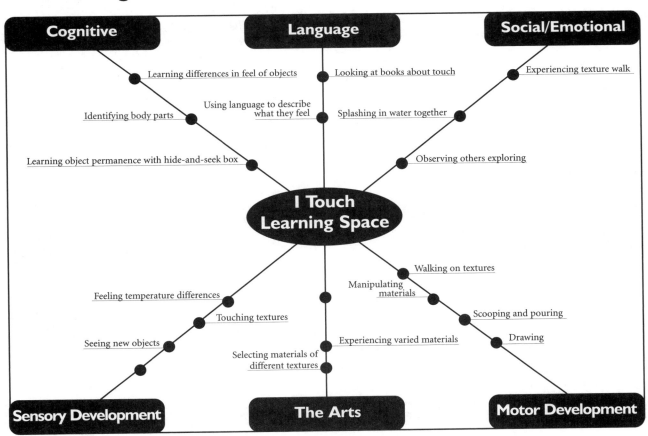

**Cognitive**

Learning differences in feel of objects

Identifying body parts

Learning object permanence with hide-and-seek box

**Language**

Looking at books about touch

Using language to describe what they feel

Splashing in water together

**Social/Emotional**

Experiencing texture walk

Observing others exploring

**I Touch Learning Space**

Feeling temperature differences

Touching textures

Seeing new objects

Selecting materials of different textures

Walking on textures

Manipulating materials

Scooping and pouring

Experiencing varied materials

Drawing

**Sensory Development**

**The Arts**

**Motor Development**

This learning space should be set up near other creative areas, such as the *Art Learning Space*. Display materials so that the young toddlers can select and use them easily. A riser or low table provides a place for toddlers to examine the materials and see them from a different perspective. An unbreakable mirror on the wall will provide another view of interesting items in the learning space.

## Vocabulary Enrichment

bumpy
cold
feel
firm
hard
rough
rub
smooth
soft
sticky
touch
warm

## Teacher- and Parent-Collected Props

sand and water table (make economical tables using
    plastic tubs on low tables or on the floor)
clear plastic boxes (to store and organize props)
cooking supplies such as flour, salt, sugar, cornstarch,
    dry beans, and uncooked rice
household items such as cotton balls, cotton swabs,
    yarn, and foil
kitchen tools such as large spoons, rolling pin, tongs,
    and ice cube trays
large paintbrushes
large plastic bowls
playdough
sandpaper (assorted grains)
scrap fabric such as corduroy, silk, satin, lace,
    netting, cotton batting, burlap, fur, and spandex
shower curtain liners or sheets of plastic (for
    tabletops and under tables and tubs)
small broom and dustpan or vacuum cleaner
stuffed animals

## ACTIVITIES

## New Materials

soap foam
rocks
seashells
ice cubes

- Change the *I Touch Learning Space* by adding different materials to the table or plastic tub, such as soap foam, rocks, seashells, and ice cubes. These unique substances will invite the young toddler to explore and manipulate.

Foam has a unique feel that toddlers enjoy exploring.

## Hide-and-Seek Box

medium-size box
scissors (adult only)
fabric
tape
variety of materials with different textures such as
    foil, sandpaper, fur, silk, corduroy, cotton balls,
    rocks, and yarn

- Cut out a hole large enough to fit a child's hand in
  one end of the box.
- Cover the hole by taping a piece of fabric over it.
- Place a variety of scrap materials inside the box.
- Encourage the toddler to reach inside and pull out
  one item.
- Ask the toddler to identify the item. Talk about
  the texture of the item.

The toddler examines the textures as the fabric is pulled from the box.

## Texture Walk

tape
variety of materials with different textures such as
    foil, sandpaper, fur, silk, corduroy, cotton batting,
    and yarn

- Tape a variety of materials on the floor of the
  learning space.
- Help the toddlers remove their shoes and socks.
- Lead them on a walk around the area.
- Talk about the different textures that they are
  feeling with their feet.
- Let the toddlers explore the textured floor on
  their own.

## New Textures with Water

large plastic tub or sink
bubble bath or liquid soap
warm or cold water

- Let the toddlers help add bubble bath or liquid
  soap to water in a large tub or sink.
- Talk about the temperature of the water (warm
  or cold).
- Talk about the slippery feel of the water.
- Allow young toddlers to experiment with the
  soapy water.
- If a toddler gets soap in his eyes, rinse with clear
  water.

**ADDING SPARK TO THE I TOUCH LEARNING SPACE**

*If children are losing interest in textures, add tools to the learning space such as large paintbrushes, a stylus (wooden writing tool), sifters, and sponges. These tools will help children explore materials in a new way.*

## The Essential Literacy Connection
(* Available as a board book)

Ehlert, Lois. (1997). *Hands.* New York: Harcourt Brace. *This uniquely shaped book shares a few of the hands-on activities a young toddler does with his/her parents.*

Hathon, Elizabeth. (2000). *Night-Night Baby.* New York: Platt & Munk. *This touch-and-feel book follows a toddler through six steps of the nightly routine.**

Kunhardt, Edith. (1989). *Pat the Cat.* New York: Golden Books. *This interactive book features Martha and Neddy making a shopping list with Mom, going to the ATM with Dad, and patting the cat along the way.*

Oxenbury, Helen. (1995). *I Touch.* Cambridge: Candlewick. *A young toddler touches a variety of different objects in his/her surroundings.**

Kindersley, Dorling. (1999). *Touch and Feel: Baby Animals.* New York: DK Publishing. *Touch the various textures of baby animals.*

Kindersley, Dorling. (1998). *Touch and Feel: Farm.* New York: DK Publishing. *Touch the various textures of farm animals.*

## Evaluation

1. Is the toddler exploring the materials and textures with his hands and/or feet?
2. Is the toddler improving fine motor coordination as he plays with materials?
3. Is the toddler attempting to use tools to manipulate materials?
4. Is the toddler making sounds or gestures to accompany his play in the learning space?

# Housekeeping Learning Space

## Overview

The *Housekeeping Learning Space* is similar to the traditional center that has been used for many years with preschool children. The *Housekeeping Learning Space* works effectively for young toddlers if the area is set up and managed to match their level of development. Active toddlers will move into a well-designed *Housekeeping Learning Space* and try out props. They will participate in beginning dramatic play and then move on to another learning space. Often they will take some of the props with them as they continue to play a role or use the prop in a new area. This is very appropriate play during the toddler period. The design and management of the *Housekeeping Learning Space* should be very flexible and open to match the changing interests and play of the young toddler.

## Learning Objectives

Young toddlers will:
1. Explore roles and props in a home setting.
2. Use gestures, actions, and language that relates to housekeeping.
3. Begin to use symbolic representation in play.
4. Develop social skills, while playing with others in the learning space.

## Time Frame

This is a very popular learning space with toddlers and should be available for their use throughout the year. The *Housekeeping Learning Space* can be changed into a related theme where many of the same props will work with just a few additions. For example, a fast-food restaurant or birthday party area could be set up in the *Housekeeping Learning Space* for short periods during the year.

## Letter to Parents

• • • • • • • • • • • • • • • •

Dear Parents,

You will notice that we have a Housekeeping Learning Space in our toddler classroom. This is a favorite of the children and they visit it frequently. In this learning space, the children are playing roles of adults and using props to support their ideas. This is important to their learning as they pretend, think, and begin to communicate in a familiar home-like environment.

It seems that we always need "new" dress-up clothes in this area. The toddlers use the items so often that we need to add clothing regularly. If you have any outgrown baby clothes, hats, bonnets, or blankets, we would appreciate your donation. These items are especially needed because toddlers love to pretend that they are babies. They see themselves as "so big" these days. We always need clothing that is small, interesting, and sturdy. We have a box in the office where you can deposit your contribution to our Housekeeping Learning Space.

# Layout of the Housekeeping Learning Space

# Web of Integrated Learning

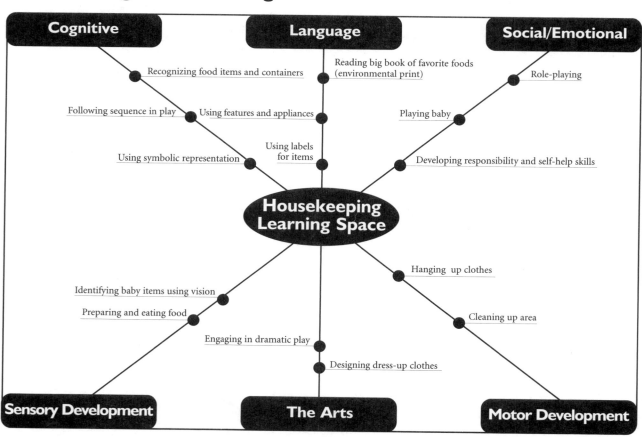

**Cognitive**
Recognizing food items and containers
Following sequence in play
Using symbolic representation

**Language**
Reading big book of favorite foods (environmental print)
Using features and appliances
Using labels for items

**Social/Emotional**
Role-playing
Playing baby
Developing responsibility and self-help skills

**Housekeeping Learning Space**

Hanging up clothes
Cleaning up area

**Sensory Development**
Identifying baby items using vision
Preparing and eating food

**The Arts**
Engaging in dramatic play
Designing dress-up clothes

**Motor Development**

This learning space needs low boundaries so young toddlers can understand where the learning space begins and ends. It should include basic housekeeping equipment, such as a stove, refrigerator, table with chairs, and baby bed. Other items that encourage dramatic play are a telephone, unbreakable dishes, cleaning equipment, and a rocking chair. A large, unbreakable mirror is essential for toddlers to observe themselves in their play. Store clothing on a wall-mounted knob hanger (see page 309 for directions), so the children can return clothing to the appropriate place easily. A soft rug, pillows, and curtains add softness to the area and absorb some of the sound produced.

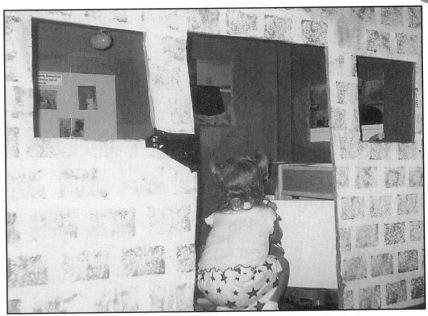

A toddler experiencing the Housekeeping Learning Space

## Vocabulary Enrichment

baby
cleanup
cooking
dishes, such as plates, cups, and spoons
dress-up
mirror
pots and pans
pretend
recipe
refrigerator
stove
telephone

## Teacher- and Parent-Collected Props

baby clothes and accessories
dress-up male and female clothes, including cultural items of the children in the classroom
empty food containers familiar to the children, such as milk, cereal, and peanut butter
old "real" telephone
rags and cloths for clean-up
"real" plastic dishes, small pots, and pans
soft washable rugs and blankets
small rocking chair

**ACTIVITIES**

# Familiar Food Items

several empty boxes and containers of food

- During group time, examine the boxes and talk about what was inside of them.
- Put the boxes that are familiar to the toddlers in the *Housekeeping Learning Space*.
- These favorites will encourage pretend play and food preparation in the learning space.
- Make a big book of the labels from the most familiar containers and place it in the *Housekeeping Learning Space* to support the children's experiences with environmental print.

# Hanging Clothing on Pegs

pegs for hanging clothes
clean, empty milk jugs, drink containers, and so on

- Toddlers should begin to be responsible for hanging dress-up items during clean-up time.
- Introduce this concept to them during their play.
- When the clean-up signal is given, return to the area and work with the toddlers in returning the clothing to the pegs.
- Talk with them about their involvement in cleanup and the importance of this work.

# Cooking and Eating Favorite Foods

ingredients, boxes, or plastic food items
kitchen utensils used in food preparation

- Talk to parents and do a survey of the young toddlers' favorite foods.
- Put ingredients, boxes, or plastic items to represent these foods in the learning space. Foods that are familiar and popular with toddlers will encourage their dramatic play.
- Go into the *Housekeeping Learning Space* and demonstrate some of the food preparation that might be associated with this food or serve the "pretend" food to the toddlers in the area.
- Leave the learning space and let toddlers prepare and eat the food in their own way.
- Observe the approaches, language, and symbols they use in their housekeeping play.

A young toddler enjoys pretending with baby dolls.

# Baby Play

songs and books about infants
baby items, such as baby clothing, baby bed, stroller, mobile, rattles, and baby toys

- Take the toddlers to visit the baby room of your program to see the babies.
- Sing songs and read books about infants during the day.
- Furnish the learning space with baby items that will encourage the toddlers to remember when they were "babies."
- Let the toddlers pretend that they are babies or use baby dolls in their play.
- The young toddler is in a transitional stage and this opportunity to play at being a baby will help him in this developmental step.

**ADDING SPARK TO THE HOUSEKEEPING LEARNING SPACE**

*A small vacuum cleaner that is rechargeable and makes a low sound will inspire new play in the Housekeeping Learning Space. Young toddlers may want to vacuum the Housekeeping Learning Space as well as the entire room.*

# The Essential Literacy Connection
**( \* Available as a board book)**

Brandt, Peter. (1998). *My Home.* New York: Star Bright. *This color photography book labels 40 different items found around the house.\**

Ellwand, David. (2001). *Big Book of Beautiful Babies.* New York: Penguin Putnam. *This black and white photography book captures the expressions of toddlers in a variety of different circumstances.\**

McGee, Marni. (2002). *Wake Up, Me.* New York: Simon and Schuster. *From bed to breakfast to outside time, toddlers can watch a young boy wake up "the world" for a new day.*

Moore, Dessie, & Moore, Chevelle. (1994). *Getting Dressed.* New York: Harper Festival. *A young toddler tells of the process of getting dressed.\**

# Other Printed Materials
A variety of printed materials can be included in the *Housekeeping Learning Space* including a phone book, cookbook, pads of paper, and washable markers.

# Evaluation
1. Is the young toddler involved in pretend play in the *Housekeeping Learning Space?*
2. Is the young toddler returning to the learning space?
3. Is the young toddler interested in communicating with others in the learning space?
4. Is the young toddler observed participating in cleanup on any occasion?

# Book Learning Space

## Overview

The young toddler period is a time of extensive language development. During this time, toddlers are storing much of the language they hear for future use. They are beginning to use gestures and words to communicate their ideas and needs. Young toddlers enjoy the sound of language, interesting phrases, or unique patterns of words. This is an ideal time to provide experiences with books and literature to help form positive attitudes about literacy, reading, and listening. An enticing *Book Learning Space* allows the young toddler to move around and manipulate items, while encouraging an interest in books, rhymes, and story reading. The toddler will begin to recognize this learning space as a place where a book can be enjoyed, a story can be read, and literature can be shared with others.

## Learning Objectives

Young toddlers will:

1. Manipulate and examine books that are appropriate for this stage of development.
2. Listen to stories, poems, or rhymes while in the *Book Learning Space.*
3. Use gestures or words to indicate a specific book they enjoy.
4. Participate when a story or fingerplay is being read.

## Time Frame

The *Book Learning Space* should be in the classroom for the entire year. Rotate books and materials in and out of the learning space so interest remains high. The young toddlers' favorite books should be retained in the learning space, so they can be revisited again and again. Add new books that support activities occurring in the classroom.

## Letter to Parents

• • • • • • • • • • • • • • • • • • • • • • •

*Dear Parents,*
*During this period of a toddler's life, a great deal of time is spent practicing motor skills. Young toddlers seem to be moving, exploring, and manipulating all the time. It is critical that we remember this is also a period of tremendous language growth. Communicating with toddlers about their daily activities and objects in their world builds their language. Books, however, expose young toddlers to words, phrases, and language that may not be used in day-to-day conversations. This more advanced "book" language stimulates development and expands their vocabulary. Toddlers need many enjoyable experiences with books and stories, as they develop positive attitudes about reading and listening.*

*In the Book Learning Space of our classroom, active toddlers can examine books and listen to stories. Sometimes people ask, "Why do you need a library in the classroom when they can't read yet?" Many language studies have shown that the early years are a critical time for language connections to be made in the brain. Hearing stories, looking at books, and interacting with responsive adults are some of the best ways to encourage language development. The Book Learning Space also nurtures an interest in "reading" and participating in the process.*

*We invite you to come and visit our Book Learning Space and see the book experiences your toddler is having. You will be amazed to see them stop for a moment to focus on a story or join in on a familiar phrase read from a book. The Book Learning Space is a very important part of our classroom.*

## Layout of the Book Learning Space

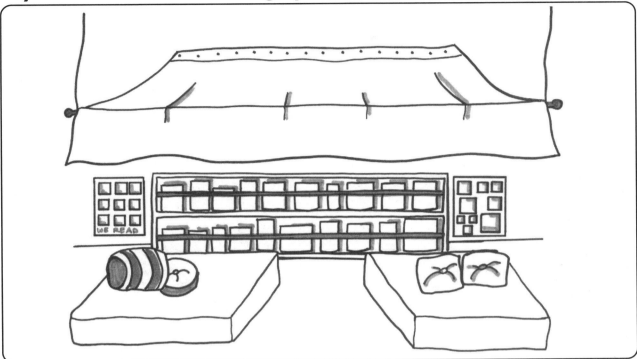

## Web of Integrated Learning

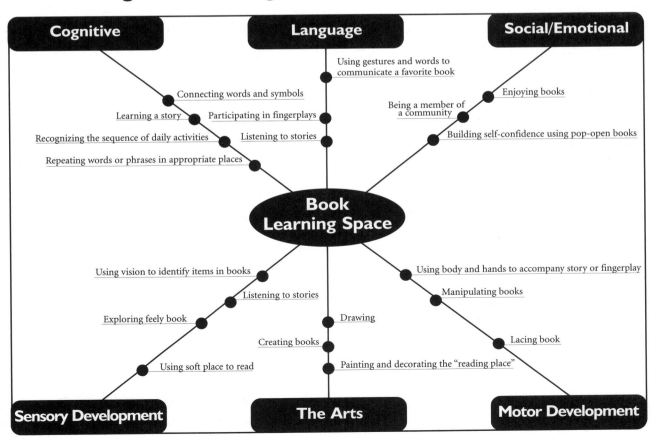

| | | |
|---|---|---|
| **Cognitive** | **Language** | **Social/Emotional** |

Using gestures and words to communicate a favorite book

Connecting words and symbols

Enjoying books

Learning a story — Participating in fingerplays

Being a member of a community

Recognizing the sequence of daily activities — Listening to stories

Building self-confidence using pop-open books

Repeating words or phrases in appropriate places

**Book Learning Space**

Using vision to identify items in books

Using body and hands to accompany story or fingerplay

Listening to stories

Manipulating books

Exploring feely book

Drawing

Creating books

Lacing book

Using soft place to read

Painting and decorating the "reading place"

| | | |
|---|---|---|
| **Sensory Development** | **The Arts** | **Motor Development** |

This learning space should be set up so active children can move around and select the materials they want to investigate. Books should be displayed so the children can see the covers, which will help them determine what they would like to "read." Include books that invite manipulation, such as handles to turn, doors to open, or mirrors to look into. Create a soft and inviting area with rugs, pillows, and throws. Of course, all of these items need to be durable and have varying textures. A canopy made from a colorful sheet or fabric (see page 306 for directions) can make this learning space feel cozy and special.

## Vocabulary Enrichment

author
book
favorite
library
listeners
stories
the end
title

## Teacher- and Parent-Collected Props

twin mattress with washable cover
soft pillows in a variety of sizes
rugs and carpet squares
collection of board books, picture books, and toy books (manipulative books)
magazines
posters of book characters
pictures of young children reading books
soft cuddly toys
soft chair or couch

## ACTIVITIES

# Creating a Pop-Open Book

cardboard or poster board
scissors (adult only)
pictures of items in the children's environment, such as food items, toys, animals, or classroom materials
glue
wallpaper, construction board, or heavyweight paper
large rings to hold pages together

- Toddlers like to look inside things, open doors, and lift flaps. A homemade toy book will build on that interest.
- Cut pieces of cardboard or poster board into pieces the size of a large picture book.
- Glue pictures of familiar items onto the cardboard pieces. Place the pictures so they will be visible when slots are cut into the front of them.
- Cover the pictures with wallpaper, construction board, or heavyweight paper. Cut openings in this top layer and fold back a "door" that can be raised by the child. Vary the shape and size of the openings.
- Make sure that the opening allows toddlers to see a major portion of the item so they can recognize it.
- Punch holes into the cardboard pages and use large rings to hold several pieces together, creating a unique book.

# A Big Book of Our Class

camera and film
cardboard
scissors (adult only)
glue
hole punch
shoelace or heavy yarn

- Take a picture of each child in the classroom. Be sure to include a picture of the teacher, aide, or any other adult that works in the classroom.

- Cut cardboard to make pages for a classroom book.
- Glue one picture on each side of the cardboard.
- Compile the cardboard pages with the pictures into a book format.
- Punch holes in the pages and use a shoelace or heavy yarn to tie the book pages together.
- Place this classroom book in the *Book Learning Space* to be enjoyed and "read" by all.

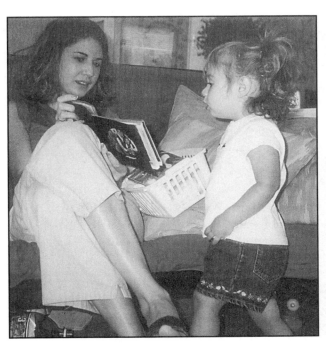

A homemade book about her classmates is of great interest to this toddler.

# Happenings in Our Class

several pictures of daily activities
materials to make a book

- Create a book of the activities that occur during the young toddlers' day.
- Take pictures during story time, lunch, outdoor play, and playtime.
- Label the pictures with the name of the activity and the toddlers who are in the picture.
- The toddlers will use this book frequently because their photographs are inside.

# A "Quiet" Reading Place

large cardboard box
materials to decorate the box
soft items to place inside the box, such as pillows, fuzzy fabric, and stuffed toys
flashlight
scissors (adult only)

- Create a special place for "reading" a book using a large cardboard box.
- Help the children paint and decorate the box.
- pillows, fuzzy fabric, and a flashlight inside of the box.
- Cut openings into the sides and top of the box so sufficient light is available for looking at the books.

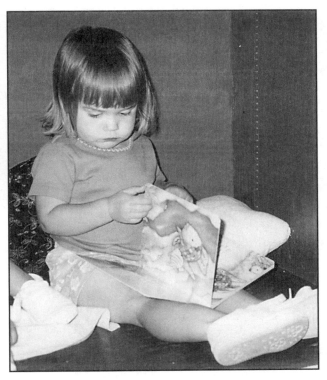

Books can be enjoyed in a small, special space.

## ADDING SPARK TO THE BOOK LEARNING SPACE

*Create a "feely" book. Bring in scraps of a variety of materials, such as sandpaper, coarse fabric, sponge, or any other textured material that is safe for toddlers to handle. With a hot glue gun (use away from the children), attach materials to poster board or art board. Include labels for how the material feels. Combine the pages to make a book.*

# The Essential Literacy Connection
**(* Available as a board book)**

Carle, Eric. (1996). *Brown Bear, Brown Bear, What Do You See?* New York: Henry Holt & Company. *Young toddlers have the chance to meet different animals in different colors.**

Degen, Bruce. (1995). *Jamberry.* New York: HarperCollins. *Enjoy the rhythmical dance of a boy and bear's adventures in Berryland.**

Freeman, Dan. (1976). *Corduroy.* New York: Scott Foresman. *Watch as a teddy bear explores a department store at night and goes home with a girl the next day.**

Guarino, Deborah. (1997). *Is Your Mama a Llama?* New York: Scholastic. *The rhymes and riddles in this book make it enjoyable for children of all ages.**

Mayer, Mercer. (1992). *Bubble, Bubble.* Roxbury, CT: Rain Bird Productions. *Comical illustrations show how a young boy uses his vivid imagination to create various animals from his magic bubble maker.*

# Evaluation

1. Is the young toddler manipulating books in the learning space?
2. Can the toddler identify his photograph in the classroom book?
3. Does the young toddler revisit a favorite book or books?
4. Is the toddler participating in story reading or storytelling?

# Construction Learning Space

## Overview

Young toddlers are interested in building, combining materials, and knocking down structures. Each aspect of this process is important because the young toddler is learning how to use blocks and understand how they work. Using a variety of building materials will help toddlers begin to organize their thinking and discover how different items respond to their manipulation. They will begin carrying and moving blocks, stacking them vertically, or placing them in a line across the floor. These early experiences with blocks provide a foundation for building structures that are more complex.

## Learning Objectives

Young toddlers will:

1. Learn how materials can be combined to build structures.
2. Investigate the responses of different materials during the construction process.
3. Attach labels to the constructions they have created.
4. Develop motor coordination as they move the blocks and stack them.

## Time Frame

This learning space can be set up at different times during the year. Reassembling it each time provides new interest in the materials and construction.

## Letter to Parents

• • • • • • • • • • • • • • • • • • • • •

*Dear Parents,*

*Your young toddler is building with blocks in our Construction Learning Space. Sometimes toddlers enjoy building structures almost as much as they enjoy knocking them down! Toddlers are learning about construction and how blocks react during this process. Building is interesting to learn about, and so is watching what happens when blocks are pushed over. This learning about "cause and effect" is important to young toddlers' thinking and problem-solving skills.*

*In the Construction Learning Space there are many different types of materials to use in building, including traditional wooden blocks, cardboard blocks, and foam blocks. However, we also have some rather unusual building materials, such as sheets of cardboard, cardboard boxes, plastic tubes, and scraps of wood. These items, combined with traditional blocks, provide an interesting challenge for developing the problem-solving skills of young toddlers. We will display pictures of some of the toddlers' building in our room and in the hall so you can admire their work.*

## Layout of the Construction Learning Space

## Web of Integrated Learning

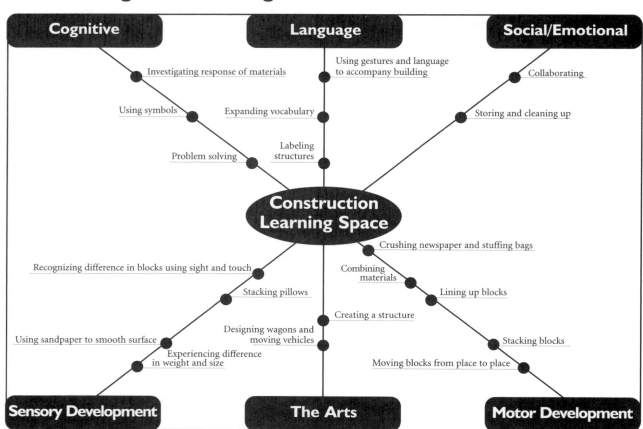

The *Construction Learning Space* is noisy and should be placed in a part of the classroom that will not disturb quiet places. A carpeted spot or a place where you can put flat area rugs works best so that some of the sound produced in this learning space is absorbed. Store blocks and building materials so that toddlers can easily identify the items they want to use. Place pictures of the toddlers' structures low on the wall for inspiration. A low table or riser is a good building surface for toddlers. This allows them to see their structure from a different perspective and work at a comfortable level.

## Vocabulary Enrichment

| | |
|---|---|
| blocks | store |
| boxes | tower |
| build | train |
| fall down | wagon |
| move | |

## Teacher- and Parent-Collected Props

brown grocery bags
foam pieces
medium-size cardboard boxes
scrap pieces of wood (sanded to remove rough splinters)
wagon

Throw-away boxes can be used for building and sorting.

# Grocery Bag Blocks

10 large, brown grocery bags
newspaper
tape

- Use large, brown grocery bags to make soft and stackable blocks.
- Ask the toddlers to scrunch newspaper to fill the bags and make them more stable.
- Fold down the tops of the bags to create a flat top and tape securely.
- Ten grocery bag blocks work well in a small *Construction Learning Space*.

# Small Props

miniature toys, such as trucks, cars, people, farm animals, zoo animals, and so on
storage tubs

- Include a set of miniature toys in this learning space to encourage new play.
- Later, add a different collection of toy props. For example, a collection of trucks and cars encourages road building, and farm animals inspire the building of a farm.
- Remember that all pieces need to pass the "choking test" because toddlers are still placing things in their mouths to discover the qualities of the toy.
- Store related items in tubs and rotate them into the learning space when the toddlers' play needs new inspiration.

# Pictures of Their Building

camera
film or digital camera memory stick

- Take pictures of the toddlers' buildings and some of their completed structures.
- Talk about these with the toddlers and show them their valued work.
- Take additional pictures each time the *Construction Learning Space* is reintroduced into the classroom.
- These pictures will document the developing block-building abilities of young toddlers during the year.

Dump trucks can carry building materials.

# Moving Vehicles

small wagon          basket with handles
cardboard box        rope or string

- One fascinating task for toddlers in the *Construction Learning Space* is trying to find ways to move the blocks from place to place.
- Young toddlers can move blocks using a small wagon, cardboard box, or basket with handles.

- Add a rope or string to the items to help the toddlers as they work to pull the blocks in the moving container.
- Toddlers enjoy both filling up and pouring out the contents of the vehicle.
- You can also use these moving items when you are working with toddlers to clean up the *Construction Learning Space*.

# Pillow Stacking

several firm couch-size pillows

- Collect and add firm pillows to the *Construction Learning Space*.
- Let the toddlers stack, climb on, and push over the pillows.
- This building material will stimulate new ways of thinking about construction as well as provide opportunities for toddlers to be active.

**ADDING SPARK TO THE CONSTRUCTION LEARNING SPACE**

*Use large tin cans to create a different kind of building material. Use empty soup or vegetable cans and large restaurant-size cans. Make sure the top has a clean cut; cover the edge with heavy tape. Spray paint (away from the children in a well-ventilated area) the cans or cover them with contact paper. These tin blocks feel different, have a different weight, and can be used for building unique structures.*

# The Essential Literacy Connection
**(* Available as a board book)**

Gibbins, Gail. (1988). *Tool Book*. New York: Holiday House. *This book illustrates a large number of tools and groups them by function.*

Grosbie, Michael J. & Rosenthal, Steve. (1993). *Architecture Shapes*. New York: Preservation. *Architectural elements are introduced through photographs of windows and simple text.**

Hutchins, Pat. (1987). *Changes, Changes*. New York: Macmillan. *Block-made characters transform structures into functional objects, such as a house and a boat.*

Royston, Angela. (1991). *Diggers and Dump Trucks*. New York: Scott Foresman. *Photographs and illustrations help to resolve children's curiosity about how things go, as they listen to the descriptions of cars, trucks, and machines.*

# Evaluation

1. Is the young toddler using different kinds of blocks in building?
2. Are gestures and language being used as the toddler works on a construction?
3. Is the young toddler moving and stacking the blocks?

# Art Learning Space

## Overview

Young toddlers are ready to explore their world using art and related media. These beginning experiences should take place in an area where toddlers can use art materials and tools in their own way. Often the toddlers' experimentation with materials is the most important aspect of their art. They have little concern about the final product; the process of doing it is everything. During this developmental period, it is essential that toddlers have sufficient time to try many different materials and discover ways of using the media.

## Learning Objectives

Young toddlers will:

1. Experiment with a variety of art materials and tools.
2. Use the tools to scribble in uncontrolled ways.
3. Learn about color and design through experimentation.
4. Recognize a growing ability to create art.

## Time Frame

This learning space should be available for use throughout the year. Remember that all the basic art materials are "new" for toddlers and that they need lots of time to explore them.

## Letter to Parents

Dear Parents,

During the early years of children's development, we are very interested in providing a wide range of possibilities for their experimentation. Art provides a very special way to learn about the world and appreciate the beauty around us. Young toddlers enjoy creating art in their own unique way. Although their work may look like uncontrolled scribbles, they often tell us about their pictures and the items they have included. We appreciate these beginning efforts because we know that they are a first step in creativity.

In our Art Learning Space your child will be painting, using clay, and gluing. He or she will want to bring these artistic works home for you to admire. When he or she shares a picture, you might say, "Tell me about your picture." Or, you could comment on the color and material they used. These supportive responses will let them know that you appreciate their work. They also enjoy seeing their art displayed, so find a special place to share their work.

# Layout of the Art Learning Space

# Web of Integrated Learning

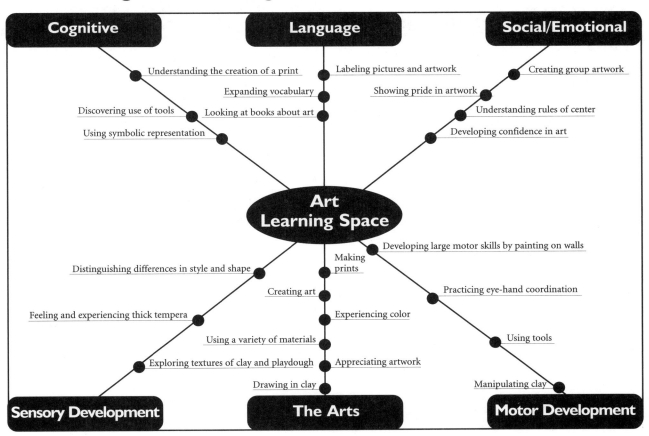

**Cognitive**

- Understanding the creation of a print
- Discovering use of tools
- Using symbolic representation

**Language**

- Labeling pictures and artwork
- Expanding vocabulary
- Looking at books about art

**Social/Emotional**

- Creating group artwork
- Showing pride in artwork
- Understanding rules of center
- Developing confidence in art

**Art Learning Space**

- Developing large motor skills by painting on walls
- Distinguishing differences in style and shape
- Making prints
- Creating art
- Practicing eye-hand coordination
- Feeling and experiencing thick tempera
- Experiencing color
- Using a variety of materials
- Using tools
- Exploring textures of clay and playdough
- Appreciating artwork
- Drawing in clay
- Manipulating clay

**Sensory Development**

**The Arts**

**Motor Development**

This learning space should be designed so that messy activities can occur and be cleaned up easily. The floor should be tile or covered with protective plastic. Tables and work surfaces should be easily cleaned or covered with plastic. Access to water will facilitate art and clean-up activities. Select tools and supplies to match the size and developmental level of young toddlers. For example, small bottles of glue and large paintbrushes work well.

## Vocabulary Enrichment

art
brush
clay
color
design
draw
glue
line
painting
shape

## Teacher- and Parent-Collected Props

butcher paper, manila paper, construction paper, and so on
containers for tools
cookie sheets or hospital trays
low easels
low table
plastic sheeting or shower curtains
plastic tub for water

## ACTIVITIES

# Clay Tray

several cookie sheets or hospital trays
potter's clay or playdough
stick, dowel rod, or unsharpened pencil
items to create interesting prints in clay

- Cover the bottom of a cookie sheet or hospital tray with potter's clay or playdough.
- Encourage toddlers to draw in the clay using a stick, dowel rod, or unsharpened pencil.
- Provide several trays so toddlers can work on their own clay.
  **Extension:** Unique items can be used to make prints in the clay. Some possibilities might include toy cars, kitchen tools, or nature items.

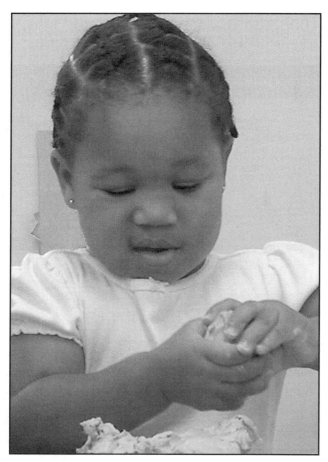

Clay provides a three-dimensional art experience.

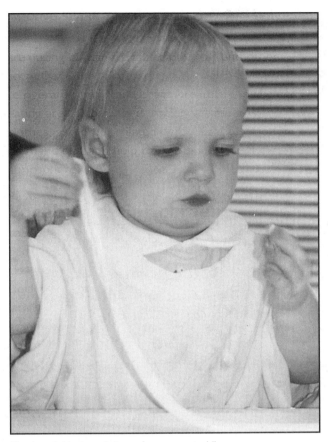

Clay is an intriguing substance for a young toddler.

# Painting on the Wall

blank wall
plastic
roll of paper
large paintbrushes
tempera paint
laundry detergent powder
3 or 4 paint smocks or small shirts

- Cover a wall and floor with plastic.
- Cut a large piece of paper from a roll and hang it so it covers a large portion of the wall.
- Toddlers can use large art brushes to paint on the wall in the big motions that they use at this stage of development.
- Add laundry detergent to the tempera paint so it is thick. This also makes it washable.

- A rule for participating in this activity is that each toddler wears a paint smock.
- Remember that great art is messy and so is the artist!

# Printing with Paint

plastic
large piece of paper
tempera paint
plastic tubs
variety of items to create interesting prints, such as a potato masher, sponge, plastic cup, measuring spoons, and so on

- Cover a section of the floor with plastic. Put the paper in the middle of the plastic.
- Mix tempera paint to a thick consistency and place it in a low plastic tub on top of the plastic.
- Provide a collection of household items that will produce an interesting print to dip into the tempera paint.
- Let the toddlers select the object they want to use in the print mural. They may choose several different items, if they desire.
- They will use these items to make one or more prints on the paper.
- Label the print with the child's name and the name of the object.
- Display the print mural low on the wall, so the toddlers can appreciate the colors and designs they helped create.

**ADDING SPARK TO THE ART LEARNING SPACE**

*Provide paper of different sizes for the toddlers to use while drawing with crayons or washable markers. Include long, skinny pieces, large pieces, curved pieces, and some colorful paper. Observe their exploration and interest in using the varied paper.*

# The Essential Literacy Connection
**(\* Available as a board book)**

Greenaway, Frank, Keates, Colin, & Young, Jerry. (1994). *Colors.* New York: DK Publishers Merchandise. *One of a series of first word books that focus on color and are filled with familiar objects and animals.*\*

Johnson, Crockett. (1981). *Harold and the Purple Crayon.* New York: HarperCollins. *See what children's minds will create after reading this inspiring tale about a toddler who draws himself into many adventures.*

Lionni, Leo. (2000). *A Color of His Own.* New York: Alfred A. Knopf. *A brightly illustrated story about a chameleon that changes colors.*\*

# Evaluation

1. Is the toddler experimenting with art materials and tools?
2. Does the toddler demonstrate that she is "proud" of her work?
3. Does the young toddler show an interest in a particular material?

# Private Place Learning Space

## Overview

Young toddlers are beginning to understand that they are separate beings from their teachers. They want to be independent and do things by themselves. They also have the very difficult task of trying to control both their emotions and their behaviors. Young toddlers can become easily over-stimulated and frustrated by too many sensory inputs, and do not know how to react. For example, you may take young toddlers on a field trip to the fire station. The fire station is filled with new sights, sounds, smells, and objects to touch. By the end of the field trip, the toddlers are tired, irritable, and prone to temper tantrums.

Children who are overwhelmed by their environment or emotions cannot put energy into learning new things. Therefore, it is very important that teachers help toddlers realize when they are over-stimulated. Young toddlers can recognize basic emotions such as afraid, happy, sad, hurt, and angry. The *Private Place Learning Space* will provide toddlers with a space to be alone and to calm down.

## Learning Objectives

Young toddlers will:
1. Begin to respond appropriately to simple emotions.
2. Learn about basic emotions, such as fear, anger, happiness, sadness, and feeling hurt.
3. Develop independence and feelings of self-worth.

## Time Frame

It is appropriate to have this learning space in the young toddler classroom during the entire year. It will take some time for the toddlers to understand the purpose of the *Private Place Learning Space*. However, it will be an area that encourages important social/emotional development for them.

## Letter to Parents

● ● ● ● ● ● ● ● ● ● ● ● ● ● ● ●

*Dear Parents,*

*We want to help your toddler grow in every area of development. As young toddlers become more independent, they learn that they have feelings separate from their teachers. For example, your toddler may be cranky and tired, while you are happy and excited. Toddlers can be easily frustrated and may have more temper tantrums during this period of development. Toddlers are unsure of how to handle their emotions in appropriate ways; they watch those around them to learn.*

*Even young toddlers sometimes need a little time and a quiet place where they can calm down. Our private place gives toddlers somewhere to go when they are feeling upset or overwhelmed. We will also be talking about basic feelings such as happiness, sadness, anger, feeling hurt, and being afraid. Please come by and visit our relaxing and soothing Private Place Learning Space.*

## Layout of the Private Place Learning Space

## Web of Integrated Learning

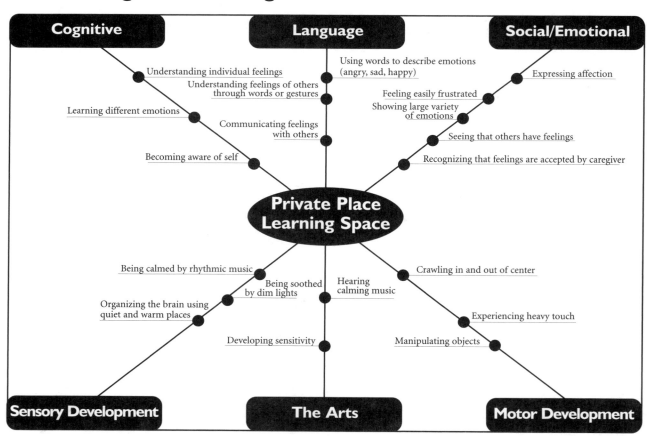

Choose a quiet part of the classroom to set up the *Private Place Learning Space.* Include a large cardboard box with a doorway to let the children in and out. Pillows, blankets, and stuffed toys can be in the area to encourage slowing down and relaxation. Soft music will also assist in creating a calm environment for the young toddler.

## Vocabulary Enrichment

afraid
angry
happy
hurt
private
quiet
sad

## Teacher- and Parent-Collected Props

large cardboard box (refrigerator, piano, or appliance boxes work well)
beanbag chair
classical music or new-age music with slow, rhythmic beats
crib mattress
pillows
soft blankets
string of white lights
tape or CD player with headphones
toddler-size rocking chair

**ACTIVITIES**

# Heavy Touch

pillows
1-lb sand pillows (see page 313 for directions)
sleeping bags
beanbag chairs
soft, heavy blankets
crib mattress

- Deep, firm touch is very calming and relaxing.
- Place objects in this area that will make the toddlers feel comfortable, warm, snuggly, and secure.
- Allow the young toddler to crawl on or under the pillows or mattress.
  **Note:** Supervise closely. Never let a child crawl completely under the mattress.
- Give a two-minute massage to soothe a child. This is useful for times other than naptime. A two- or three-minute massage should be adequate to help calm a child who is having difficulty getting organized. Slowly and firmly massage the toddler's arms, legs, and back. You may speak softly and talk about each body part as you massage it or just be quiet. Do not massage a child's face or stomach unless he asks you to do so.

# Calming Music

several music selections, such as classical, new age, jazz, and so on
headphones

- Music with a steady, rhythmical beat helps little brains get organized.
- Classical or new age music works best for calming.
- Headphones allow one child to quietly listen to music in the learning space, while not disturbing the rest of the class.
- Young toddlers can select where to relax and what music to listen to.

# Dim Lights

large cardboard box
sheet or blanket
small string of white lights

- Select a large cardboard box for the learning space.
- Hang a sheet or blanket over one end as the entranceway.
- If desired, hang a small string of white holiday lights on the ceiling. This will allow just enough light for a toddler to look at a book while inside the *Private Place Learning Space.*

Toddlers need a private space for unwinding.

## GUIDELINES FOR THE PRIVATE PLACE LEARNING SPACE

**Special Note:** *In order for this learning space to work effectively in the classroom, you must allow each toddler to use the learning space when he or she feels it is necessary. Respect the child's right to feel angry, sad, or afraid. Always help toddlers use words to label their emotions. It is recommended that you carefully monitor how the children are using the learning space. It will take time and direction for young toddlers to learn when and for how long they need to stay in the learning space. Be patient and consistent with them; this area may lead to a lifelong tool for managing their emotions.*

*It is important that you set a few simple rules for young toddlers. Tell the toddlers the rules for the Private Place Learning Space before opening it. Some suggested rules for toddlers using this learning space are as follows:*

* *Only one child at a time is allowed in the learning space.*
* *The child must tell the teacher before entering the area.*
* *This learning space is to be used when the child is feeling _____ (angry, sad, hurt, scared, and so on).*

# Name That Feeling

- Try to name the emotions as you or the children demonstrate them throughout the day.
- Begin with simple emotions such as feeling happy, sad, angry, scared, and hurt.
- You might say, "I can see that you are feeling hurt because you fell down."
- Children learn from observing others around them. Demonstrate appropriate ways to express your feelings.
- When you are sad, talk about why you are sad and how you are going to sit in a "private place" for a few minutes to be quiet.

Toddlers need a place to be alone in the busy classroom.

### ADDING SPARK TO THE PRIVATE PLACE LEARNING SPACE

*Some new items to introduce in the Private Place Learning Space include fake furs or soft materials, a ticking clock, stuffed animals, flashlights, and carpet samples. These add to the secure and safe feeling of the area.*

## The Essential Literacy Connection
(* Available as a board book)

Alborough, Jez. (2001). *Hug.* Boston: Horn Book. *Enjoy the adventure of following a baby chimpanzee's pursuit of his mother's hug.**

Brown, Margaret Wise (1991). *Runaway Bunny.* New York: HarperCollins. *Young toddlers will feel the security of a mother's love as they look at this book.**

Katz, Karen. (2001). *Counting Kisses.* New York: Margaret McElderry. *This book allows toddlers to share the kisses a baby receives from all the members of the family.**

Parr, Todd. (2000). *The Feelings Book.* Boston, MA: Little Brown and Company. *Adults can validate toddlers' feelings as they share their own feelings through the pages of this book.*

## Evaluation

1. Is the young toddler going into the *Private Place Learning Space* at appropriate times?
2. Is the young toddler beginning to verbalize basic emotions?
3. Is the young toddler attempting to control his own behavior?

# Music Learning Space

## Overview

Music captures the interest of young toddlers. They enjoy listening and participating in the creation of music. If toddlers have music around them, they will begin to "sing" or make sounds to accompany the musical patterns they hear. Many will have music that they especially like and want to hear repeated many times. A *Music Learning Space* is a planned environment where toddlers are free to experiment with sounds, create their own music, and enjoy the sounds.

## Learning Objectives

Young toddlers will:

1. Enjoy making music and participating in musical activities.
2. Listen to a variety of music.
3. Find new ways to express thoughts and ideas using music and instruments.

## Time Frame

The *Music Learning Space* can be rotated in and out of the classroom throughout the year, remaining approximately two weeks at a time. By observing the toddlers' participation, you will be able to determine whether the learning space and materials should remain longer or if a shorter period is needed.

## Letter to Parents

● ● ● ● ● ● ● ● ● ● ● ● ● ● ● ● ● ● ● ●

*Dear Parents,*

*Music delights young toddlers! The Music Learning Space is designed to give your young child an opportunity to hear a variety of music and sing along with the songs that they hear. In this learning space, they will be experimenting with different homemade instruments and some rhythm band instruments. This active participation with music will add to their enjoyment and learning.*

*We will be adding some string instruments to the Music Learning Space to provide other interesting experiences. If you have an old guitar, ukulele, Autoharp, or other string instrument that could be strummed and plucked by toddlers, please let us know. These would be wonderful additions for their musical experimentation in the Music Learning Space.*

## Layout of the Music Learning Space

## Web of Integrated Learning

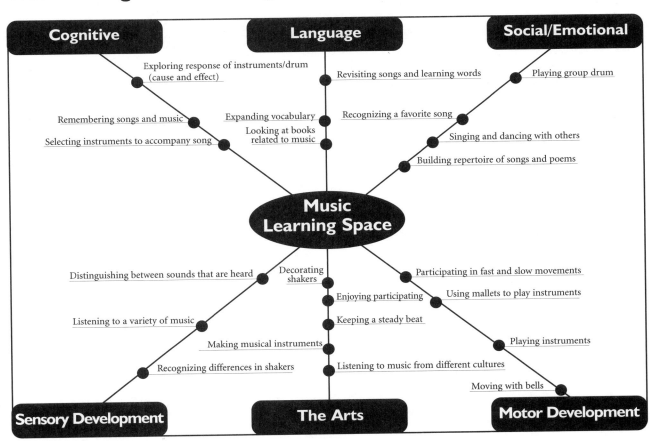

**Cognitive**
- Exploring response of instruments/drum (cause and effect)
- Remembering songs and music
- Selecting instruments to accompany song

**Language**
- Revisiting songs and learning words
- Expanding vocabulary
- Looking at books related to music

**Social/Emotional**
- Playing group drum
- Recognizing a favorite song
- Singing and dancing with others
- Building repertoire of songs and poems

**Music Learning Space**

**Sensory Development**
- Distinguishing between sounds that are heard
- Listening to a variety of music
- Recognizing differences in shakers

**The Arts**
- Decorating shakers
- Enjoying participating
- Keeping a steady beat
- Making musical instruments
- Listening to music from different cultures

**Motor Development**
- Participating in fast and slow movements
- Using mallets to play instruments
- Playing instruments
- Moving with bells

The *Music Learning Space* should be located away from quiet activities such as the *Book Learning Space* (page 132-136). Sound can be contained in the area by including soft items and surfaces to absorb the music produced. A toddler-size tape player encourages toddlers to select and play recordings on their own. A small couch or stuffed chair provides a relaxing place to enjoy music.

## Vocabulary Enrichment

drum
fast and slow
guitar or ukulele
instrument
listening
musician
recordings
singing
sounds
steady beat

## Teacher- and Parent-Collected Props

boom box
CDs or tapes of music from different cultures, such as Irish, African, Native American, and so on
collection of CDs and tapes (Include a variety of recordings, such as children singing, professional singers, band, orchestra, and guitar.)
drum
posters or pictures of musical events
rhythm instruments, such as rhythm sticks and shakers
soft items to add to the learning space, such as pillows, rugs, fabric, and so on
triangle
**Note:** Toddlers LOVE to pull the tape out of the cassettes. Supervise children closely as they handle cassette tapes!

## ACTIVITIES

# Responsive Musical Bracelet

jingle bells (medium size)
½" wide elastic
needle and nylon thread

- Toddlers are very active and in constant motion. Elastic bands with attached bells will respond to their movements and encourage them to produce more sounds.
- Select bells that are used during holidays or other times.
- Cut the ½" wide elastic into strips that will go around a young toddler's ankle or wrist.
- Securely sew the bells to each elastic strip with nylon thread.
- Sew the elastic strip ends together, like a bracelet.
- Toddlers can wear these when they are listening and moving to music. The bells will respond to the toddlers' movement and provide an accompaniment to the songs.

# Shakers

6 to 8 empty aluminum cans
materials to make sounds, such as rice, beans, nuts, rocks, and large buttons
duct tape, contact paper, or electrical tape
contact paper or washable markers

- Create shakers from empty aluminum cans.
- Fill each can with a selected material. Let the young toddlers help with putting items inside the cans.
- Cover the opening with duct tape, contact paper, or electrical tape.
- Label the bottom of each can with the name of the material inside so you know what is inside each can.
- Toddlers can decorate the cans with scraps of contact paper or washable markers.
- Each shaker will produce a different sound. The toddlers can use these to accompany their singing and/or movement.

A community drum can be used by several toddlers to make music.

# Community Drum

community drum (see page 306 for directions)
2 dowel rods
2 rubber balls
hot glue gun (teacher only)

- Create a large drum that can be played by several children at the same time.
- To improve the quality of the sound, place the drum on a long block or piece of lumber while toddlers are playing it.
- Let the toddlers play the community drum first with their hands. Later, they can use mallets to produce a different tone.
- Effective mallets can be made using a dowel rod for the handle. Punch a hole in a rubber ball and hot glue (teacher only) it to the dowel rod.
- These mallets produce a deep clear tone when used by the toddlers.
- Several toddlers can play this drum at the same time and eliminate disagreements that usually occur when only one drum is available for them. **Note:** After the toddlers play the drum a number of times, you may need to tighten the lacing so a good tone will continue to be produced.

# Favorite Songs

several recordings of songs
child's tape player

- Make a recording of the toddlers' favorite songs.
- Place the recording with a child's tape player in the *Music Learning Space*.
- The toddlers will be able to stop and start the music for themselves, and they will be able to control the amount and times they listen to the song.
- This encourages independence, while letting toddlers make choices about the music they hear.

# Musical Story

stories that encourage musical participation
drum or rhythm sticks, optional

- Tell a story that encourages participation in the telling. One that works well with this age group and invites sounds to accompany the telling is *The Little Red Hen* (Isbell & Raines, 2000, pp. 65-69).
- When the animals are asked to help, the toddlers can respond, "Not me" or "No, I won't help."
- If desired, use a drum, rhythm sticks, or clapping to accompany this phrase.
- The toddlers can help decide what sounds and instruments should accompany the story.

# Rhythm Sticks

wooden dowel rods of varying diameters (½" to ¾" sizes work best)
saw (adult only)
sandpaper
spray paint in different colors (adult only)

- Buy dowel rods at home building supply stores or art stores.
- Cut the rods into six-inch lengths (adult only).
- Be sure to sand the ends of the rods after they are cut.
- Spray paint the rods with different colors (adult only).
  **Note:** Do this away from the children in a well-ventilated area.
- Young toddlers can handle these rods and use them to tap with the steady beat of a song.
- Keeping a steady beat is a basic musical concept that should be nurtured during this period of development. Many toddlers will be able to imitate this pattern.

Toddlers use rhythm sticks to play a steady beat.

## ADDING SPARK TO THE MUSIC LEARNING SPACE

*A child's tape player with a microphone will encourage toddlers to sing and dance. These are very durable and easy for young toddlers to operate. The microphone will inspire toddlers to perform and watch others singing. Interesting dress-up items can add to their performance.*

# The Essential Literacy Connection

**(* Available as a board book)**

Adams, Pam. (2000). *Old MacDonald*. Bridgemead, Swindon: Child's Play International. *An illustrated version of the familiar song complete with cutouts of animals and their sounds.*

Baer, Gene. (1991). *Thump, Thump, Rat-a-Tat-Tat*. Illustrations by Lois Elhert. New York: HarperCollins. *Bright photographs and vivid word choices make this book a lively sensory experience.*

Brown, Marc. (1985). *Hand Rhymes*. New York: Sutton Children's Books. *This book consists of various nursery rhymes and includes diagrams showing children and teachers how to reproduce the fingerplays.*

Greenfield, Eloise. (1991). *I Make Music*. London: Writers and Readers. *A toddler explores the sounds of various instruments including the drum and piano.**

Spier, Peter. (1990). *Crash! Bang! Boom! A Book of Sounds*. New York: Doubleday. *This book includes illustrated sounds of everyday noises including those from the kitchen to those in outdoor building projects.*

## Other Printed Materials

Additional printed materials include music books with children's songs and catalogues for ordering musical instruments.

## Evaluation

1. Is the young toddler enjoying the music in the learning space?
2. Is the young toddler experimenting with different types of sounds he can produce?
3. Is the young toddler returning to the learning space to listen to favorite recordings?

# Nature Learning Space

## Overview

Toddlers are curious about the world around them. They want to examine things they collect outdoors and on walks using all of their senses. They enjoy revisiting the items, each time gathering new information.

This learning space can inspire budding naturalists and provide them with a safe place to experiment with real items from nature. It also nurtures an appreciation of things in nature and a concern for taking care of their world.

## Learning Objectives

Young toddlers will:

1. Explore items from nature using the senses—vision, touch, hearing, and smell.
2. Manipulate nature items using their developing fine motor skills.
3. Learn language labels for items collected and examined in the *Nature Learning Space*.
4. Begin to appreciate the natural environment in which they live.

## Time Frame

This learning space will be most appropriate when young toddlers are able to go on walks outside and collect items in nature that interest them. It may be set up from two weeks to a month. When toddlers' interest is decreasing, remove the learning space and store interesting items to use at another time.

## Letter to Parents

• • • • • • • • • • • • • • • • • • • • • • •

*Dear Parents,*
*Your toddler enjoys going on short walks and collecting nature items. We often take small bags with us on our walks, so we can bring "treasures" back to our Nature Learning Space. Toddlers find many interesting items that adults don't notice. Take time to examine these fascinating items with your young toddler and talk about what you find.*

*If you discover a special item that your toddler would like to bring to school, place it in a bag, label it, and note where it was found. This "treasure" will be added to our Nature Learning Space for other toddlers to examine and enjoy. We believe that an appreciation of beauty and nature begins during the early years. We are working to start that important process with our young toddlers.*

# Layout of the Nature Learning Space

# Web of Integrated Learning

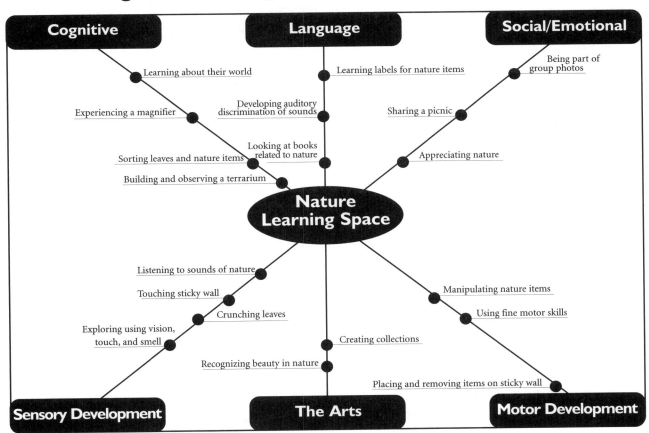

**Cognitive**

Learning about their world

Experiencing a magnifier

Sorting leaves and nature items

Building and observing a terrarium

**Language**

Learning labels for nature items

Developing auditory discrimination of sounds

Looking at books related to nature

**Social/Emotional**

Being part of group photos

Sharing a picnic

Appreciating nature

**Nature Learning Space**

Listening to sounds of nature

Touching sticky wall

Crunching leaves

Exploring using vision, touch, and smell

Recognizing beauty in nature

Creating collections

Manipulating nature items

Using fine motor skills

Placing and removing items on sticky wall

**Sensory Development**

**The Arts**

**Motor Development**

A low table is needed to display interesting nature items. Active toddlers will be able to walk around the table and manipulate items frequently. Include good lighting in the area so they can use their vision as well as touch to explore the materials. Use small plastic tubs to hold the items, so the toddlers can choose what they want to examine.

## Vocabulary Enrichment

collect

examine

feel

names of items collected

nature

picnic

pretty, beautiful

smell

texture

treasure

## Teacher- and Parent-Collected Props

large magnifier

low table

picnic basket and plastic utensils for eating outdoors

pictures of nature items that are collected during the season

plastic covers for table and/or floor

plastic zipper-closure bags for collecting and containing items

small plastic tubs or baskets for storing nature items

## ACTIVITIES (EXAMPLES INCLUDED ARE FOR THE FALL SEASON)

# Crunching Leaves

leaves and evergreen needles

containers

* Make a collection of all types of leaves and needles from trees around the school and in the neighborhood. Include some leaves that are already dry, others that are not.
* Place the leaves in a container that will allow the toddlers to crunch the leaves with their hands.
* Let the toddlers discover that some dry leaves make a crunching sound, while others make very little sound.

# Collection on Sticky Wall

blank wall

contact paper

tape

collection of nature items, such as grass, leaves, flowers, small sticks, bark, ferns, and moss

* Attach a long piece of contact paper to the wall with the sticky side out.
* Make sure the paper is securely attached and placed at the toddlers' level.
* Encourage the toddlers to stick nature items to this sticky wall.
* Continue to add items to the wall during the entire time the learning space is up in the classroom.

# Sounds of Nature

several recordings of nature sounds

tape or CD player to play the recordings

* Play recordings of nature sounds that the toddler might hear in the environment. This creates a more natural environment in the learning space.

# Picnic

basket
eating utensils
tableware
plastic tablecloth
small cooler

- A picnic is exciting for toddlers, so set up this possibility in the *Nature Learning Space*.
- Use an old basket to put items that the young toddler can use for eating outdoors, such as paper plates, cups, and forks/spoons.
- Let them use a plastic tablecloth to determine where they will have their picnic.
- A small cooler that they can open and shut adds interest to the area.
- Take pictures of the children as they take part in the "pretend" picnic.
- Later, carry the tablecloth and basket outside to have a picnic outdoors.

A toddler collecting nature items

- For example, if the toddlers live where there are birds, crickets, and wind chimes blowing, they will recognize these sounds. On the other hand, if the toddlers live in an urban environment, they will recognize crows "cawing" and dogs barking.
- At this stage of development, it is important to include sounds of nature that toddlers have experienced or that are within their world.

Camping and picnicking occurs in the Nature Learning Space.

**ADDING SPARK TO THE NATURE LEARNING SPACE**

*Create a terrarium (see page 313 for directions) where bugs and insects could come inside for a visit. When the Nature Learning Space is closed, let the toddlers take the bugs and insects back outdoors where they can live in their "real" environment. This provides an opportunity to talk about animals, bugs, and insects that need to live outdoors.*

# The Essential Literacy Connection
**(* Available as a board book)**

Carle, Eric. (1990). *The Very Quiet Cricket*. New York. Philomel Books. *A young cricket is greeted by various bugs and cannot respond until it meets another cricket.**

Cristini, Ermanno. (1991). *In the Woods*. Saxonville, MA: Neugebauer. *This wordless picture book shows the animals, insects, and flowers that can be found in the forest.*

Florian, Douglas. (1989). *Nature Walk*. New York: Greenwillow. *Illustrations guide the reader through a nature walk with familiar and unfamiliar animals, flowers, insects, and birds.*

Keats, Ezra Jack. (1971). *Over in the Meadow*. New York: Scholastic. *Illustrations and simple text describe various woodland animals and their young.*

McCully, Emily. (1999). *Picnic*. New York: HarperCollins. *A young mouse is left behind on the family picnic. No one is happy until she is found.*

# Other Printed Materials

Additional printed materials to have in the *Nature Learning Space* include books with pictures of items in nature around the area and catalogues of outdoor supplies.

# Evaluation

1. Is the young toddler interested in collecting items to add to the learning space?
2. Is the young toddler experimenting with the nature items in the learning space?
3. Which nature items are most interesting to the young toddler?
4. Can the young toddler be observed appreciating and being careful with nature items?

# Push and Pull Learning Space

## Overview

Once young toddlers have mastered standing and walking, they will begin practicing the new skills of pushing and pulling objects. Pushing toys in front will give toddlers support that assists them as they walk. Pulling toys is a little more difficult because it requires more balance. As a child pulls a toy, he or she can learn to stop, go, and change directions. Toddlers can also learn to walk while turning their bodies to look at toys pulled behind them.

The *Push and Pull Learning Space* is an important addition to a young toddler classroom. It is designed to encourage motor development and enhance cognitive skills. It is relatively simple to set up and provides toddlers with appropriate stimulation for active learning.

## Learning Objectives

Young toddlers will:

1. Improve eye-hand coordination through push-and-pull activities.
2. Gain experience in gross motor development.
3. Begin learning about directions (forward and backward).
4. Improve upper body strength by pushing and pulling objects.

## Time Frame

Young toddlers will benefit from this learning space for two or three weeks. You may want to revisit this learning space later in the year, as toddlers' development changes.

## Letter to Parents

Dear Parents,

We are pleased to announce the opening of a new learning space in our classroom, the Push and Pull Learning Space. Often, a young toddler will try to push objects in front of him or her to provide support before walking independently. After toddlers learn to walk, they will start pulling items behind them. This learning space will help your young toddlers with important motor skills such as bending down, stopping, going, and changing directions while walking. It contains many toys and objects to push or pull such as rolling toys, toys with strings attached, and a toy vacuum cleaner.

Some of the best things to push and pull are objects you probably have around your home such as cardboard boxes, chairs, towels, and large balls. Toddlers also like to imitate things they have seen you do, such as sweeping, vacuuming, or washing off the table. Enjoy watching your child as he or she practices pushing and pulling objects over and over again. Appreciate the wonderful motor skills he or she is developing.

# Layout of the Push and Pull Learning Space

# Web of Integrated Learning

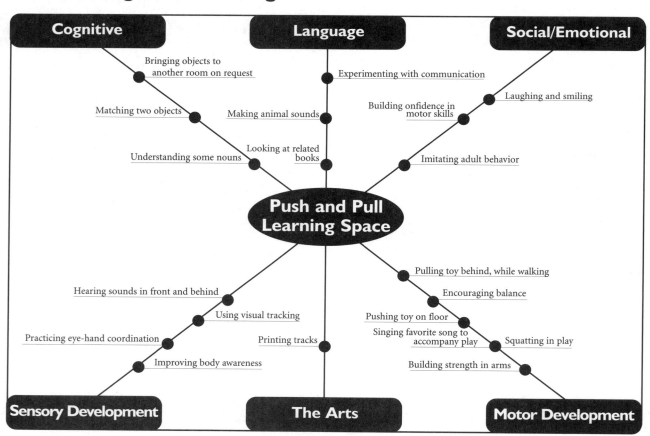

**Cognitive**

**Language**

**Social/Emotional**

Bringing objects to another room on request

Experimenting with communication

Laughing and smiling

Matching two objects

Making animal sounds

Building confidence in motor skills

Understanding some nouns

Looking at related books

Imitating adult behavior

**Push and Pull Learning Space**

Pulling toy behind, while walking

Hearing sounds in front and behind

Encouraging balance

Using visual tracking

Pushing toy on floor

Practicing eye-hand coordination

Printing tracks

Singing favorite song to accompany play

Squatting in play

Improving body awareness

Building strength in arms

**Sensory Development**

**The Arts**

**Motor Development**

The *Push and Pull Learning Space* will work best as an addition to the Motor Learning Space (page 112). Young toddlers need plenty of room to practice pushing and pulling objects. Put out riding toys, boxes, and wagons. Then, watch as the young toddlers select objects to move.

## Vocabulary Enrichment

box
go
lawnmower
pull
push
stop
vacuum cleaner
walk

## Teacher- and Parent-Collected Props

cardboard boxes in a variety of
        sizes
corn popper
large gymnastic balls
ramp
riding toys
rolling push toys
small plastic toys
stuffed animals
toy lawnmower and vacuum cleaner
toys that make a sound when they
        are pushed or pulled, such as
        a duck that quacks or an
        alligator that snaps
wagon
wheeled toys with strings

## ACTIVITIES

# Box Play

medium and small cardboard boxes
string, rope, or strong ribbon
small toys and stuffed animals

- Cardboard boxes make great, inexpensive push and pull toys.
- Attach string to the bottom of small boxes for pulling.
- Show the toddlers how to put a few toys inside the box to pull or push "for a ride."

A cardboard box makes a great wagon for moving stuffed animals.

## Just Like You

toy vacuum and broom
towels and washcloths
child-size chairs

- Toddlers love to imitate everyday activities.
- They like to sweep with a broom or follow you with their vacuum cleaner as you clean.
- Give them dry or wet washcloths and let them wipe off tables, the floor, or windows.
- Ask them to help you push the chairs to and from the table at snack time.

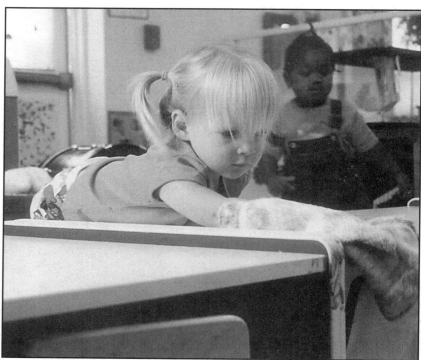

A toddler imitating the cleaning of a table—push and pull

## Animal Push and Pull

plastic farm animals and barn
tape
string or yarn

- Choose toy farm animals that are medium or large in size.
- Tape a piece of string or yarn to the toy for pulling.
- Demonstrate how to push and pull the animal across the floor, walking them back to their barn.
- Name the animal and make the appropriate animal sound as you go.
- Incorporate favorite songs into this game, such as "Old MacDonald Had a Farm" or "The Farmer in the Dell."

## Making Tracks

newspaper or black trash bags
tape
tempera paint, soap foam, or flour
old and/or washable push and pull
    toys

- This activity is best suited for an area of the room that is easy to clean up.
- Cover the floor with newspaper or black trash bags and tape them down securely.
- Place several different objects for pulling and pushing on the covered floor.
- Put a few "puddles" of paint, soap foam, or flour on the covered floor.
- Allow the toddlers to push and pull the objects through the "puddles" to make "tracks" on the covered section of the floor.

**ADDING SPARK TO THE PUSH AND PULL
LEARNING SPACE**

*Help toddlers do simple sorting.
Give them two different types of
objects such as stuffed animals
and blocks to "clean up." Put a
stuffed animal in one box and a
block in the other. Ask them to
place objects in appropriate boxes
to push or pull back to their
storage place.*

## The **Essential Literacy Connection**

Gay, Michael. (1983). *Take Me for a Ride*. New York: William Morrow. *A young toddler gives various animals a ride in his stroller until he gets tired and the roles are reversed.*

Hoban, Tana. (1972). *Push. Pull. Empty. Full.* New York: Macmillan. *Black and white photographs of day-to-day life help children identify and read 15 different opposites.*

Hoban, Tana. (1990). *Exactly Opposites*. New York: Greenwillow. *A colorful wordless picture book of opposites.*

Schaefer, Lola. (1999). *Push and Pull*. Mankato, MN: Capstone. *This book of color photography illustrates various push and pull movements.*

## **Evaluation**

1. Can the young toddler push toys or objects on the floor?
2. Can the young toddler pull a toy on a string?
3. Can the young toddler squat to pick up or move a toy?

# Hat Learning Space

## Overview

In this stage of development, the beginnings of dramatic play can be observed. Some young toddlers will pretend to be "baby" or "Mommy" in the *Housekeeping Learning Space* (pages 127-131). They will be playing a simple sequence in an activity, for example, as they prepare and eat food. This dramatic play is important and should be encouraged in the toddler classroom. In dramatic play, toddlers are developing symbols to represent real items. During this period, they need props that clearly resemble the real thing. Hats are a great way to encourage dramatic play and take on roles that relate to them.

In the *Hat Learning Space*, the props are easily identified and often relate to a specific role. Toddlers will be able to select and play with hats that interest them. This encourages their participation in the very important activity of dramatic play. Although much of the hat play is short in duration and may include a restricted view of the related role, this is a beginning step of development. As they participate in this play, young toddlers will be developing cognitive abilities, social skills, language, and motor skills. This integrated learning makes important brain connections that will positively affect the toddlers' development.

## Learning Objectives

Young toddlers will:
1. Try on hats and play the roles of people who might wear them.
2. Be involved in role-play.
3. Repeat actions, gestures, or words that relate to the wearing of hats and/or a specific role.
4. Watch and participate in play with others.

## Time Frame

This unique learning space adds interest to the toddler classroom. Rotate it into the area for two to three weeks and then store it away for future use. Hats can be collected throughout the year and added to the prop box for the next set-up in the classroom.

## Letter to Parents

Dear Parents,
Next week, we will be introducing a new learning space—the Hat Learning Space. This learning space will contain some unique hats that will be of interest to your toddler. In this learning space, toddlers will be able to try on the hats and view themselves in this new piece of clothing. They will begin to use "pretend play" as they experiment with the actions the hat inspires. It is so interesting to observe this play and the activity that it encourages. We will share with you some of the play that we observe transpiring in the Hat Learning Space so you can share in this learning experience.

We are looking for hats to add to our collection. We will be rotating a variety of hats into the learning space during the next two weeks. If you have a hat that toddlers can wear and play with, let us know. We can add it to the Hat Learning Space.

## Layout of the Hat Learning Space

## Web of Integrated Learning

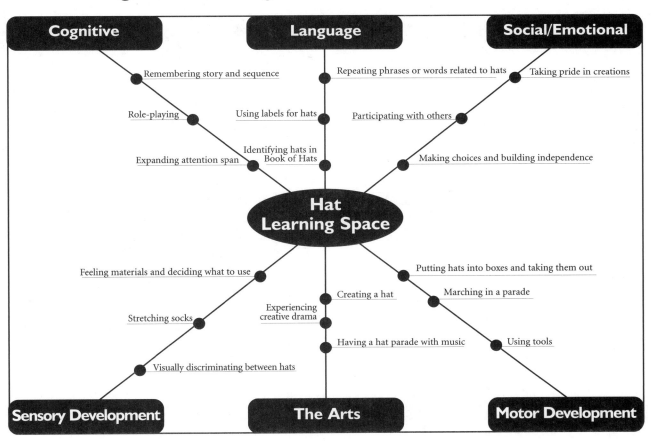

**Cognitive**

Remembering story and sequence

Role-playing

Expanding attention span

**Language**

Repeating phrases or words related to hats

Using labels for hats

Identifying hats in Book of Hats

**Social/Emotional**

Taking pride in creations

Participating with others

Making choices and building independence

**Hat Learning Space**

Feeling materials and deciding what to use

Stretching socks

Visually discriminating between hats

Creating a hat

Experiencing creative drama

Having a hat parade with music

Putting hats into boxes and taking them out

Marching in a parade

Using tools

**Sensory Development**

**The Arts**

**Motor Development**

The *Hat Learning Space* will be set up in the *Housekeeping Learning Space* for a few weeks. This learning space will be transformed to include a collection of hats. Put hat racks, pegs, and places to clearly display the hats available for use in the area. Hatboxes or containers that can be used for storing hats will also add interest to the play. A full-length mirror, as well as some non-breakable hand or stand mirrors, should be in the area so toddlers can see themselves in the hats. Include pictures on the wall that show hats being worn by different people. Hats can be either ordinary or unique—both types will interest young toddlers.

## Vocabulary Enrichment

| | |
|---|---|
| baby bonnet | glue |
| fancy | hard hat |
| farm | hats |
| firefighter | tape |
| fit | wearing |

## Teacher- and Parent-Collected Props

baby bonnet

fancy hats

firefighter's helmet

foam wig heads

full-length mirror and small mirrors

hard hat

hatboxes or other boxes for hats

hats that are a part of the local culture, such as
    fishing hat, baseball cap, band hat, cowboy hat,
    and so on

helmets, such as ones used for riding a bicycle,
    motorcycle, horse, and so on

knit hat

man's hat

peg racks

rain hat

straw hat

sunbonnet

## ACTIVITIES

# Book of Hats

scrapbook

pictures of hats from magazines

scissors (adult only)

- Use a scrapbook to create a handmade book about hats.
- Cut out pictures of hats from magazines, including hats that are part of the toddlers' experience. Include a few unique items, but primarily focus on hats that they have seen.
- Include the hat book in the learning space for the children to look through and identify the hats.

# Caps for Sale

tape recorder

blank tape

A brown paper grocery bag becomes a great hat for a toddler.

- Tell the story "Caps for Sale" in the *Hat Learning Space* during story time.
- Adapt the story so that the peddler (salesperson) sells hats that are available in the learning space.
- For example, "On his head he had a baby bonnet, a farmer's straw hat, a fancy hat," and so on.
- After the telling of the adapted story, open the *Hat Learning Space* for play.
- Make a recording of your telling of the story so the children can listen to it again, if they wish

# Create a Hat

several small brown paper bags (enough for each child)
materials, such as scraps of paper, ribbon, fabric, contact paper, feathers, net, pipe cleaners, and plastic flowers
washable markers
glue
several foam mannequin heads

- Use brown paper bags to form the foundation for a hat. Use the smaller size that will fit the toddler's head.
- Roll up the edge, so it will stay on their head when the creation is completed.
- Have a variety of materials available for the toddlers to use in decorating their hat.
- Foam wig heads can help by holding the hat while the toddler is working.
- Place the toddlers' creations in the *Hat Learning Space* for children to see.
- Toddlers can add decorations to the hats for several days, if they are interested in continuing the process.
- Take a picture of the child in her hat creation to display and share with parents.

# Sock Hat

several adult-size stretch socks
materials to decorate sock hats, such as yarn, flowers, pompoms, trim, scraps of fabric, and netting

- Use adult-size stretch socks to create interesting caps.
- The stretch end of the sock will fit the young toddler's head.
- The foot portion of the sock can be stuffed, left loose, or removed, depending on the child's choice.
- Let the children decorate them or wear as they are.

# Hat Parade

hats
marching music

- Encourage the young toddlers to select a hat from the area to wear in a parade. Some may want to wear the hat they have created in the *Hat Learning Space*.
- Play a march, such as John Phillip Sousa's "Stars and Stripes Forever."
- Marching music with a strong steady beat will encourage toddlers to participate in the hat parade.
- Toddlers will enjoy "showing off" their hats and marching to the music.

Hats helps toddlers take on a role.

**ADDING SPARK TO THE HAT LEARNING SPACE**

*Add a collection of baby caps and hats. Young toddlers enjoy playing "baby." These new props will encourage their participation in the play and the use of sounds to mimic a baby.*

# The Essential Literacy Connection

Adams, Pam. (1999). *Mrs. Honey's Hat.* Bridgemead, Swindon: Child's Play. *Young toddlers will delight in watching Mrs. Honey's hat transform each day of the week.*

Keats, Ezra Jack. (1966). *Jennie's Hat.* New York: HarperCollins. *When Jennie receives a rather plain hat from her aunt, she works hard to make it the prettiest hat ever.*

Morris, Ann. (1993). *Hats Hats Hats.* New York: Mulberry Books. *A multicultural book of color photographs showing people and hats from around the world.*

Slobodkina, Esphyr. (1987). *Caps for Sale.* New York: Harper Trophy. *The classic tale of a peddler who outwits the monkeys that took his hats.*

Smith, William J. (1993). *Ho for a Hat!* Boston, MA: Little, Brown, and Company. *A young boy and his dog try on a variety of hats.*

# Other Printed Materials

The *Hat Learning Space* also should have catalogues that contain pictures of hats.

# Evaluation

1. Is the young toddler trying on hats and viewing himself in the mirror?
2. Can the toddler be observed using actions, gestures, or words inspired by the hats?
3. Has the toddler created hats to wear and/or display?

# Ball Learning Space

## Overview

Young toddlers are fascinated by balls of all different sizes, colors, and textures. Throwing balls is a motor skill that they work diligently to learn during this stage of development. By the end of the second year, most toddlers will be able to throw a ball under-handed while sitting down. Some young toddlers will be able to throw a ball over-handed and forward. Young toddlers may attempt to kick a ball. Some toddlers will walk toward a ball and move it forward by bumping into it. A few toddlers will even stand and kick a ball with one foot.

As with most developmental skills, throwing and kicking a ball takes a lot of practice. The *Ball Learning Space* will provide these experiences for toddlers while allowing them to use balls in new and different ways.

## Learning Objectives

Young toddlers will:

1. Improve eye-hand coordination by using balls.
2. Develop eye-foot coordination.
3. Learn labels for balls and accompanying activities.

## Time Frame

This learning space is effective in a young toddler classroom for two or three weeks. Observe the toddlers' activities in the *Ball Learning Space* to decide when appropriate play has ended. You may revisit this learning space later in the year. This learning space will also work well when weather restricts outdoor play.

## Letter to Parents

• • • • • • • • • • • • • • • • • • • •

*Dear Parents,*

*We have just opened our new* Ball Learning Space. *Toddlers love to play with balls of all sizes and shapes. They like to throw, kick, roll, pick up, and carry balls. By 18 months old, some toddlers may be able to throw a ball forward. They usually learn how to catch a ball sometime after they have learned to throw a ball.*

*The* Ball Learning Space *will help our young toddlers with their eye-hand coordination, balance, and gross motor skills. Please bring in any inner tubes or cardboard boxes that you could share with us. The toddlers can use them for target practice using foam balls, paper balls, and beanbags, which are safe for indoor play.*

## Layout of the Ball Learning Space

## Web of Integrated Learning

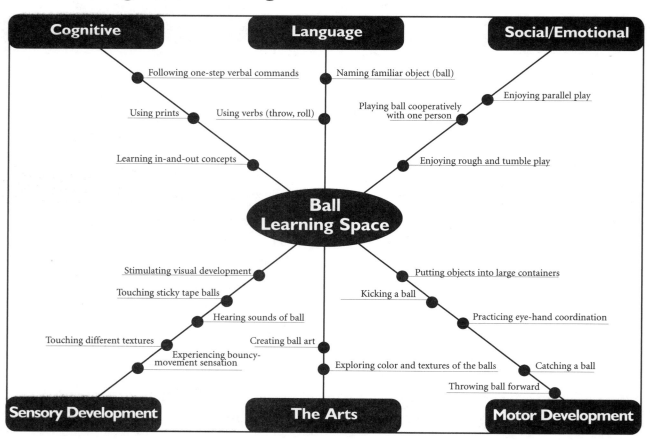

**Cognitive**

- Following one-step verbal commands
- Using prints
- Learning in-and-out concepts

**Language**

- Naming familiar object (ball)
- Using verbs (throw, roll)
- Playing ball cooperatively with one person

**Social/Emotional**

- Enjoying parallel play
- Enjoying rough and tumble play

**Ball Learning Space**

**Sensory Development**

- Stimulating visual development
- Touching sticky tape balls
- Hearing sounds of ball
- Touching different textures
- Experiencing bouncy-movement sensation

**The Arts**

- Creating ball art
- Exploring color and textures of the balls

**Motor Development**

- Putting objects into large containers
- Kicking a ball
- Practicing eye-hand coordination
- Catching a ball
- Throwing ball forward

The *Ball Learning Space* is best suited for a part of the room where there is ample floor space, such as the *Motor Learning Space*. Toddlers will be very active in this area, so it is best to place it away from quiet places. A carpeted floor will help decrease the noise level. Keep smaller balls in storage containers to be readily available.

## Vocabulary Enrichment

ball
carry
catch
kick
large
roll
small
throw

## Teacher- and Parent-Collected Props

beanbags
bowling pins
cardboard boxes and plastic containers in a variety
    of sizes
foam balls
hula-hoops
large gymnastic balls (One ball should be very large
    and another should be small enough for young
    toddlers to sit on with their feet touching
    the floor.)
large net or basket for ball storage
medium-size balls, such as soccer balls
nubby balls
playdough
scented balls
small balls, such as tennis balls
small baby swimming pool filled with plastic balls
tire inner tubes

## ACTIVITIES

# Big Ball Fun

various gymnastic (therapy) balls, 21" or larger

- Large gymnastic balls can create many new challenges for young toddlers.
- Do not completely inflate the gymnastic balls. Leave them a little soft so that they do not move as quickly.
- You may hold a toddler very firmly as he sits or bounces on top of the ball on his stomach, back, or bottom.
- Young toddlers can sit alone on large balls, if their feet touch the floor.

Teachers can help toddlers sit on the gymnastic ball.

# Balls In and Out

large and medium cardboard boxes
scissors (adult only)
beanbags
foam balls
string, rope, or wide ribbon

- Cut a large circular hole into one side of large boxes. Leave the top open in medium-size boxes.
- Attach one end of a string to each beanbag and/or ball used in the activity.
- Attach the other end of the string to the inside edge of the box.
- Demonstrate how young toddlers can throw the attached balls or beanbags into the boxes.
- Toddlers can pull the strings to remove balls or beanbags from inside the box, and the strings help keep the box and balls together.
- Begin by placing the boxes close to the children (one foot away) and giving them many soft balls for throwing.
- Push the boxes farther away, as the toddlers improve their aim.

A toddler places a textured ball into a box.

# Ball Art

large paper
tape
medium-size paintbrushes
small and medium washable plastic or rubber balls
tempera paint in several colors
pie tins

- This is a messy and fun activity. Ball Art works best in the *Art Learning Space* or outside for easy cleanup.
- Tape paper to the floor.
- Give the toddlers a ball and a paintbrush.
- Pour tempera paint into pie tins.
- Demonstrate how to use the paintbrush to paint their ball.
- Let them complete the painting of their ball and "roll" or "bounce" the ball onto the paper to make ball art.
- Display the ball art in the learning space for all to appreciate.

# Tape Balls

many long strips of tape, such as masking, packing, electric, duct, and so on
foil or wax paper, optional

- Young toddlers love the new sticky experience of playing with tape.
- Give toddlers long strips of tape and show them how to squeeze the tape together to form a ball. You may use a variety of types of tape to make balls.
- Watch young toddlers explore the tape balls.
- Ask them to try to throw or roll the balls.
- If desired, put foil or wax paper on walls or tabletops for targets.
- Watch how the tape balls stick to surfaces.

## ADDING SPARK TO THE BALL LEARNING SPACE

*Encourage the toddlers to crumple paper to make balls. Put out large coffee cans or clean, plastic trashcans for targets to throw or drop balls into.*

# The Essential Literacy Connection
**(* Available as a board book)**

Asquith, Ros. (2000). *Ball!* New York: Dorling Kindersley. *A rhythmic tale about a toddler's journey after his bouncy ball.*

Breeze, Lynn. (1998). *Pickle and the Ball.* Boston: Houghton Mifflin. *A toddler explores all the activities he can do with a ball.**

Nelson, Mary Beth. (2000). *Balls.* New York: Random House. *An interactive book of Elmo's World that has large flaps to open, uncovering different types of balls.**

Tafuri, Nancy. (1989). *The Ball Bounced.* New York: Greenwillow. *Young readers can follow the sequence of events that occur when a toddler drops a bouncy ball.*

# Evaluation

1. Is the young toddler throwing balls?
2. Is the young toddler attempting to kick balls while standing?
3. Is the young toddler placing balls in and out of containers?

# Sand Learning Space

## Overview

Sand is a wonderful natural material that young children enjoy. Young toddlers appreciate the feel, the manipulation, and the responsiveness of the sand. In the *Sand Learning Space,* toddlers can develop their fine motor skills as they pour, sift, and build with this intriguing substance. When tools are added, new discoveries occur and the learning changes. This interesting area draws young toddlers to participate and explore in special ways.

## Learning Objectives

The young toddler will:
1. Investigate the properties of the natural material of sand.
2. Develop fine motor skills using sand and tools.
3. Build a longer attention span, while using sand in a personally meaningful way.
4. Learn vocabulary that accompanies activity in the *Sand Learning Space.*

## Time Frame

The *Sand Learning Space* is a high interest area and toddlers will be drawn to play there. First, introduce the sand in the learning space without any tools and toys. This allows the toddler to explore sand and its unique qualities. After this investigation has taken place, add a few simple tools that encourage pouring, sifting, and building. This learning space can also be transformed into a water area or dirt area, when a change is needed. Many of the same tools that work in the *Sand Learning Space* will work in these areas, too.

## Letter to Parents

• • • • • • • • • • • • • • • • • • • •

*Dear Parents,*

*We are setting up a Sand Learning Space for our young toddlers. Sand is a natural material that most young children enjoy using. Since sand is very responsive, they can observe an immediate reaction to their movements. This allows them to see what they are doing and get feedback from their activity. The interest in sand is so high that many toddlers will remain in this learning space for long periods exploring, practicing pouring, and sifting.*

*The coordination of hands and eyes is an important ability that begins to develop during early childhood. In the Sand Learning Space, this development will be encouraged in meaningful ways. As they pour sand into a bottle, young toddlers coordinate their hands with what they see. As they sift, they watch how the sand comes through the opening. Toddlers want to participate because the sand is such a unique substance, and they learn a great deal during the process.*

# Layout of the Sand Learning Space

# Web of Integrated Learning

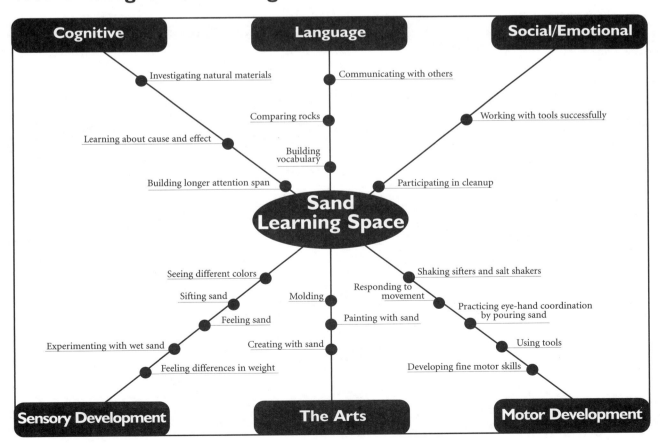

**Cognitive**

Investigating natural materials

Learning about cause and effect

Building longer attention span

**Language**

Communicating with others

Comparing rocks

Building vocabulary

**Social/Emotional**

Working with tools successfully

Participating in cleanup

**Sand Learning Space**

Seeing different colors

Sifting sand

Feeling sand

Experimenting with wet sand

Feeling differences in weight

Molding

Responding to movement

Painting with sand

Creating with sand

Shaking sifters and salt shakers

Practicing eye-hand coordination by pouring sand

Using tools

Developing fine motor skills

**Sensory Development**

**The Arts**

**Motor Development**

Place a low sand and water table in the *Sand Learning Space*. If no table is available, use plastic tubs to hold the sand. Place plastic under the table to catch sand spills and simplify cleanup. Keep a hand-held vacuum or broom with dustpan in the area. Toddlers enjoy using these tools in their cleanup. Pictures of deserts and beaches displayed on the wall add to the visual interest in the *Sand Learning Space*. Storage tubs can hold some of the tools that are used with sand after the initial exploration period.

## Vocabulary Enrichment

| | |
|---|---|
| cleanup | sift |
| dip | texture |
| feel | tools, such as a sifter, funnel, |
| fill | shovel, tube, and so on |
| pour | turn |
| sand | watch |

## Teacher- and Parent-Collected Props

bag of sterilized white sand
broom (with short handle) and dustpan
hand-held vacuum cleaner
plastic tubs for sand and tools
roll of clear plastic
tools for use with sand, such as sifters, funnels, plastic cups, tubes, shovels, spoons of various sizes, plastic bottles with large openings, plastic flower pots, plastic nested measuring cups, measuring spoons, and sand toys

## ACTIVITIES

## Homemade Sifter

aluminum pie plates or frozen food containers
pencil or pen

- Make a few holes in the bottom of the containers with a pencil or pen (adult only).
- Place the containers in the sand for the toddlers to experiment with. Watch the sifting that occurs.
- Young toddlers can make their own sifter by punching holes in aluminum plates and comparing the different flows of sand that occur with a few holes or many.
**Note:** Supervise closely.

## Wet Sand

plastic spray bottle
plastic cups, gelatin molds, muffin pans, and other objects
- Spraying water on sand changes the feel and responsiveness of the sand.

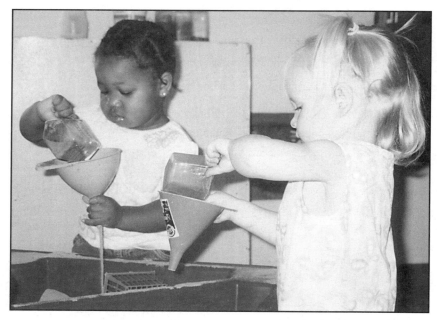

Toddlers practice pouring, which helps develop fine motor skills.

- Toddlers can use various items to mold wet sand.
- Let the young toddlers spray the sand with water. Then, encourage them to experiment with wet sand to determine the characteristics that are different from dry sand.

# Rocks

several rocks of various sizes and colors

- Provide an interesting collection of different types and colors of rocks in the *Sand Learning Space*.
- Make sure the various-size rocks are larger than a quarter in size. Include some rocks that are rough and others that are smooth.
- Some of the tools that are used to explore sand can also be used with rocks.
- Ask the young toddlers, "How do they feel?" "Are they heavy?" "Can you pour and sift them?"

# Colorful Sand

white sand
dry tempera paint
large plastic bottle with lid

- Combine white sand with some dry tempera paint in a plastic bottle with lid.
- Young toddlers can shake the bottle and watch the sand change color.
- After you have created enough colored sand, add a tub of colorful sand to the learning space.
  **Note:** Add more tempera paint to create more intensely colored sand.
- Toddlers will be interested in finding out if colorful sand responds in the same ways the white sand responds.

# Sand Painting

white glue
cardboard or heavy paper
large plastic or metal saltshaker filled with colored
    sand
large paintbrush

- Paint a piece of cardboard or heavy paper with white glue.
- Let the toddlers sprinkle colored sand onto the glue surface using a large plastic or metal saltshaker.
- Some sand will stick to the glue and dry; some will not.
- Hand-made sifters mentioned in other activities are also effective for sand painting.
- Display these unique sand creations in the *Sand Learning Space* for the toddlers to appreciate.

# Shredded Paper Art

paper
paper shredder
sand and water table or plastic tub
large brushes
white glue
dark paper

- **Experimenting First:** Shred paper. The long, thin pieces of shredded paper are very interesting to young toddlers. They can feel, move, and examine the shredded pieces of paper, which respond very differently from the sand that is usually in the learning space.
- **Creating Art:** Shredded paper can also be used to create art. Give the toddlers large brushes and watered-down white glue to attach the pieces to a background of dark paper. Some pieces will stick, some will overlay, and some will fall off the paper. The shredded paper and glue produces a three-dimensional work of art.

**ADDING SPARK TO THE SAND LEARNING SPACE**

*Collect plastic animals that might live in sand and add these to the Sand Learning Space. Create tunnels and caves to provide hiding places for the animals in the sand. Young toddlers will enjoy burying and finding these plastic animals.*

## The Essential Literacy Connection

Hubbell, Patricia. (2001). *Sea, Sand, Me!* New York: HarperCollins. *Rhythm and repetition make this story of going to the beach a colorful adventure.*

Oxenbury, Helen. (1982). *Tom and Pippo on the Beach.* New York: Dial. *The illustrations in this wordless picture book depict a toddler's adventures in the sand on the beach.*

Prager, Ellen. (2000). *Sand.* Washington, DC: National Geographic Society. *A sandpiper bird discovers how sand is created in this simple story with collage illustrations.*

## Other Printed Materials

In addition to books, put the postcards of beaches or deserts in the *Sand Learning Space*.

## Evaluation

1. Is the young toddler interested in manipulating the sand?
2. What kinds of fine motor skills is each toddler developing?
3. Does the young toddler participate in the cleanup of the tools and learning space?

# Friends Learning Space

## Overview

During this period of development, young toddlers are very egocentric. They view the world from their perspective and in relation to how things affect them. Young toddlers often work and play independently, having little interaction with others. They are just beginning to become aware of other children and their needs. Social development can be encouraged during this period by providing non-threatening possibilities for working with others. Toddlers also need the flexibility to leave an activity or group when they become frustrated or tired.

The planned *Friends Learning Space* focuses on the possibility of making friends and beginning to appreciate their importance. While these early social experiences are occurring, young toddlers are attempting to answer some important questions. What is a friend? How does a friend act? How can I be a friend to other toddlers?

In the *Friends Learning Space,* toddlers will be able to find some answers to these questions as they participate in group projects and observe the behaviors of other toddlers. This area is flexible enough that young toddlers can continue to play as long as they are interested and leave the space when they are ready. This allows toddlers to influence their environment and the length of their social involvement.

## Learning Objectives

Young toddlers will:
1. Recognize the possibility of having friends.
2. Begin to use vocabulary related to friends.
3. Begin to consider the needs of friends as they play in the area.
4. Discover ways to be a friend.

## Time Frame

This learning space can be rotated into the classroom throughout the year. When the composition of the class changes and/or new members are added, this learning space can help introduce new friends to the group.

## Letter to Parents

• • • • • • • • • • • • • • • • • • • • • •

*Dear Parents,*

*During the second year of children's lives, they become more social. They are interested in other people and children in their environment. However, toddlers remain very egocentric and often say "mine" or "no." Learning to live in the world requires that they learn social skills and how to get along with others. This is a long journey and takes many years for most children.*

*Next week, we will be setting up a new learning space about friends. In this Friends Learning Space, we will focus on developing friendships and behaviors that support relationships such as sharing and helping. At home, talk with your toddler about his or her friends in the classroom. This is a beginning step for learning about friends and how important they are in our lives.*

# Layout of the Friends Learning Space

# Web of Integrated Learning

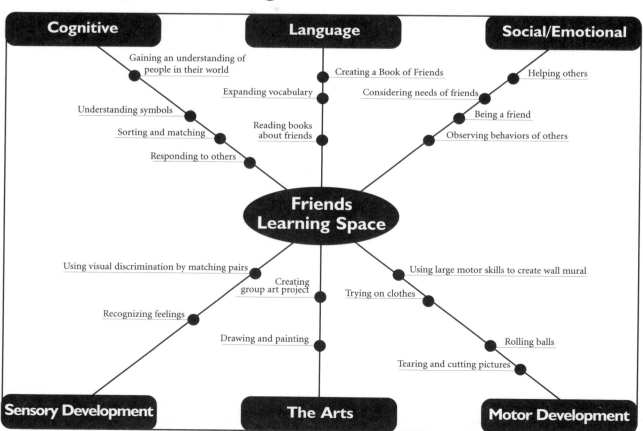

**Cognitive**

Gaining an understanding of people in their world

Understanding symbols

Sorting and matching

Responding to others

**Language**

Creating a Book of Friends

Expanding vocabulary

Reading books about friends

**Social/Emotional**

Helping others

Considering needs of friends

Being a friend

Observing behaviors of others

**Friends Learning Space**

Using visual discrimination by matching pairs

Creating group art project

Recognizing feelings

Drawing and painting

Using large motor skills to create wall mural

Trying on clothes

Rolling balls

Tearing and cutting pictures

**Sensory Development**

**The Arts**

**Motor Development**

The *Friends Learning Space* can be small and used in a variety of ways. A flat wall can be covered with plastic for group artwork. A low table or riser can be used for activities such as pairing of objects. Display pictures of toddlers in the classroom at a low level in the space, so they can recognize class members.

## Vocabulary Enrichment

friends
help
kind
"Look at their faces, see how they feel."
sharing
work together

## Teacher- and Parent-Collected Props

old magazines that might show
    pictures of friends
pairs of clothing, such as gloves;
    two matching hats, shoes,
    socks; two matching toys;
    matching salt and pepper
    shakers; and two matching
    books
photographs of each toddler

# Book of Friends

pictures of the toddlers
materials to make a book, such as construction
    paper, glue, and markers

• Create a book that includes pictures of each of the young toddlers in the class.
• Include the toddler's name, pictures of things they like to do, or some of their favorite foods.
• Place this book in the *Friends Learning Space*. It can also be used in the *Book Learning Space*.

Friends talking and responding to each other

# Collection of Pairs

plastic tub
several items that come in pairs, such as gloves,
    socks, shoes, and hats that are the same
unbreakable mirror

• Place the collection of paired items in a plastic tub.
• Place an unbreakable mirror in the learning space, so the toddlers can try on the clothing items.

**GROUP ART PROJECTS**

*One of the ways a toddler can successfully experience working with others is through group artwork.*

Friends working on the same art project.

- Comment that they are matching the gloves, shoes, or hats.
- If young toddlers are helping someone pair items, comment on this positive behavior.

## Group Art Project—Wall Mural with Friends

tape
plastic roll
large sheet of butcher or construction paper
liquid tempera paint
laundry detergent powder
pie pans
paper towels/cloths for cleanup
marker

- **Personal Print**: Tape plastic on a large wall space. Tape a large sheet of paper on top of the plastic. Mix tempera paint with laundry detergent and put it into pie pans. Young toddlers, guided by the teacher, can determine what they would like to contribute to the mural. Possibilities include prints of their hand, foot, or finger. Label the prints with the young toddlers' names.

- **Object Print:** A variation of this idea is creating a print mural using a sponge, potato masher, comb, feathers, and dish scrub brush. Let toddlers choose the color and item to use. They can paint the object of their choice with tempera paint, and then determine where they will place their prints on the mural. Label the contribution of each toddler, so they can visually see their part and the work of the other toddlers. Display the group project in the *Friends Learning Space*.

# Group Art Project–Magazine Collage

old magazines, such as parenting, children's, catalogs, and others that have pictures of friends
glue
large art paper

- Ask the young toddlers to look through magazines and find pictures of "friends."
- Help the toddlers tear out or cut the pictures from the magazines and glue them to the art paper.
- Ask the toddlers what the friends are doing and talk about the pictures they selected.
- If two toddlers are working together, comment on this and label the artwork with both names.
- Display this group art in the *Friends Learning Space*.

**ADDING SPARK TO THE FRIENDS LEARNING SPACE**

*Rolling balls with friends encourages interacting between toddlers. Two young toddlers can sit on the floor with legs outstretched and the soles of their feet touching. They can roll a rubber ball to each other, using their legs to contain the path of the ball. By working together, they are able to roll the ball back and forth.*

## The Essential Literacy Connection

Blegvad, Lenore. (2000). *First Friends*. New York: HarperCollins. *A rhyming book that shows children playing, sharing, and getting along together.*

Isadora, Rachel. (1990). *Friends*. New York: Greenwillow. *Simple illustrations and one-word labels help young children identify what friends might do on a typical day.*

Parr, Todd. (2000). *The Best Friends Book*. Boston: Little, Brown, and Company. *Celebrate friendship with this boldly illustrated book that shares how friends are friends no matter what.*

Pfister, Marcus. (2001). *Where Is My Friend?* New York: North-South. *While searching for a friend, a porcupine first meets a cactus, a hairbrush, and many other prickly objects.*

## Evaluation

1. Is the toddler beginning to observe the actions of other children?
2. Is the toddler using the word "friend" during the day?
3. Is the toddler participating in positive interactions with other toddlers in the classroom? Does the teacher or another toddler appreciate these interactions?

# CHAPTER FIVE

# Older Toddler
## 24-36 months

## Developmental Considerations

In the first two years of life, children learn the basic motor and sensory skills that are needed throughout the rest of their life. Older toddlers are now spending more time refining these motor skills and sensory skills, rather than learning many new skills. This allows older toddlers to focus more energy on cognitive, language, and social-emotional development.

Older toddlers are going through a critical period of cognitive and emotional growth. Their language is exploding and it seems as though they learn a new word every day. They are able to distinguish between a variety of emotions such as anger, fear, love, and joy. Yet, they are not able to express their feelings effectively. In addition, older toddlers continue to be self-centered (egocentric). An older toddler is concerned about herself and has a difficult time taking others' feelings into consideration. The older toddler is striving to be independent and may become quite frustrated when she cannot do what she wants to do "by myself." This may lead to emotional outbursts. Older toddlers are developing autonomy and can see themselves as capable when teachers support their beginning efforts.

Older toddlers need caregivers that understand their special developmental considerations. Toddlers need and respect rituals and routines. They do best when they are given a flexible time frame for their daily schedule. It is important that teachers follow the pace of the toddler. Carefully observing toddlers' play and interactions will also help teachers prevent over-stimulation. Guiding, rather than demanding that toddlers complete a task, will promote their learning process.

## Cognitive
- Recognizes self in photograph
- Knows full name
- Demonstrates use of common objects
- Engages in simple make-believe
- Understands complex sentences
- Listens to stories
- Identifies more body parts
- Matches shapes, such as circle, square, and triangle
- Matches one primary color, such as red, yellow, green, or blue
- Pretend (symbolic) play begins

## Social/Emotional
- Imitates adult activities
- Plays beside another child (parallel play)
- Relates best to one adult at a time
- Initiates own play but requires supervision to carry out ideas
- Is very possessive of loved ones
- Displays both dependent and independent behavior (whines, clings, and pushes away)
- Tends to be physically aggressive
- Is becoming aware of sex differences
- Participates in toilet training
- Plays in similar activities (associative play)

## Gross Motor
- Stands on tiptoes
- Runs safely
- Goes up and down stairs, one at a time
- Kicks large ball
- Walks backwards
- Pedals tricycle
- Throws ball overhead

## Language
- Calls self by name
- Uses simple sentences ("more cookie")
- Uses 10-20 words
- Repeats requests (echoes)
- Constant questions ("What's that?")
- Asks for food and drink appropriately
- Answers simple questions

## Sensory
- Notices sounds in the environment
- Finds objects at far distances

## Fine Motor
- Builds tower of six to seven large blocks
- Imitates circular stroke
- Imitates vertical stroke
- Good spoon control
- Drinks from open cup
- Unzips zipper
- Snips with scissors
- Copies a circle

The learning spaces presented in this chapter have been especially designed to promote the development of older toddlers. The learning spaces address each developmental area, while respecting older toddlers' special developmental considerations. The activities provided help expand toddlers' knowledge about themselves, others, and the world around them. In the learning spaces, older toddlers can influence their environment and learning process.

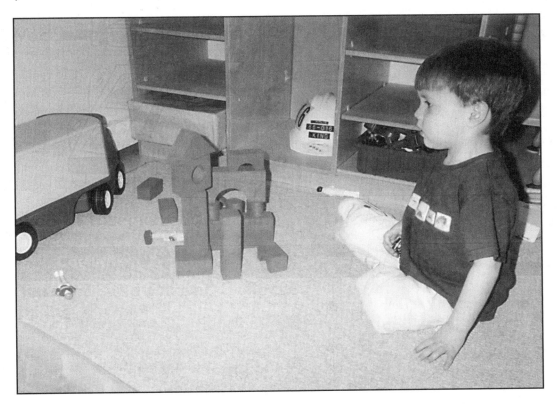

Older toddler building a town with blocks.

# Motor Learning Space

## Overview

Older toddlers are refining the movement skills they mastered during their second year. They have more confidence and try more difficult actions such as climbing and jumping. They can complete new motor activities such as an obstacle course or outdoor climbing structure. Two-year-olds can also imitate more bilateral (both sides) arm and hand movements, as in dance.

Toddlers need time every day to spend in motor activities. Often, physically active young children attend better to cognitive tasks and are less distracted in general. Children can be active inside or outside, but they should receive a minimum of 30 minutes of physical activity in an 8-hour period. The *Motor Learning Space* will use fun games and appropriate equipment to meet this need, while promoting gross motor skills.

## Learning Objectives

Older toddlers will:

1. Expand their repertoire of body movements.
2. Improve coordination in fine motor tasks.
3. Improve balance and coordination in gross motor movements.

## Time Frame

This learning space may remain available for the entire year, with equipment and materials changing throughout the year.

## Letter to Parents

• • • • • • • • • • • • • • • • • • • • • • •

*Dear Parents,*

*Two-year-olds continue to practice their motor skills and now their movements begin to look more smooth and coordinated. Toddlers are known for being brave and adventurous. They like to climb and jump off of anything and everything. They need safe and appropriate activities that will help them learn more advanced motor skills such as throwing a ball into a large container, jumping forward, hopping on one foot, and stepping with one foot at a time up and down stairs. They are also getting better at imitating your movements. A fun thing to do is put on music, let your child imitate you, and then take a turn copying his or her "new dance."*

*Our indoor Motor Learning Space will have fun activities designed to improve large motor skills. We will have an obstacle course, go on "animal walks," and do fingerplays, such as "Where Is Thumbkin?" and "Here is the Beehive." Come by and let us teach you a new fingerplay game to try at home with your toddler.*

## Layout of the Motor Learning Space

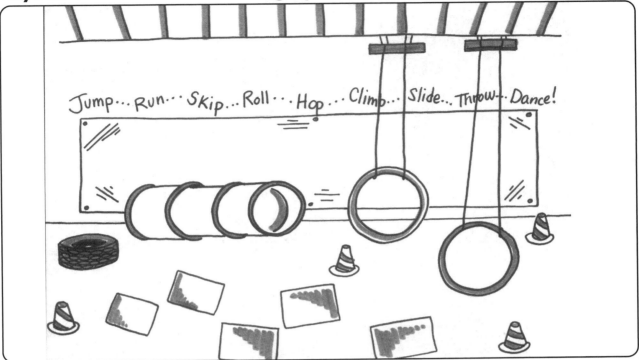

## Web of Integrated Learning

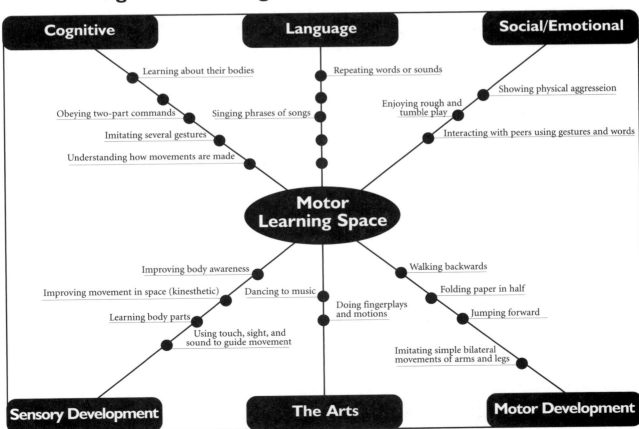

The *Motor Learning Space* requires a large open space. Toddlers will experience frequent falls in this space, so a carpeted area is good idea. Hang a large net from the ceiling to store large and small balls. Use a clothing hook on the wall to hang hula-hoops, and place other items inside a carpeted cylinder standing upright against a wall or corner of the room. A large unbreakable mirror, low on the wall, will encourage movement that the toddlers will watch and imitate.

## Vocabulary Enrichment

down
finger
hop
imitate
inside
jump
move
obstacle course
outside
up

## Teacher- and Parent-Collected Props

carpet samples
carpeted cylinders (see page 307 for directions)
collapsible tunnel
foam wedges (see page 309 for directions)
hula hoops
large and small soft balls
large unbreakable mirror adhered to the wall
mats
riding toys
rubber tire
tricycles

## ACTIVITIES

# Fingerplays

Various fingerplays:
- "The Eensy Weensy Spider"
- "Here Is the Beehive"
- "This Is the Way We..."
- "Where Is Thumbkin?"
- "Five Little Monkeys"

- Demonstrate the movements to several fingerplays each day.
- Select fingerplays with more difficult movements for older toddlers.
- Let the toddlers select their favorites. Keep in mind that they may want to repeat the same fingerplays many times.

# Obstacle Course

suggested obstacle course options:
- crawl through tunnels
- climb over wedges or cylinders
- jump into the "water" (tires or hula hoops)
- crawl under mats
- hop on one foot
- throw small balls into medium-size containers
- roll over or under large ball
- push toys
- ride tricycle
- step from one carpet sample to the next
- jump on a mini-trampoline

- Use the teacher- and parent-collected props to set up an obstacle course. Design the course to have three or four different activities (see suggestions above).
- Take a few minutes to introduce the course to the toddlers and to demonstrate how to complete it. Use your imagination and the children's interests to describe the course as a lake, ocean, mountain, tree, cave, or tall building.

- Toddlers will want to practice the obstacle course until they conquer it.
- Change the obstacle course when you see that the toddlers are losing interest.
- Later, the toddlers can help in redesigning the obstacle course for different routes.

Toddler jumps into a hula hoop on an obstacle course.

# Animal Walks

- Demonstrate how a particular animal "walks." Ask the children to follow you.
- Select animals such as an elephant, frog, cat, snake, monkey, bear, bird, dog, and fish.
- Allow the children to choose animals, too. They can even make up their own "animal walks."
- If desired, add music to this activity.
- This activity improves older toddlers' ability to plan and implement motor actions.

# "Simon Says..."

Commands for use with "Simon Says...":
- put your finger on your nose
- touch your ears
- stand on one foot
- don't move
- jump up and down
- make your body a straight line
- put your hand on your knee
- clap your hands two times
- turn around and then sit down
- shake hands with a friend
- make your body a circle

- Modify this simple game and use it to help young children improve their body awareness.
- If desired, use your own name instead of "Simon says..." and ask the children to do simple actions.
- Start with one-step commands and, as children improve, add more steps and more difficult actions.
- Older toddlers may not understand why you sometimes say, "Simon says..." and other times you do not. Therefore, it is recommended that you always say, "Simon says...."

Toddlers can imitate motions of others.

**ADDING SPARK TO THE MOTOR LEARNING SPACE**

*Read* We're Going on a Bear Hunt *to the toddlers. Design your obstacle course as a "bear hunt." Hide several small stuffed bears under a box or in a container at the end of the course.*

# The Essential Literacy Connection

**(\* Available as a board book)**

Ancona, George. (1998). *Let's Dance.* New York: William Morrow & Co. *This color photography book illustrates and describes various full-costume dances of different cultures.*

Carle, Eric. (1999). *From Head to Toe.* New York: HarperCollins. *Toddlers can mimic the actions of the animals in the book while discovering their own body parts.\**

Cauley, Lorinda Bryan. (2001). *Clap Your Hands.* New York: Penguin USA. *This book shows children and animals involved in clapping, hopping, wiggling, and moving in a variety of ways.\**

Croll, Carolyn, & Cross, Carolyn. (2001). *Fingerplays and Songs for the Very Young.* New York: Random House. *Children will enjoy looking at and learning the 25 new and traditional fingerplays illustrated in this book.\**

Pinkney, Andrea, & Pinkney, Brian. (1997). *Watch Me Dance.* New York: Harcourt. *A preschooler entertains a baby by teaching him to dance.\**

Rosen, Michael. (1997). *We're Going on a Bear Hunt.* New York: Simon & Schuster Children's. *This is a delightfully funny and exciting story of a brave family's journey through beautiful landscapes.\**

Wood, Audrey. (1999). *Silly Sally.* New York: Harcourt. *This humorous tale shares a cumulative rhyme about how a girl gets from here to there.\**

# Evaluation

1. Is the older toddler able to isolate her fingers for a simple fingerplay?
2. Is the older toddler able to jump forward?
3. Is the older toddler able to imitate simple movements of the arms, legs, head, and trunk?

# I See Learning Space

## Overview

Older toddlers' visual skills are more like adults. By age three, some toddlers can match blocks by color, even though they cannot name the colors. They can place a circle, square, and triangle in the correct position in a puzzle. Toddlers' visual perceptual skills are still developing. They may continue to name all older men wearing hats "Papa." As they grow, toddlers begin to visually analyze whole areas, and will tell you if a chair or toy is out of place. A toddler can even find a favorite toy truck that he hid several hours before.

The *I See Learning Space* will be a place where toddlers can continue to develop the important sense of vision and use it more functionally. This learning space will include visual-perceptual activities such as bead stringing, puzzles, and sorting.

## Learning Objectives

Older toddlers will:

1. Learn about the world through vision.
2. Begin sorting by color and basic shapes.
3. Develop fine motor skills, by experimenting with simple puzzles and drawing.

## Time Frame

The *I See Learning Space* can be available to toddlers during the entire year. You may include a planned art activity, described during circle time, for toddlers who want to participate later in the learning space.

## Letter to Parents

• • • • • • • • • • • • • • • • • • • •

*Dear Parents,*

*In the* I See Learning Space, *your toddler will be developing his or her sense of vision. He or she will be experimenting with shapes, colors, and lines. He or she will be discovering ways to sort objects and complete simple puzzles. We will be reading and looking at the colorful illustrations of simple books. Feel free to bring in your child's favorite book to share with the other toddlers.*

## Layout of the I See Learning Space

## Web of Integrated Learning

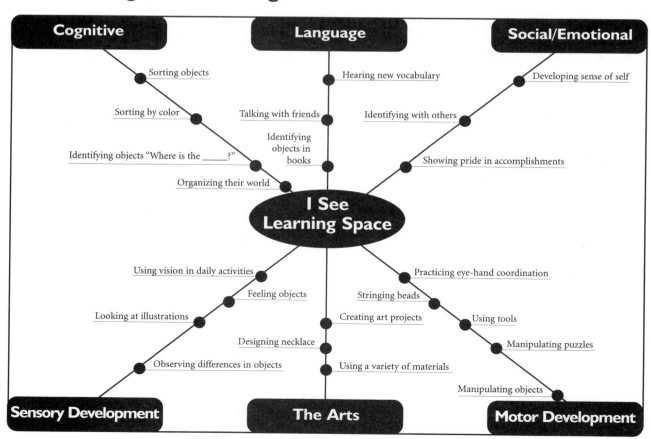

The *I See Learning Space* should be located in an area of the room where toddlers can manipulate objects and complete planned art projects. It would be useful to have this learning space where there is natural light. Also, consider that you may be turning out the lights in this part of the room.

## Vocabulary Enrichment

behind
color
dark
down
flashlight
in front
inside
light
outside
shape
sort
sunglasses
up

## Teacher- and Parent-Collected Props

3- to 12-shape sorter
3- to 8-piece jigsaw puzzles
books with uncluttered pictures
bubbles
clear plastic containers
colorful beads and blocks
colorful plastic wrap
dry cereal for stringing
flashlights
medium-size pegs and pegboard
paper
pipe cleaners
simple parquetry boards
single-piece puzzles
string or yarn
sunglasses
tape
washable markers
white sheet
wooden or plastic shapes

## ACTIVITIES

# Color Flashlights

several medium-size flashlights
colorful plastic wrap
tape
white wall or white sheet

- Use flashlights with easy on/off switches.
- With assistance, let the toddlers cover the head of the flashlights with colorful plastic wrap or thin colored plastic. Tape the plastic around the edges.
- Use a white wall or hang up a white sheet.
- Turn out the lights and let the toddlers do a light show with the color flashlights. See if they can identify the colors on the wall.
- They can also shine the colored flashlights onto objects, to see what color the objects become.

# Face Puzzles

photographs or magazine pictures of children's faces, approximately 8" x 10"
cardboard or poster board
glue
scissors

- Help the toddlers glue the photographs or pictures to poster board or cardboard.
- Cut the pictures into three to four pieces.
- Help the older toddlers complete the puzzles or even mix and match pieces to make new faces.
- Toddlers' photographs could also be enlarged and used as personal face puzzles.

# Cleanup

coffee cans with lids
paper
labels

- Clean-up time is the perfect time to experience sorting.
- Make containers for small objects by covering coffee cans with paper and cutting holes in the lids, or use shelves or purchased containers for sorting.
- Make sure to label all containers or shelves with both pictures and words.
- With your help, older toddlers can learn to match objects to the pictures on their appropriate containers.

# Sorting

several different sizes and colors of objects, such as blocks, beads, connecting blocks, pegs, and shapes

- Have a variety of materials available for sorting.
- Demonstrate how to sort objects.
- Ask the toddlers to sort the objects by color.
- As they become skilled with sorting by color, suggest that they sort the objects by shape.

# Bead Necklace

several pieces of yarn, stiff string, or pipe cleaners
variety of large colorful beads (at least 1" in diameter)

- Demonstrate how to make a necklace using beads, and then let the toddlers create their own.
- Give the toddlers pieces of yarn or stiff string with knots at one end.
- Provide large beads of different colors and shapes to string.
- Assist the toddlers in making their own necklaces to wear.

# Object Identification

books with pictures

- Select books with simple, realistic drawings that are not too cluttered.
- While reading to toddlers, encourage them to point to pictures. Questions such as, "Show me the cow," or "Where is the tree?" will involve the toddlers in noticing the drawings and illustrations in the book.
- Remember that sometimes toddlers have a short attention span, so don't strain story time by asking too many questions.
- Observe the older toddlers' involvement and close the activity when their interest fades.

Plastic tubing works well for stringing beads.

**ADDING SPARK TO THE I SEE LEARNING SPACE**

*Providing older toddlers with new materials to sort and string will encourage them to think creatively. It will also help them maintain their attention to these tasks. Start collecting miscellaneous objects for sorting and keep them in a box. Materials to sort include plastic fruits or vegetables, shoes, hats, and cans. Items for stringing include pipe cleaners, shoelaces, dry cereal, spools, plastic lids with holes, large buttons, and CD's.*

## The Essential Literacy Connection
**(\* Available as a board book)**

Brandenberg, Aliki. (1998). *My Five Senses.* New York: HarperCollins. *An older toddler discovers how he uses his five senses in a variety of ways and combinations.*

Cousins, Lucy. (1997). *What Can Pinky See?* Cambridge: Candlewick. *This lift-the-flap book allows toddlers to see what Pinky the rabbit spies in a day while encouraging them to become more aware of what they may see during their day.*

Marzollo, Jean. (1997). *I Spy Little Book.* New York: Scholastic. *Toddlers will enhance their observation skills as they find the hidden objects in this book.\**

Zarin, Cynthia. (1998). *What Do You See When You Shut Your Eyes?* Boston: Houghton Mifflin. *Children's imaginations are illustrated through the pictures of what happens when they begin to use their senses.*

## Evaluation

1. Is the older toddler able to complete simple puzzles?
2. Is the older toddler imitating large bead stringing?
3. Is the older toddler able to identify some pictures in a book by pointing or by name?

# I Touch Learning Space

## Overview

Toddlers learn about the world through their senses (vision, hearing, taste, smell, and touch). It is important to encourage older toddlers to use their sense of touch for discovery. This learning space allows toddlers to explore and experiment with a variety of textures and materials. Toddlers should not only use their hands, but also their feet, face, and limbs to feel. Older toddlers should also use tools to help them manage and learn about new substances and textures. This will encourage their creativity as well as their motor skills.

Toddlers in the *I Touch Learning Space* will be active and messy. This learning space should be a place where children feel free to explore and create.

## Learning Objectives

Older toddlers will:

1. Understand their world through the sense of touch.
2. Learn about different textures.
3. Become creative as they participate in sensory activities.
4. Develop independence in using tools to manipulate materials.

## Time Frame

Keep the *I Touch Learning Space* set up for at least two to three weeks. Observe toddlers in the learning space to determine when they stop exploring. Then, close the *I Touch Learning Space* and bring it back at a later time. You may keep this learning space in operation for a longer period of time, if the toddlers' interest remains high.

## Letter to Parents

• • • • • • • • • • • • • • • • • • • • • • •

*Dear Parents,*

*Our* I Touch Learning Space *gives older toddlers the opportunity to learn about the world through their sense of touch. In this learning space, toddlers will explore a variety of textures such as smooth, hard, soft, rough, bumpy, slippery, and squishy. Toddlers will also be able to use tools such as funnels, measuring cups, and paintbrushes. This learning space will be a fun and educational way for your child to develop knowledge about the environment.*

*Please bring in any fabric scraps, such as silk, satin, lace, fur, or corduroy, or materials that you may have at home, such as cotton balls, cotton swabs, lengths of rope, sandpaper, or bubble wrap. This will help us create an exciting* I Touch Learning Space *for your toddler.*

# Layout of the I Touch Learning Space

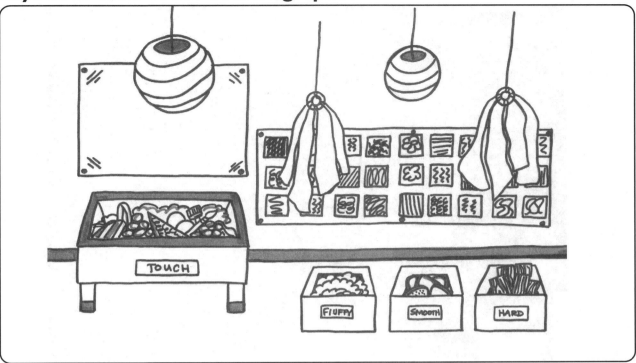

# Web of Integrated Learning

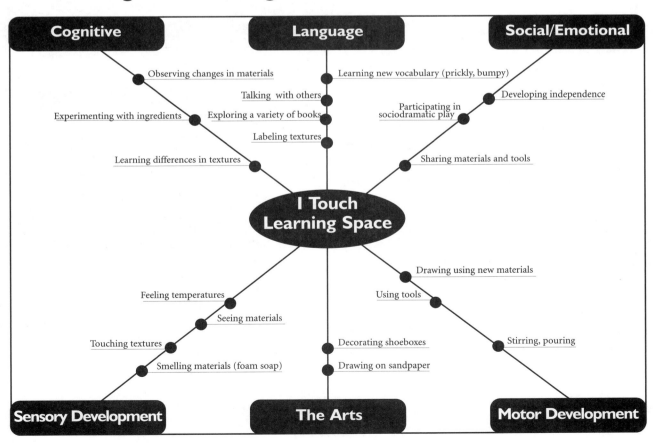

**Cognitive**

Observing changes in materials

Experimenting with ingredients

Learning differences in textures

**Language**

Learning new vocabulary (prickly, bumpy)

Talking with others

Exploring a variety of books

Labeling textures

**Social/Emotional**

Developing independence

Participating in sociodramatic play

Sharing materials and tools

**I Touch Learning Space**

**Sensory Development**

Feeling temperatures

Seeing materials

Touching textures

Smelling materials (foam soap)

**The Arts**

Decorating shoeboxes

Drawing on sandpaper

**Motor Development**

Drawing using new materials

Using tools

Stirring, pouring

The *I Touch Learning Space* is best suited to an area of the room used to create art and manipulate materials. It should be placed near other creative learning spaces, such as the *Art Learning Space*. A sand/water table is useful for allowing older toddlers to explore new materials through touch; a toddler-size table can also work well. Scrap fabrics, textured objects, and other items may be stored in separate clear plastic containers. The *I Touch Learning Space* can be easily transformed into another learning space, such as the *Sand and Water Learning Space* or the *Science and Nature Learning Space*.

## Vocabulary Enrichment

| | | |
|---|---|---|
| bumpy | hard | smooth |
| cold | prickly | soft |
| different | rough | sticky |
| feel | same | touch |
| firm | slippery | warm |

## Teacher- and Parent-Collected Props

clear plastic boxes (to store and organize props)

cooking supplies, such as flour, salt, sugar, and cornstarch

fabric scraps, such as corduroy, silk, satin, lace, denim, cotton, polyester, taffeta, netting, cotton batting, burlap, fur, and spandex

household items such as cotton balls, cotton swabs, yarn, and foil

kitchen tools, such as large spoons, rolling pin, tongs, and ice cube trays

large paintbrushes

large plastic bowls

plastic toys such as animals, cars, and trucks

playdough or modeling clay

sand and/or water table (make economical tables with plastic tubs on low tables or on the floor)

sandpaper (several different grains)

shower curtain liners or sheets of plastic (place on tabletops and under tables and tubs)

small broom and dustpan or vacuum cleaner

stuffed animals

## ACTIVITIES

# New Materials

several new items for older toddlers:
- soap foam
- bubble wrap
- rocks
- seashells
- dirt
- tree bark
- ice cubes
- dog toys with textures (wash before using)

- Change the *I Touch Learning Space* by adding different materials, one at a time, to the sand/water table or plastic tub.
- Each new material will stimulate the older toddler's exploration and learning.

Birdseed in the sand/water table stimulates new play for toddlers.

# Sociodramatic Play

sand/water table or plastic tub

medium-size plastic animals

small toys with wheels

soap foam or cornstarch

- Put soap foam or cornstarch into the sand/water table or a plastic tub.
- Add plastic animals and toys with wheels to encourage dramatic play in the *I Touch Learning Space*.
- Encourage older toddlers to push a tractor through the "snow" (soap foam or cornstarch).

Drawing with chalk on sandpaper

## New Textures with Water

large bowl
cornstarch
water
spoon

- Pour cornstarch into a large bowl.
- Encourage the toddlers to touch the cornstarch. Talk about its smooth, soft, fluffy texture.
- Add water to the cornstarch and mix with a spoon.
- Talk about how the wet cornstarch feels in your hands.
- Encourage the toddlers to notice how the wet cornstarch changes shape in their hands. This unique substance responds to toddlers' touch in new ways.

## Texture Writing

chalk
large pieces of sandpaper
paper

- Toddlers can use chalk to draw on sandpaper, or on a piece of paper placed on top of the rough sandpaper.
- The sandpaper will add an interesting texture to their drawings.
- Talk about how the sandpaper feels to their hands as they draw and how it changes their picture.

# Texture Box

various materials, such as burlap, foil, yarn, bark, cotton balls, and satin
several shoeboxes
glue

- Collect a variety of materials with interesting textures.
- Give each toddler her own shoebox.
- Let the toddlers select materials and glue them on the outside of their boxes.
- Ask the toddlers to identify the different textures on their boxes.
- These special boxes can be used to store their treasures or personal items.

### ADDING SPARK TO THE I TOUCH LEARNING SPACE

*If toddlers are losing interest in textures, add tools such as paint sponges, scissors, stylus (wooden writing tool), funnels, and sifters. These tools will help children explore materials in a new way.*

## The Essential Literacy Connection
**(* Available as a board book)**

Bryant-Mole, Karen. (1996). *Texture.* Parsippany, NJ: Silver Burdett Press. *Colorful photography is used to teach toddlers some of the vocabulary used when discussing textures.*

Carter, David A. (1995). *Feely Bugs.* New York: Simon & Schuster Children's. *This book includes bugs with a variety of textures to touch and feel, while labeling each illustration.*

Sclavi, Tiziano. (1994). *Touch and Read.* Honedale, PA: Boyds Mills Press. *Older toddlers are encouraged to guess what is coming next by listening to questions and feeling die-cut pages.**

## Evaluation

1. Is the older toddler exploring materials and textures with his body, including hands and/or feet?
2. Is the older toddler improving in fine motor coordination as she plays with materials?
3. Is the older toddler using simple tools to manipulate materials?
4. Is the older toddler beginning to use simple words to identify the textures and/or materials in the *I Touch Learning Space?*

# Housekeeping Learning Space

## Overview

Home is a place that older toddlers understand. They have experience with the people who live there, the roles they perform, and the activities that occur in this setting. This provides a level of understanding that can be used by older toddlers in their play. The traditional *Housekeeping Learning Space* has been used in early childhood programs for more than 100 years. Housekeeping has long encouraged active participation in a safe environment that toddlers can relate to and understand. It is an essential learning space in the older toddler classroom. In this environment, they can take on roles that are familiar to them, such as mother, father, grandparent, or baby. Often, toddlers, who may be new to the classroom or unfamiliar with the other learning spaces, will begin in this area and return to it again and again.

## Learning Objectives

Older toddlers will:

1. Expand oral language while they participate in activities.
2. Build on their current understanding of family and home.
3. Begin to understand the roles and responsibilities of other people.
4. Develop a positive view of their capabilities as they work in a familiar environment.

## Time Frame

This learning space will be set up in the classroom throughout the year. In some classrooms where space is very limited the *Housekeeping Learning Space* can be transformed into other learning spaces that will rotate into the area for two to three weeks at a time. For example, the *Cooking Learning Space* can work well in the space, while using many of the same materials.

## Letter to Parents

• • • • • • • • • • • • • • • • • • • • •

*Dear Parents,*
*The* Housekeeping Learning Space *is an essential part of our toddlers' classroom. This traditional learning space has been included in early childhood programs for more than 100 years. The* Housekeeping Learning Space *has been so important because it enables toddlers to develop language skills, participate in dramatic play, and begin to understand about the work of other people. Older toddlers also begin to learn about taking care of others, cooking meals, and cleaning up—skills they will need throughout their lives.*

*We are always looking for new items to add to our* Housekeeping Learning Space. *If you would like to contribute any props, we would greatly appreciate it. Some possibilities include men's and women's hats, shawls, scarves, ties, dress-up clothes, gloves, boots, and pieces of interesting fabric. Thank you for your continuing support.*

# Layout of the Housekeeping Learning Space

# Web of Integrated Learning

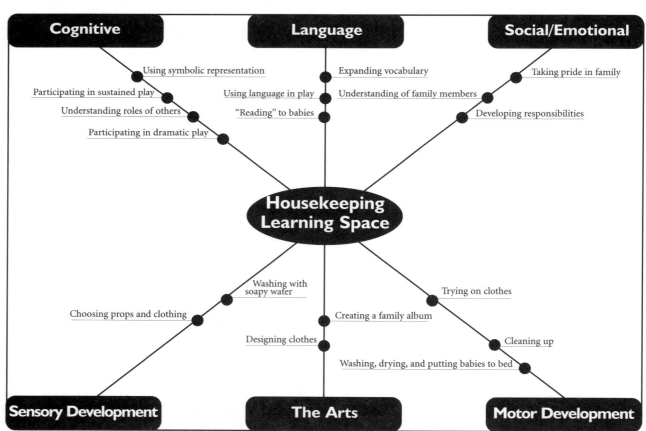

**Cognitive**
- Using symbolic representation
- Participating in sustained play
- Understanding roles of others
- Participating in dramatic play

**Language**
- Expanding vocabulary
- Using language in play
- Understanding of family members
- "Reading" to babies

**Social/Emotional**
- Taking pride in family
- Developing responsibilities

**Housekeeping Learning Space**

**Sensory Development**
- Washing with soapy water
- Choosing props and clothing

**The Arts**
- Creating a family album
- Designing clothes

**Motor Development**
- Trying on clothes
- Cleaning up
- Washing, drying, and putting babies to bed

The *Housekeeping Learning Space* should resemble the kitchen and bedroom in a home. Decorate the area using curtains, a tablecloth, rug, and other attractive items. Basic equipment, such as stove, refrigerator, table, and chairs create a cooking and eating area. A baby bed, rocking chair, dress-up clothes, and other related items set the stage for dramatic play and help to create a home-like atmosphere.

## Vocabulary Enrichment

babies
bed
cleanup
clock
family
grandparents
home
vacuum

kitchen
parents (or names used by older toddlers)
relatives
responsibilities
storage
toddlers

## Teacher- and Parent-Collected Props

baby doll, bed, and high chair
bowls (unbreakable)
cleaning tools and materials, such as a sponge, vacuum cleaner, broom, dustpan, mop, and bucket.
collection of dress-up clothes for men, women, and children
telephone, intercom, walkie-talkie, and other communication props
cookie sheet
cooking utensils
empty food containers, such as cereal, crackers, soup, pasta, milk, and juice
full-length unbreakable mirror
hand eggbeater
kitchen appliances, such as a stove, refrigerator, and sink (these can be made from cardboard boxes)
pots and pans
sink with cabinet for washing and storing "real" plastic dishes
skillet
small table with chairs

**ACTIVITIES**

Toddlers wearing dress-up clothes and making a grocery list

## Design Your Own Clothes

various pieces of interesting fabric, approximately ½ yard or less
colorful scarves and ties
clothespins and belts
baskets
full-length unbreakable mirror

- Provide pieces of interesting fabric, scarves, and ties for the toddlers to use to design clothing.
- Clothespins and belts can be used to hold pieces of fabric on the toddler.
- Place all the materials in baskets so they can be seen and used easily.
- Be sure to include a full-length mirror so the older toddlers can observe their unique clothing.
- Display photographs of the toddlers' creations in the *Housekeeping Learning Space* as inspiration to others.

# Cleaning House

cleaning supplies and materials, such as a vacuum
   cleaner (upright and hand), broom/dust pan,
   spray bottles with water, mops, sponges, bucket,
   rags and cloths, polish cloths and mitts, pieces of
   tarnished silver, and toothpaste (white paste)

- Add a few of the cleaning supplies to the
  *Housekeeping Learning Space.*
- Talk to the toddlers about the need to do a big
  cleaning of the home.
- Demonstrate some of the techniques that can be
  used, such as mopping, washing tables and dishes,
  cleaning silver, and polishing the furniture.
- Help the toddlers get started on the cleaning.
- Return to admire their "squeaky" clean
  *Housekeeping Learning Space.*
  **Note:** Closely supervise use of any cleaning
  material.

A toddler reads to a baby doll.

# Cooking a Pizza

pizza box
pizza pan
purchased or homemade dough, or sliced English
   muffins
tomato sauce
shredded cheese
pepperoni, hamburger meat (cooked), or peppers
oven or toaster oven (adult only)

- Toddlers can help make a pizza in the
  *Housekeeping Learning Space.*
- Place the ingredients on a table in the learning
  space.
- Place the dough or muffins on a pizza pan.
- Let the toddlers choose and place the ingredients
  for their pizza on the dough.
- Bake or toast the pizza (adult only).
  **Note:** Closely supervise use of oven or toaster
  oven.
- Toddlers will enjoy eating their pizza for snack.

# Washing the Babies and Putting Them to Bed

tub for washing dolls
items for bathing, such as washcloth, tear-free liquid
   soap, bath toys, and towels
plastic to cover the floor
water
baby dolls
pajamas for dolls
rocking chair
books
doll bed

- Provide a baby bathtub in the *Housekeeping
  Learning Space.* Include items that can be used for
  washing baby dolls.
- Place plastic on the floor or on the table where
  the tub will be placed.
- Add a small amount of water and some liquid
  soap to the tub.

**Note:** Closely supervise whenever activities include water.

- The toddlers can wash the baby dolls and dress them for bed.
- Have a rocking chair available so the toddlers can rock the babies.
- Books will encourage them to read to the babies before they are put to bed.

**ADDING SPARK TO THE HOUSEKEEPING LEARNING SPACE**

*A collection of hats can inspire new interest in the* **Housekeeping Learning Space.** *Some that might be included are baseball hats, fancy hats, hats for cold weather and hats to keep the sun out. Place these in a hat box and add them to the* **Housekeeping Learning Space.**

## The Essential Literacy Connection
**(* Available as a board book)**

Hines, Anna Grossnickle. (1999). *Daddy Makes the Best Spaghetti.* Boston: Houghton Mifflin Company. *Follow Corey and his father through the adventures they have in preparing a meal for his mother including shopping, cooking, and serving.**

Hoberman, Mary Ann. (1982). *A House Is a House for Me.* New York: Penguin Putnam Books. *The rhyming text describes the various dwellings of people, animals, vehicles, and many other imaginative things.*

Rockwell, Harlow. (1987). *My Kitchen.* New York: Greenwillow Books. *The child in this story takes the older toddler on a tour of his kitchen, where he shows how his lunch is prepared.*

## Other Printed Materials

The *Housekeeping Learning Space* should also include a phone book next to the telephone. Include familiar children's books so the toddlers can use them to "read" bedtime stories. This adds another literacy opportunity.

## Evaluation

1. Is the older toddler taking on roles in his dramatic play?
2. Is the older toddler's play in the *Housekeeping Learning Space* lasting longer?
3. What props does the older toddler use frequently and in what way?
4. Is the older toddler using more language, as she plays with other toddlers?

# Library Learning Space

## Overview

Older toddlers who have positive experiences with books are very interested in "reading" and looking at the pictures in books. The *Library Learning Space* provides a special place for toddlers to examine books and literacy materials. This learning space should be home-like and inviting. It may include puppets and audiotapes, two very popular items for active toddlers. To help the toddlers understand the *Library Learning Space,* read stories and encourage parents to read in the learning space when they come to pick up their child.

The *Library Learning Space* should be designed so older toddlers are able to select and manipulate books for themselves. It is a place where a story can be read or told by an adult. This cozy and attractive learning space will draw older toddlers to books and sharing stories with others.

## Learning Objectives

Older toddlers will:
1. Enjoy looking at and manipulating books.
2. Develop auditory abilities as they listen to stories or tapes.
3. Appreciate books and stories they experience in the learning space.
4. Participate in beginning literacy activities.

## Time Frame

This learning space should be available to toddlers throughout the year. The contents of the learning space should change from time to time, but favorite books should remain. Older toddlers enjoy revisiting favorite books and gathering additional information with each reading visit. Books should be displayed so toddlers can see the covers, because this is how they decide if they want to look at the contents.

## Letter to Parents

• • • • • • • • • • • • • • • • • • • • • • • •

*Dear Parents,*
*In our older toddler classroom, we have a very important area called the* Library Learning Space. *Toddlers enjoy listening to stories and looking at the books for themselves in this area. This special learning space encourages toddlers to examine books and hear them read. They will also enjoy the puppets and props that they can use to accompany their literacy experiences.*

*We are looking for parents, grandparents, or family friends to come to our classroom to read books in the* Library Learning Space. *If you have an hour or a morning that you could join us for reading, let us know. Currently, we are preparing a schedule for guest readers and we would like you to participate. Toddlers learn a great deal when they see important people in their lives reading and enjoying books.*

## Layout of the Library Learning Space

## Web of Integrated Learning

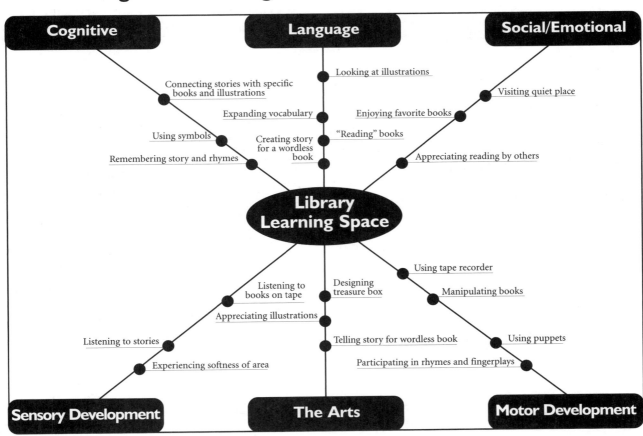

**Cognitive**

Connecting stories with specific books and illustrations

Using symbols

Remembering story and rhymes

**Language**

Looking at illustrations

Expanding vocabulary

Creating story for a wordless book

"Reading" books

**Social/Emotional**

Visiting quiet place

Enjoying favorite books

Appreciating reading by others

**Library Learning Space**

Listening to books on tape

Appreciating illustrations

Listening to stories

Experiencing softness of area

Designing treasure box

Telling story for wordless book

Participating in rhymes and fingerplays

Using tape recorder

Manipulating books

Using puppets

**Sensory Development**

**The Arts**

**Motor Development**

The *Library Learning Space* should be located in a quiet area of the classroom, away from the *Block Learning Space* or *Motor Learning Space*. The area may have a special feature that will draw the toddlers to it. For example, a small tent, draped fabric, an air mattress, or lawn cushions may be just the things that help the toddlers identify this learning space as an interesting place to visit. A small collection of puppets adds interest when combined with a small cardboard stage. Rugs, cushions, and soft stuffed animals create softness in the learning space and make it inviting. Be sure to include illustrations or posters from popular toddler books on the wall for them to recognize.

## Vocabulary Enrichment

| | |
|---|---|
| board book | listen |
| books | read |
| favorite | share |
| guest | special |
| illustrations/pictures | story |
| library | visit |

## Teacher- and Parent-Collected Props

cardboard box
children's tape player and books
    on tape
hand puppets
pictures from toddler books
rocking chair
shelf for displaying books
soft pillows and rugs
soft stuffed animals
soft transparent fabric

## ACTIVITIES

## Treasure Box

cardboard box with lid
materials to decorate the box, such as paint, contact
    paper scraps, small pieces of fabric, foil, trim,
    stickers, ribbons, and tissue paper
selected books

• Create a treasure box using a cardboard box with a lid. Toddlers can paint and decorate the box. This helps them identify that this box contains a very special item.
• Each week, select a book to place inside the treasure box.
• During the early morning welcoming time, read the book to the toddlers.
• When you are finished reading, let the toddlers see the featured book placed inside the treasure box in the *Library Learning Space*.
• They will be able to "discover" the treasure box with the special book inside when they go to the learning space.

A soft cozy chair invites a toddler to read a book.

# Teacher-Made Tape

blank cassette tape
tape recorder
various books

Sharing a special story in the Library Learning Space

- Observe the toddlers in the *Library Learning Space* to see which books they like best.
- Make a recording of these stories.
- Include an interesting sound for turning the page, such as a click, a bell, or say, "Turn the page."
- Label the tape with the name of the book that is included.
- Have a simple-to-operate tape player in the learning space with some books-on-tape. Add this teacher-made tape to the collection.
- The toddlers will quickly determine who is reading the book and will play it many times.

# Wordless Book

camera and film
materials to make a large scrapbook

- Take pictures of people and items in the toddler classroom, including pictures of adults and toddlers reading books. Take pictures of special guest readers, if possible.
- Be sure to include the director, custodian, aide, and assistants—all with their favorite books.
- Place the pictures in a large scrapbook and put it in the *Library Learning Space*.
- Toddlers who use the area will enjoy this wordless book.

# Books of Familiar Rhymes

various books with illustrations that clearly relate to the rhyme

- There are many excellent board books available for toddlers that include familiar nursery rhymes and fingerplays.
- Some toddlers will "read" the book, making the gestures or saying some of the words from the rhyme.
- This familiar text combined with effective illustrations may become some of the first reading material that connects with the older toddler.
- These beginning efforts with books should be appreciated and valued as an important step in the "reading" process.

## ADDING SPARK TO THE LIBRARY LEARNING SPACE

*Invite the director, cook, or custodian into the classroom to share a book. Make sure you explain to the guest that toddlers listen, move away, and later return to hear the story. This is expected from active toddlers and does not mean they are disinterested, but that they simply need to be active. Toddlers will often return to listen to interesting parts, phrases, or the conclusion. So, it is important to keep reading the story. These special guests will provide another opportunity for toddlers to observe an important person reading, an activity they will imitate.*

# The Essential Literacy Connection
**(* Available as a board book)**

Adams, Pam. (2000). *This Is the House that Jack Built.* Bridgemead, Swindon: Child's Play International. *The story's cumulative sequence allows toddlers to follow the story and learn to recite this classic tale.**

Ga'g, Wanda. (1997). *Millions of Cats.* New York: Putnam Publishing Group. *This rhythmic read-aloud tells of a man and wife who try to find the perfect cat.*

Keats, Ezra Jack. (1998). *Snowy Day.* New York: Viking Children's Books. *Enjoy the magic of waking up to snow in the morning.**

Wood, Audrey. (2000). *The Napping House.* New York: Harcourt. *Rhythmic, repetitive text and hilarious pictures tell the story of a house full of sleeping people and animals that are awakened by a flea.**

# Other Printed Materials

Additional materials for the *Library Learning Space* include puppets, books with tapes, index cards, and pencils to sign out books.

# Evaluation

1. Is the older toddler going to the learning space and looking at books?
2. Can the older toddler be observed listening and participating in the stories?
3. Is the older toddler using tapes and puppets?
4. Does the older toddler enjoy hearing stories read and told?

# Construction Learning Space

## Overview

Block play promotes cognitive, language, social emotional, sensory, and motor development. Therefore, blocks are a necessary component of every toddler classroom. The *Construction Learning Space* will include a variety of building materials for toddlers to use in their creations. This learning space is designed to encourage older toddlers in becoming active builders, as they work alongside each other to pile, stack, push, carry, and knock over building materials.

Stick with three or four types of blocks in the learning space at one time. Too many different types of building materials may be overwhelming for some older toddlers. Visit the *Construction Learning Space* with the toddlers. Comment as they build, saying, "You are stacking one block on top of the other." This will help older toddlers understand the building process and relate language to their construction. Help the toddlers work, to demonstrate cooperation. Observe the play that is occurring in the *Construction Learning Space* and determine when to change the building materials to keep toddlers interested.

## Learning Objectives

Older toddlers will:
1. Begin to respect the other children's buildings.
2. Follow simple directions.
3. Begin learning basic math skills.
4. Play beside other children.

## Time Frame

This learning space will be effective for two to three weeks at a time. It is appropriate to bring this learning space back many times during the year, following the interest of the older toddlers. New building materials will encourage expanded building, when the learning space is reintroduced.

## Letter to Parents

• • • • • • • • • • • • • • • • • • • • • • • • • •

*Dear Parents,*
*When toddlers play in our Construction Learning Space, they are learning many new things. They are learning to problem solve as they decide which blocks to put where, and they are developing social skills as they work beside other toddlers to construct buildings. In addition, they are learning simple math and science concepts, such as selecting blocks one by one, and determining which blocks are heavy or light. Many toddlers enjoy knocking over their buildings and starting over. But, toddlers do not want others to mess up their creations. They want to come back and look at their accomplishments from time to time. In our Construction Learning Space, we will be helping the toddlers learn to respect their friends' buildings.*

*The toddlers are going to make shoebox blocks for our Construction Learning Space. Would you please send any extra shoeboxes to school with your toddler? Look for pictures of our toddlers' buildings next time you visit!*

# Layout of the Construction Learning Space

# Web of Integrated Learning

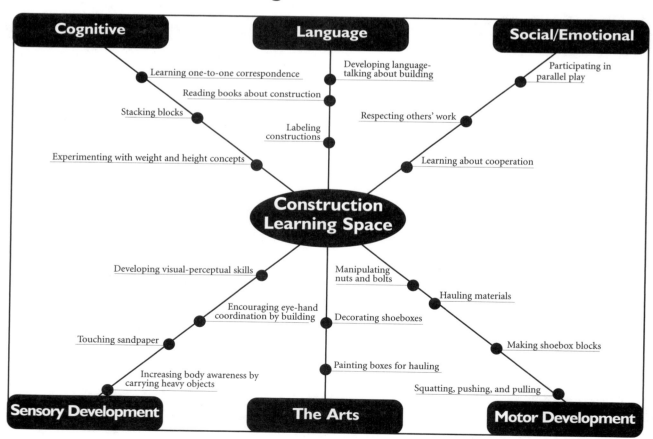

**Cognitive**

Learning one-to-one correspondence

Reading books about construction

Stacking blocks

Experimenting with weight and height concepts

**Language**

Developing language-talking about building

Labeling constructions

**Social/Emotional**

Participating in parallel play

Respecting others' work

Learning about cooperation

**Construction Learning Space**

Developing visual-perceptual skills

Encouraging eye-hand coordination by building

Touching sandpaper

Increasing body awareness by carrying heavy objects

Manipulating nuts and bolts

Decorating shoeboxes

Painting boxes for hauling

Hauling materials

Making shoebox blocks

Squatting, pushing, and pulling

**Sensory Development**

**The Arts**

**Motor Development**

The *Construction Learning Space* is a place where older toddlers can be very active in their play. Block play stimulates conversation, and toddlers often use loud voices to "discuss" their accomplishments. Rugs, pillows, and other soft materials help absorb the "busy" noise. Display a variety of building materials so toddlers can view their options and make selections. A raised area, 6 to 12 inches high, can provide a different place for building and an opportunity to see the structures from another perspective.

## Vocabulary Enrichment

| | |
|---|---|
| blocks | light |
| build | respect |
| cardboard | sandpaper |
| construction | short |
| cooperate | tall |
| equipment | tower |
| heavy | under |
| house | |

## Teacher- and Parent-Collected Props

2" x 2" pieces of wood (use with blocks under one side to make a ramp)
Bristle blocks (blocks that stick together)
camera
cardboard boxes of all sizes
cobbler's bench and hammer
couch pillows
large, clear, plastic containers for storage
large, plastic toy bolts and screws
Lego building blocks
milk carton blocks (see page 310 for directions)
PVC pipe pieces and connectors
small wooden blocks
sponges
very fine-grain sandpaper

## ACTIVITIES

# Shoebox Blocks

several shoeboxes with lids
newspaper
tape
contact paper
washable markers or materials to decorate boxes

- Let each toddler select a box.
- Ask the toddlers to crumple newspaper and fill their boxes with the paper.
- Help the toddlers securely tape the lid on the shoebox and cover it with contact paper.
- Toddlers may use washable markers to decorate the shoebox blocks.
- These are a good size and weight for toddlers to use in their building.

A low canopy makes the Construction Learning Space special.

# Building under a Tent

flat sheet (king or queen size)
tape
four chairs
various blocks
flashlights

- Because toddlers like to play in small spaces, make a tent in the learning space using a king- or queen-size flat sheet.
- Tape the sheet to the backs of four chairs, spread evenly apart.
- Place one or two types of blocks underneath the tent.
- Add flashlights for play.
- This special area will encourage more building by toddlers.

# Hauling Blocks

several medium-size cardboard boxes
paint and paintbrushes to decorate boxes

- Fold down or remove the box tops.
- Toddlers can paint the boxes or use their imagination to decorate the sides.
- Demonstrate how they can fill up a box to "haul" their blocks around the learning space.
- The filling of boxes and emptying of their contents adds a new dimension to the *Construction Learning Space*.

# Respect My Work

paper
tape
camera and film

- While some toddlers will readily knock over their buildings, others will really value their creations and want to leave them up. It is important to model respect for others' work to the toddlers.
- Find an area of the *Construction Learning Space* where a toddler may choose to leave his work in progress or completed building.
- Tape a piece of paper with the child's name in large letters to the construction.
- Take a picture of the building to document the child's work.
- Collect and post pictures you have taken as a record of each child's progress in construction during the year.
- Help the toddler decide when the work can be cleaned up.
- Respect for the property of others takes a long time to learn; this is an important first step.

Working together with blocks in the Construction Learning Space

# Prop Box

large, plastic container
props, such as toys with wheels (cars and trucks), small plastic people, plastic farm animals, plastic zoo animals, plastic trees and houses

- Fill plastic containers with related props, such as farm animals, people, trees, and houses.
- Rotate a prop box into the space, one at a time, and keep the others stored for future use.
- The props will often stimulate older toddlers to build using a specific theme. For example, farm animals might encourage construction of a barn, while plastic people might suggest a house or community.
- Toddlers may also use these props in other ways.

## ADDING SPARK TO THE CONSTRUCTION LEARNING SPACE

*A small wagon is a wonderful piece of equipment for toddlers to pile or stack blocks inside. They can use it to pull the blocks from place to place.*

## The Essential Literacy Connection
(• Available as a board book)

Barton, Byron. (1990). *Building a House.* New York: William Morrow & Company. *Complete with blueprints, this book depicts the steps involved in the construction of a house from digging the foundation to the completion of the project.*

Hoban, Tana. (1999). *Construction Zone.* New York: Greenwillow Books. *Thirteen photographs of machines shown from two different angles are sure to inspire the older toddler's earth-moving work.\**

Vainio, Pirkko. (1997). *The Dream House.* New York: North South Books. *Watch as Lucas builds his house into a home with the help of some friendly children.*

## Evaluation

1. Is the older toddler building with materials in the learning space?
2. Can the older toddler complete one-to-one correspondence?
3. Does the older toddler demonstrate parallel play skills in the learning space?
4. Is the older toddler beginning to respect the buildings that other children have built?

# Art Learning Space

## Overview

Toddlers are creative and enjoy experimenting with art materials. The *Art Learning Space* should be a place where they are free to examine, try new materials, and do things in their own way. The process of participating in an art activity is the most important aspect of the *Art Learning Space*. At this point, **doing** is the focus for the toddlers, not the product. Painting, molding, gluing, and combining are what is supported in the *Art Learning Space*. This is a place where being messy is accepted and beginning efforts are valued. Individuality is accepted—everyone's art should not be the same!

## Learning Objectives

Older toddlers will:

1. Explore a variety of art media and materials.
2. Expand their creative thinking as they participate in the *Art Learning Space*.
3. Build self-confidence as they use art to express their ideas.
4. Develop fine motor skills as they use the tools provided in the *Art Learning Space*.

## Time Frame

This creative *Art Learning Space* should be set up in the older toddlers' classroom most of the year. Different materials and activities should be added every now and then, but the basic tools should remain predictably available.

## Letter to Parents

• • • • • • • • • • • • • • • • • • • • • • •

*Dear Parents,*

*In the older toddler classroom, we have an Art Learning Space. This area provides a place where older toddlers can use basic art materials, such as crayons, washable markers, glue, clay, and a variety of types of paper. During this stage, toddlers are using scribbles and simple symbols to represent their ideas, which is a very important step in their development. We value each of these masterpieces and often display them in the Art Learning Space. Of course, many of them will be brought home for you to see. You might ask your toddler questions about their work ("Tell me about your picture." or "How did you make this?"), or simply comment on the colors and lines you see. The most important thing for toddlers is that you appreciate their work.*

*Art with toddlers can be messy; this is part of the process. We have added laundry detergent to the tempera paint so it will wash out more easily, and will do our best to minimize messy stains. However, the best help is for your toddler to wear an old shirt or paint smock while working in the Art Learning Space. If you have not sent one for your child, we would appreciate this addition. As we frequently say, "Young children are hands-on learners; dress them so they can actively participate." This is certainly true in the Art Learning Space.*

## Layout of the Art Learning Space

## Web of Integrated Learning

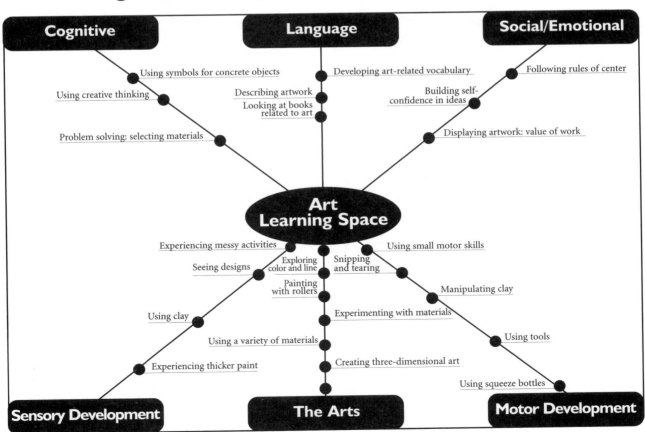

**Cognitive**
- Using symbols for concrete objects
- Using creative thinking
- Problem solving: selecting materials

**Language**
- Developing art-related vocabulary
- Describing artwork
- Looking at books related to art

**Social/Emotional**
- Following rules of center
- Building self-confidence in ideas
- Displaying artwork: value of work

**Art Learning Space**

- Experiencing messy activities
- Seeing designs
- Exploring color and line
- Snipping and tearing
- Using small motor skills
- Painting with rollers
- Manipulating clay
- Using clay
- Experimenting with materials
- Using a variety of materials
- Using tools
- Experiencing thicker paint
- Creating three-dimensional art
- Using squeeze bottles

**Sensory Development**  **The Arts**  **Motor Development**

This is a messy learning space, so it will work best if placed on a tile floor. A water source would be helpful, although a plastic tub can be used if water is not available. A low table is needed for scissor cutting and other activities that need a workspace. To help with cleanup, cover the area under the table with paper or plastic. A flat wall surface is helpful for wall painting. Place a large basket in the learning space to collect scraps of paper for future projects.

## Vocabulary Enrichment

| | |
|---|---|
| art | display |
| artist | easel |
| brush | glue |
| clay | marker |
| color | mold |
| cut | paint |
| decorate | paper |
| design | smock |

## Teacher- and Parent-Collected Props

child-safe scissors
dry laundry detergent
glue
newspaper
old brushes
old shirts or paint smocks
plastic for floor and tables
scraps of paper, foil, contact paper, trim, and so on
shower curtain liners
tempera paint
tools for painting, such as feathers, turkey baster, foam paintbrushes, pastry brush, sponges, deodorant roll-on bottles, and paint rollers
variety of types of clay
washable markers

Toddlers' paintings on bubble wrap

**ACTIVITIES**

Toddler experimenting with cutting sandpaper

## Snip and Tear

child-safe scissors (non-loop, blunt-end)
materials that are easy to cut, such as stiff paper,
    card inserts from magazines, inexpensive
    wallpaper pieces, newspaper, heavyweight
    computer paper, index cards, construction
    paper, and brown paper bags
playdough
clear plastic containers

- One of the tools that older toddlers may begin to use is scissors.
- Because scissor use is a difficult skill to learn, it is important to select materials that will make the process easier for older toddlers. When the going

gets rough, they may become frustrated and resort to tearing what they are trying to cut. This is an acceptable approach for toddlers.

- Non-loop scissors are good for beginning cutters. These easy-to-use scissors have no finger holes and work by squeezing.
- Blunt-end scissors should be sharp enough to work properly and actually cut items. They should be a size that fits the older toddler's hand and have small finger holes.
- Playdough can be cut with scissors and is easy to work with.
- Place scissors and materials for cutting on a low table in clear plastic tubs so older toddlers can select the tool and paper that they will use. They will do a lot of experimenting as they try to figure out how scissors work.

  **Special Note:** Progression of cutting with scissors for older toddlers usually follows this sequence:
  1. Cutting, using two hands to hold scissors
  2. Holding scissors with thumb on the bottom and fingers on top
  3. Snipping paper with thumb in top hole and fingers in bottom hole of scissors
  4. Cutting across paper

## Tennis Shoe Print

roll of white butcher paper
tape
paint rollers or brushes
thick tempera paint in two or three colors
pie pans or trays
old tennis shoes

- Make a long path with white butcher paper on the floor. Tape it securely, so it will not move.
- Pour tempera paint into pie pans or trays. Add rollers or brushes.
- Collect several old tennis shoes that have interesting designs on the soles.
- Check the toddlers' tennis shoes and determine if they will produce a print.

- Let the toddlers decide if they will use their own shoes or one from the tennis shoe collection.
- Roll or brush paint on the soles of one toddler's tennis shoes.
- Help the toddler walk down the paper path. At the end of the path, wash her shoes.
- Next, another toddler can add his tennis shoe prints by walking down the white paper path.
- Label each print with the name of the toddler who created it.
- Display the tennis shoe art in the *Art Learning Space,* so all can appreciate the interesting mural they have created.

## Squeeze Bottle Paint

½ cup all-purpose flour (not self-rising)
¼ cup salt
1 tablespoon dry laundry detergent
water
two bowls
½ cup dry tempera paint
several squeeze bottles, such as small ketchup bottles, small shampoo bottles, mustard bottles, and travel bottles
cardboard or poster board

- Mix flour, salt, water, and detergent in a bowl. The mixture should be as thick as paste or glue.
- Divide the mixture into two parts.
- Add a different color tempera paint to each bowl of the mixture.
- Pour the thick paint into squeeze bottles that are easy for toddlers to use.
- Use cardboard pieces or poster board as the base for the painting.
- Toddlers squeeze the paint onto the board and create interesting designs and combinations.
- The thickness of the paint will require more time to dry before hanging the artwork.

## Clay Sculpture

earth or potter's clay
materials for placing in the clay, such as straws, sticks, pinecones, stones, leaves, pine needles, dried flowers, and other collected nature items

- Let toddlers explore and mold the earth or potter's clay for a long time before presenting a planned activity.
- After much experimentation, create a large mountain of clay with the help of the toddlers in the learning space.
- Let the toddlers select what they want to stick in the clay.
- Once the clay has hardened, all can admire the three-dimensional sculpture.

## Roller Painted Wall

blank wall
plastic
tape
butcher paper
various paint rollers (thick, thin, patterned)
tempera paint
several shallow buckets or trays

- Cover a wall and the floor with plastic.
- Tape a large, long sheet of butcher paper at the toddlers' arm height onto the wall.
- Collect paint rollers in a variety of sizes and textures.
- Pour several colors of tempera paint into shallow buckets or trays.
- Toddlers dip their rollers into the paint and roll it on the paper. Several older toddlers can work at the same time on the wall.
- This roller painting creates a big, bold mural that is beautiful for the toddlers to admire.

## ADDING SPARK TO THE ART LEARNING SPACE

Toddlers using eyedroppers to create artwork

*Use a large turkey baster or large medicine dropper as paint tools. The toddlers can use these tools to pick up watery tempera paint in a bowl. Use several pieces of paper towel or coffee filters as the canvas. Toddlers drop paint on the absorbent paper, creating interesting designs, colors, and patterns. Allow them to dry before displaying the abstract artwork in the Art Learning Space.*

## The Essential Literacy Connection

Germein, Katrina. (2000). *Big Rain Coming*. Boston: Houghton Mifflin Company. *Bright paintings tell the tale of a village awaiting rain.*

Hubbard, Patricia. (1999). *My Crayons Talk*. New York: Henry Holt & Company, Inc. *Hear what crayons "say" in this two-line, rhythmic chant.*

Snyder, Carol. (2002). *We're Painting*. New York: HarperCollins Children's Books. *This book illustrates and identifies the process of painting.*

## Other Printed Materials

Additional materials for the *Art Learning Space* include catalogs of children's art supplies and equipment.

## Evaluation

1. Is the older toddler experimenting with art materials and tools?
2. Does the older toddler value her work and want to display it or take it home?
3. Can you observe improvement in the older toddler's fine motor coordination: cutting, painting, and gluing?
4. Is the older toddler demonstrating creativity as she works in the *Art Learning Space*?

# Private Place Learning Space

## Overview

Older toddlers are egocentric. It is normal for an older toddler to try to be independent and become easily frustrated when he or she cannot do a task "by myself." Older toddlers demonstrate more variety in their emotions. They may become jealous when their caregiver holds another child or excited when they find out they are going swimming. There are many difficult social tasks for older toddlers to learn during their "twos." These include learning boundaries and rules, and understanding the routines of daily living with other people.

Caregivers need to remember that each toddler has his or her own disposition, such as "easy-going," "slow-to-warm-up," or "active," and this will influence his or her emotional development. In addition, the environment has a great impact on how toddlers handle their emotions. Toddlers do best when they have a structured environment. Following a consistent schedule will help make their life more predictable and easier for them to understand. They also need a few very simple rules to follow such as, "We don't hit!" The *Private Place Learning Space* will provide older toddlers with a space to be alone and to calm down, so they may return to classroom activities. Activities to help older toddlers learn about their emotions are also included in this learning space.

## Learning Objectives

Older toddlers will:
1. Begin developing control of simple emotions, such as fear, anger, happiness, and sadness.
2. Begin obeying simple rules.
3. Learn simple and appropriate coping techniques.

## Time Frame

This learning space can remain set up throughout the year. It may take a few weeks for the older toddlers to begin using the *Private Place Learning Space* for its designated purpose.

## Letter to Parents

• • • • • • • • • • • • • • • • • • • • • • •

*Dear Parents,*

*The toddler period is often called the "terrible twos." This is because toddlers have the very difficult task of learning how to be independent, while following the rules of society. The environment influences your older toddler's behavior. Toddlers learn how to interact with others by watching those around them. Here are a few simple ideas to help your toddler learn how to handle his or her emotions:*

1. *Follow simple routines in your daily life. For example, brushing teeth before bed or taking a nap after lunch.*

2. *Use simple words to describe the emotions you see in your toddler. You could say, "I see you are feeling sad because Mommy is leaving."*

3. *Try to stay calm and relaxed during your child's crisis. This will help an already upset toddler feel more secure.*

*Our Private Place Learning Space gives toddlers a safe, quiet place to spend time. We will be talking about feeling happy, sad, angry, hurt, calm, and afraid. We will help toddlers learn how to identify their emotions and react appropriately. Please come by and visit our relaxing and soothing Private Place Learning Space.*

## Layout of the Private Place Learning Space

## Web of Integrated Learning

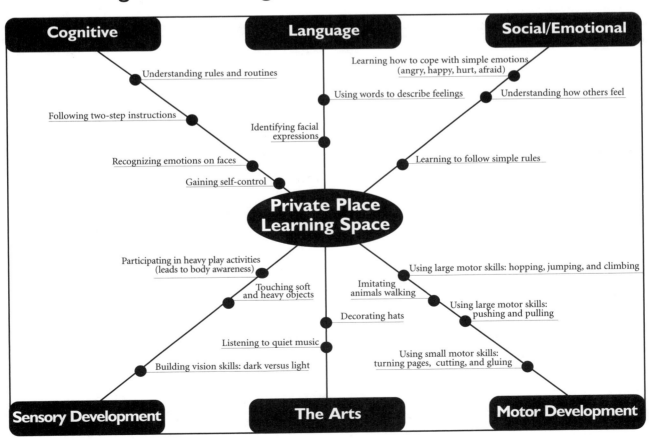

Use a very large cardboard box as the *Private Place Learning Space*. Place the box in an area of the room where quiet activities occur. Make sure to face the opening of the box outward, so you can easily observe what is going on inside without having to go in the space. You may decorate the outside of the box to make it appealing to older toddlers.

## Vocabulary Enrichment

afraid

angry

calm

excited

feelings

happy

patient

private

quiet

sad

## Teacher- and Parent-Collected Props

beanbag chair

books about feelings

classical music or new-age music with slow, rhythmic beats

crib mattress

flashlights

large cardboard box (refrigerator or piano boxes work well)

pillows

soft blankets

string of white lights

tape or CD player with headphones

Private area next to the Library Learning Space

### ACTIVITIES

# Rules for the Private Place Learning Space

Before opening the *Private Place Learning Space*, sit down with the toddlers, explain the purpose of the learning space, and make "rules" for its use. Make only three or four rules that will work in your classroom. Write them down on a piece of paper and post them outside the *Private Place Learning Space*. Read the rules to the older toddlers whenever necessary. Some suggested rules for toddlers using this learning space are as follows:

• Only one child at a time is allowed in the learning space.

• The child must tell the teacher before entering the learning space.

• This learning space is to be used when a child is feeling _____ (angry, sad, tired, hurt, scared, and so on).

Remember a few simple things when using this learning space in your classroom:

- Allow each child to enter the learning space when he or she feels it is necessary.
- Respect each toddler's right to feel angry, sad, or afraid.
- Always help toddlers use words to label their emotions.
- Carefully monitor how older toddlers are using the learning space. It will take time and direction for toddlers to learn when and for how long they need to stay in the learning space.
- **Most important:** Be patient and consistent with older toddlers. Eventually, this learning space may lead to a lifelong tool for managing their emotions.

## "Angry" Hat

hats
art materials, such as paper, glue, tape, scissors, fabric pieces, washable markers, and sparkles

- Allow each child to pick out his own hat and use art materials to decorate it.
- Tell the toddlers that this is an "Angry Hat" and it is to be worn when they are upset or angry.
- Place each child's hat in her own cubby.
- When you observe that an older toddler is angry, help him get his "Angry Hat" to wear.
- When the toddler is no longer angry, help him return his hat to its place for safekeeping.
- The goal is for each child to put on the hat to help demonstrate feelings of anger in an appropriate manner.

## Heavy Play Activities

- Heavy play activities are activities that are hard work for older toddlers. This type of activity is calming and organizing for young children.
- Use these activities before you want the toddlers to be seated or quiet for a little while. Remember that sitting for a short period seems like a very long time to a toddler.
- Let the toddlers "help" you by cleaning and moving furniture.
- Have them push or pull large toys or furniture, such as beanbag chairs, adult chairs, mats, large balls, or push toys.
- Let them roll around and jump into a crash pad (see page 307 for directions on fabrication of crash pad).
- Encourage them to climb on appropriate structures.
- Play the animal-walk game and imitate how different animals walk, such as a cat, elephant, crab, or monkey.
- Ask them to hop, skip, jump, run, and crawl.
- Give older toddlers a bucket and a cloth to wash windows, walls, or tabletops.

232

# Can You Make a _____ Face?

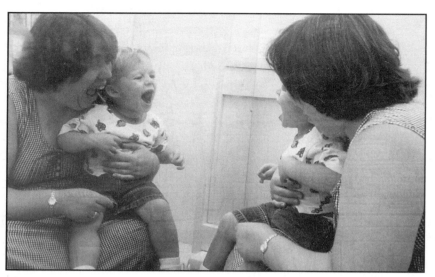

Imitating emotions with a caregiver while looking in a mirror

books or magazines with faces showing different
    emotions
mirrors

- Show toddlers pictures or books of children with different facial expressions and tell them about the emotions.
- Ask older toddlers to make each face and then look at themselves in the mirror.
- Ask them if they have ever felt the emotion.
- See if they can tell you a time when they felt that way.

**ADDING SPARK TO THE PRIVATE PLACE LEARNING SPACE**

*Add items such as mirrored contact paper on the walls of the learning space, paper and washable markers, a ticking clock, and stuffed animals to the Private Place Learning Space to add interest.*

## The Essential Literacy Connection
(* Available as a board book)

Dejoie, Paula. (1997). *My Hair Is Beautiful: Because Its Mine.* New York: Black Butterfly Children. *Rhymes and illustrations promote the older toddlers' positive self-image.**

Krauss, Ruth. (1999). *You're Just What I Need.* New York: HarperCollins Children's Books. *A heartwarming story of a hide-and-seek game between a mother and child.*

McCourt, Lisa. (2002). *I Love You Stinky Face.* Memphis, TN: Troll. *Hilarious illustrations reassure older toddlers that they will be loved no matter what.**

Scott, Ann Herbert. (2000). *On Mother's Lap.* Boston: Houghton Mifflin. *Cuddle up with this cheerful book that demonstrates there is always room on mother's lap.**

Viorst, Judith. (1989). *Alexander and the Terrible, Horrible, No Good, Very Bad Day.* New York: Scott Foresman. *Endearing illustrations and colorful text help older toddlers identify with Alexander and realize that they are not alone on their bad days.*

## Evaluation

1. Is the older toddler using the learning space at appropriate times?
2. Is the older toddler beginning to obey and respect simple rules?
3. Is the older toddler verbalizing basic emotions?

The Complete **Learning Spaces** Book for Infants and Toddlers

# Music Learning Space

## Overview

Music and toddlers are a great combination for a learning space. In the *Music Learning Space,* musical materials and instruments will be grouped to allow older toddlers to choose what they want to explore. They will also be able to determine how long to focus on items that interest them. Toddlers enjoy a variety of music and often sing along with familiar tunes. They sing the songs and play the recordings they like repeatedly, as they develop a musical repertoire.

Toddlers often add body movements and gestures to the music they hear. This active participation makes the musical experience more powerful for developing toddlers, who are using multiple ways of learning: music and movement. The *Music Learning Space* is a planned environment where older toddlers can experiment with sounds while creating their own music. Through their positive involvement, many toddlers will develop an interest and appreciation of music they have experienced.

## Learning Objectives

Older toddlers will:

1. Enjoy making music and participating in the process.
2. Listen to a variety of music while developing auditory abilities.
3. Experiment with sounds and different ways of producing them.

## Time Frame

This is a high-interest learning space for older toddlers and can be enjoyed throughout the year. The *Music Learning Space* can be moved into the classroom monthly or remain set up over a longer period. New materials should be added to the learning space to maintain the toddlers' interest in making music in different ways.

## Letter to Parents

• • • • • • • • • • • • • • • • • • • •

*Dear Parents,*

*You have probably noticed that we have a special Music Learning Space in our classroom. Older toddlers enjoy listening and moving to music. They also create music using instruments and their voices. Toddlers love to sing their favorite songs again and again. This helps them build confidence in their musical abilities, as they continue to learn the song.*

*Does your toddler have a recording, CD, or tape he or she enjoys at home? If so, we would like to include that music in our Music Learning Space. Do you have a musical instrument that could be examined by the toddlers? Let us know, so we can plan for that addition to our learning space. You are always invited to join us in our musical activities in the Music Learning Space.*

## Layout of the Music Learning Space

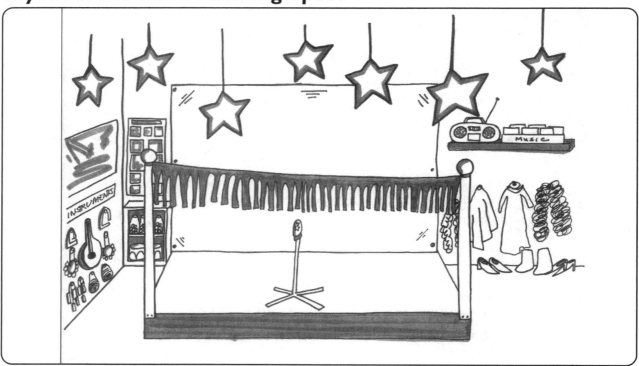

## Web of Integrated Learning

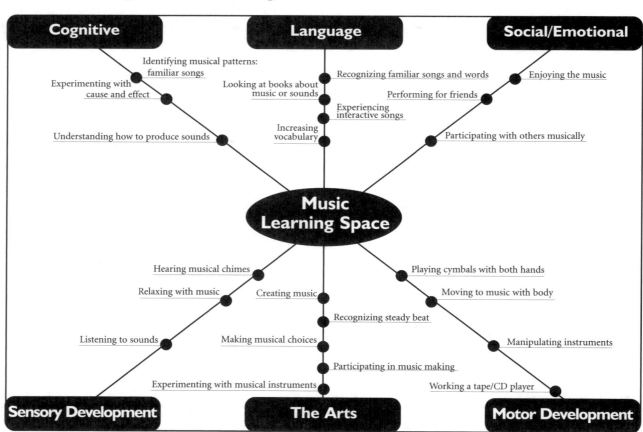

**Cognitive**

Identifying musical patterns: familiar songs

Experimenting with cause and effect

Understanding how to produce sounds

**Language**

Looking at books about music or sounds

Recognizing familiar songs and words

Experiencing interactive songs

Increasing vocabulary

**Social/Emotional**

Enjoying the music

Performing for friends

Participating with others musically

**Music Learning Space**

Hearing musical chimes

Relaxing with music

Creating music

Playing cymbals with both hands

Moving to music with body

Recognizing steady beat

Listening to sounds

Making musical choices

Manipulating instruments

Participating in music making

Experimenting with musical instruments

Working a tape/CD player

**Sensory Development**

**The Arts**

**Motor Development**

The *Music Learning Space* is a place where many sounds are produced. For this reason, it should be placed away from quiet learning spaces such as the *Library Learning Space*. In this area, attention must be paid to absorbing and retaining as much sound as possible. Soft items, such as rugs, pillows, and fabric or sound panels in the learning space will absorb sound and contain the music. Chime mobiles and other musical mobiles will add both visual and sound interest to the area. Place a tape recorder/player in the learning space so older toddlers can hear and see the source of the music. Store instruments in clear, plastic containers so the toddlers can see what is available. For this age group, it is helpful to rotate instruments in and out of the learning space so they are not overwhelmed with all of the musical choices.

## Vocabulary Enrichment

| | |
|---|---|
| bells | moving |
| cymbals | music |
| drum | rhythm |
| enjoy | singing |
| instruments | songs |
| listen | sounds |
| movement | xylophone |

## Teacher- and Parent-Collected Props

boom box or CD player

commercial and/or homemade rhythm instruments

drum

microphone

old instruments that can still be played, such as a guitar, ukulele, drum, brass instrument, keyboard, and maracas

pillows

recordings of a variety of music, such as classical, bluegrass, jazz, and children's songs

soft rug

xylophone that is designed from low to high

## ACTIVITIES

# Musical Mobile for Playing

medium-size quilting hoop or embroidery hoop

yarn

objects that produce a musical sound when tapped, such as a metal fork, cowbell, pan lid, large nails, and large bolts

mallets

- Use the quilting hoop as the base for the mobile.
- String selected objects from the hoop with heavy yarn. Hang about four or five objects around the loop. Tie on the objects securely.
- Attach yarn to the top of the hoop for hanging.
- Suspend the mobile so older toddlers can comfortably hit the objects.
- Demonstrate how to tap the mobile to produce sound. Older toddlers can experiment with this approach.
- Later, provide mallets for new sounds and playing techniques.
- Seeing objects that produce sound is fascinating for the older toddler.

## Body Sounds

- Ask older toddlers to find ways to make music with their bodies, such as clapping their hands or legs, stomping their feet, and any other movement that creates a sound.
- Encourage the toddlers to use these sounds to create music and patterns of rhythm.
- Toddlers will continue to investigate sounds they can produce.

## Music from Plastic Bottles

small, plastic drink bottles

- Blowing into the neck of the bottle can produce various musical sounds.
- Blowing is a new experience for toddlers. Some will be able to produce a sound, while others will simply enjoy experimenting with this technique.

## Cymbals for Both Hands

four medium-size metal pot lids
rhythm sticks
mallet

- Toddlers can clap two lids together to make sounds or tap one lid with a rhythm stick or mallet.
- These home-collected lids demonstrate that music can be created from everyday items.
- Older toddlers will be able to clap the lids together using both hands.

Making music with rhythm instruments, including a tambourine hat

## Musical Instruments

various musical instruments, such as rhythm sticks, small drum, triangle, maracas, gyro, and sand blocks
musical recordings that invite participation, such as marches, up-tempo pieces, and folk music from familiar cultures
boom box or CD player

- When introducing the instruments to the toddlers, demonstrate how each one works.
- Encourage the toddlers to experiment with the instruments.
- After this exploration, they will begin to use the instruments to accompany music or make their own musical patterns.

# Live Performances for Toddlers

guest musician

- Invite a local musician to visit the *Music Learning Space*. Middle school or high school band and orchestra members are great, as are parents who play instruments.
- Toddlers appreciate simple performances, and nothing inspires young musicians like experiencing a live performance by a musician.
- Be sure the visiting musicians understand that toddlers want to touch the instruments and sit with the musician. This is, of course, the way older toddlers learn about music.
- If a musical group performs at the center or school, ask the members to come for a short visit to the *Music Learning Space*.
- Remember that it should be a short performance—perhaps one song and a longer period of exploration with the instrument and/or performer.

**ADDING SPARK TO THE MUSIC LEARNING SPACE**

*Include a xylophone or resonator bells in the Music Learning Space. Select a xylophone that has bars arranged in a stair design, from lowest note to highest. These help toddlers make a connection to both see and hear the lowest or highest note. Resonator bells come in separate pieces and can be used by toddlers to produce beautiful and clear tones. Display three or four resonator bells in the learning space; select distinctively different notes. These bells encourage older toddlers to experiment with tones, notes, and rhythm.*

## The Essential Literacy Connection
(* **Available as a board book**)

Adams, Pam. (2000). *This Old Man.* Bridgemead, Swindon: Child's Play International. *The brightly colored photos and rhythmic word patterns make this classic song a delight for toddlers, as they begin to understand numbers.*

Carle, Eric. (1996). *I See a Song.* New York: Scholastic, Inc. *This colorful, wordless picture book sparks the imagination, as it illustrates the song of a violinist.*

Hillenbrand, Will. (2002). *Down by the Station.* New York: Harcourt, Inc. *Toddlers can sing along with the story, as they watch a diverse group of children and animals play together.*

Moss, Lloyd. (2000). *Zin! Zin! Zin!: A Violin.* New York: Aladdin Paperbacks. *This rhythmical, rhyming book introduces ten different instruments to children.*

Pinkney, Andrea, & Pinkney, Brian. (1997). *Shake Shake Shake.* New York: Harcourt. *Siblings practice moving to the rhythm, while listening to the sound of a shekere, an African percussion instrument made from a gourd.**

## Other Printed Materials
The *Music Learning Space* should also include music books with songs.

## Evaluation
1. Is the older toddler actively listening to music?
2. Can the older toddler be observed selecting favorite songs or recordings to hear again?
3. Is the older toddler "singing" and "dancing" to the music in the learning space?
4. Is the older toddler creating music using her voice or instruments?

# Science and Nature Learning Space

## Overview

Toddlers are little scientists who are interested in exploring, experimenting, and finding out about things in their immediate surroundings. The *Science and Nature Learning Space* provides a safe place to participate in this exploring process. In this learning space, older toddlers are encouraged to examine the nature materials and see interesting features, feel the textures, smell the scents, and compare the items. Exploring interesting items and questioning provides a positive base for the beginning of scientific inquiry.

## Learning Objectives

Older toddlers will:

1. Learn about the natural environment in which they live.
2. Experiment with materials using their senses.
3. Develop problem-solving and questioning skills.
4. Appreciate the natural materials that are around them.

## Time Frame

This learning space is especially effective when related to the current season. For example, during the winter months, display items relating to winter in the *Science and Nature Learning Space*. When exploration and interest in these items fades, pack up the learning space and revisit when spring arrives. Collect natural materials during each new season.

## Letter to Parents

• • • • • • • • • • • • • • • • • • • • • • • • • • • •

*Dear Parents,*

*Have you noticed how your older toddler is interested in the ice and snow that he or she sees outdoors these days? We are setting up a Science and Nature Learning Space so the older toddlers in our classroom can have the opportunity to examine, observe, and learn about nature and the winter season. When you are outdoors or driving in your car, talk with your toddler about things he or she sees in nature, such as the bare trees, the fog on the window, and visible breath.*

*We will keep our class pet in the Science and Nature Learning Space. The older toddlers will be learning about what our pet needs to live: water, food, a clean home, and a gentle touch. On some weekends and holidays when school is closed, our pet needs a home to visit. If you would like to have our pet visit, let us know. We will furnish a book about how to care for the animal. We will also send a camera home for you to take pictures of our pet's visit with your family.*

# Layout of the Science and Nature Learning Space

# Web of Integrated Learning

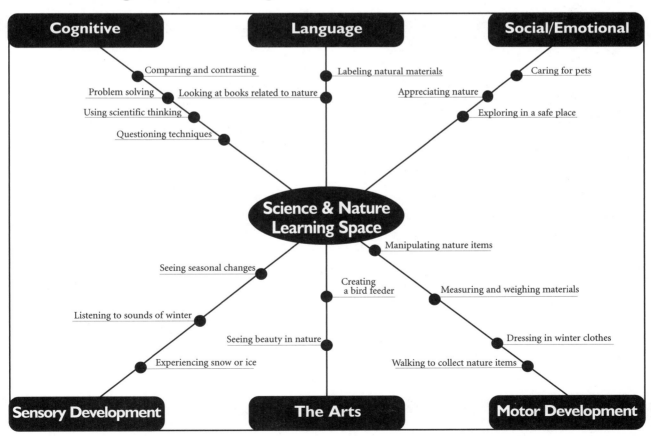

This learning space should be designed to invite toddlers to explore and manipulate nature materials. Put a low table in the area to display materials so toddlers can see and examine the materials while standing. Attractively display beautiful things from nature, such as a hanging limb with leaves, fall flowers in a vase, or a collection of feathers in a basket.

## Vocabulary Enrichment

care
class pet
collect
explore
fish
guinea pig
nature
questions
scientist
smell
texture
white mouse

A class guinea pig helps toddlers learn about caring for a pet.

## Teacher- and Parent-Collected Props

aquarium (for growing plants)
clamp-on light or floor lamp
clear plastic jars with lids
gloves
growing plants, such as a cornflower, peace lily, or other hardy non-poisonous type
items for the class pet, such as cage, food, toys, and so on
large magnifying glasses (at least two)
low table for display
pie pans and aluminum pans
plastic containers for collections
scale
sponges

**ACTIVITIES**

# Rocks for Comparing and Contrasting

various medium-size rocks
scale for weighing
tape measure or ruler

- Collect rocks that are varied in color, size, texture, and weight.
- Encourage the older toddlers to explore the rocks using their senses.
- Include a scale, tape measure, or ruler for toddlers to experiment with and determine properties of the rocks. At this stage, tools are used in an experimental way and are not used to produce accurate measurements.

# A Bird Feeder for the Winter

pinecones or apples
peanut butter or lard (also known as hard fat or suet)
birdseed
string or yarn
clean, plastic milk jugs

- Toddlers create birdfeeders by coating pinecones or apples with peanut butter or lard and then rolling them in birdseed.
- After these are made, older toddlers can hang them outside and watch for birds to enjoy their treat.
- Make another type of birdfeeder by cutting out a hole in a plastic milk jug for birds to enter. Be sure to poke tiny holes in the bottom of containers for rainwater to drain out. Place birdseed in the milk jug and hang outside. **Special Note:** Check for peanut allergies before doing this activity.

# Winter Cold

winter dress-up clothes, such as rubber boots, gloves, hats, heavy coats, wool scarves, raincoat, and mittens
large unbreakable mirror

- Bring in dress-up clothes that could be worn in the winter cold.
- Be sure to include a large, unbreakable mirror so older toddlers can admire their winter attire.
- Toddlers will examine the clothes, try them on, and learn from the process.

# Sounds of Winter

recording of winter sounds, purchased or made

- In the *Science and Nature Learning Space,* play a tape or CD of sounds from winter.
- This will help toddlers connect with the auditory world of winter and provide another way of learning about the season.

Nature items invite toddlers to explore.

## ADDING SPARK TO THE SCIENCE AND NATURE LEARNING SPACE

*Bring snow or ice into the Science and Nature Learning Space. Place it in a large plastic tub or water table so the older toddlers can see, touch, and experience it. Later, add food coloring to create new interest in the snow. Use small plastic shovels and spoons as tools for moving the snow.*

## The Essential Literacy Connection
**(\* Available as a board book)**

Brett, Jan. (1999). *Annie and the Wild Animals.* Boston: Houghton Mifflin Company. *Annie faces many surprises in the woods as she searches for her lost cat.*

McPhail, David. (2000). *The Puddle.* New York: Farrar, Straus & Giroux. *An older toddler enjoys a rainy day adventure, even though his mother has warned him to stay out of puddles.*

Pandell, Karen. (1994). *I Love You, Sun. I Love You, Moon.* Illustrated by Tomie dePaola. New York: Putnam Publishing. *Toddlers from around the world express their feelings toward nature and caring for their environment.\**

## Other Printed Materials

The *Science and Nature Learning Space* should include nature magazines (such as *Big Backyard* or *Ranger Rick*) and camping equipment catalogues.

## Evaluation

1. Is the older toddler interested in examining items included in the *Science and Nature Learning Space?*
2. Can the older toddler be observed caring for the pet and plants?
3. Is the older toddler interested in nature and the seasonal items that exist?
4. Is the older toddler finding new ways to learn about nature?

# Transportation Learning Space

## Overview

Toddlers are interested in movement. They are refining the use of their bodies, as they move from place to place. They are also questioning how objects move and what makes this happen. The *Transportation Learning Space* will focus on things that move and have wheels. As they manipulate these props, older toddlers will begin to understand the cause and effect of movement. While they are experimenting with representations of cars, trucks, wagons, buses, and other forms of transportation, they will discover similarities, differences, and possibilities for making things move.

## Learning Objectives

Older toddlers will:

1. Learn ways of moving people and things.
2. Use new vocabulary as they learn labels for props.
3. Discover cause-and-effect relationships with wheeled toys.
4. Identify things in their environment that move.

## Time Frame

This unique learning space will match the older toddlers' interest in movement. It should remain in the classroom for two to three weeks and then be stored away. Later, the toys and props can be reintroduced into the learning space. Many of the props can also be added to the *Construction Learning Space* when the *Transportation Learning Space* is put away.

## Letter to Parents

• • • • • • • • • • • • • • • • • • • • •

*Dear Parents,*

*Older toddlers enjoy walking, running, and moving around. They are interested in many forms of transportation that they see in their world: the big yellow school bus, the big truck, the train, or a wagon. Our* Transportation Learning Space *will build on older toddlers' fascination with movement and vehicles. In this learning space, they will experiment with toy dump trucks, miniature trains, buses, and cars. Older toddlers will learn the names of these things, how they move, and how to make them go.*

*When you are with your toddler and see interesting forms of transportation, talk with them about what you see. Ask them questions, "What makes that truck go?" "Look at the train; where is the engine?" or "What is that?"*

## Layout of the Transportation Learning Space

## Web of Integrated Learning

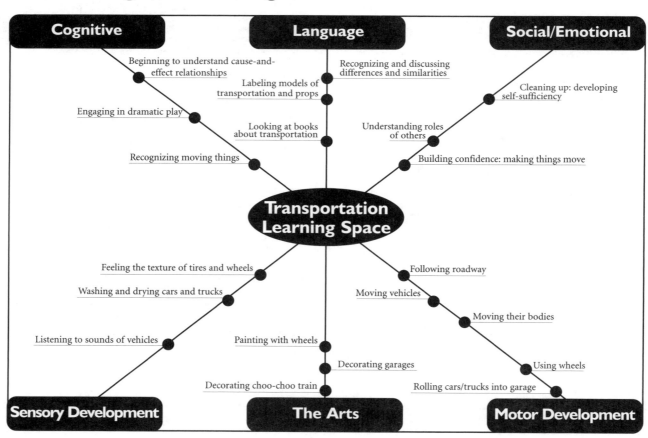

**Cognitive**

Beginning to understand cause-and-effect relationships

Engaging in dramatic play

Recognizing moving things

**Language**

Recognizing and discussing differences and similarities

Labeling models of transportation and props

Looking at books about transportation

Understanding roles of others

**Social/Emotional**

Cleaning up: developing self-sufficiency

Building confidence: making things move

**Transportation Learning Space**

Feeling the texture of tires and wheels

Washing and drying cars and trucks

Listening to sounds of vehicles

Following roadway

Moving vehicles

Moving their bodies

Painting with wheels

Decorating garages

Using wheels

Decorating choo-choo train

Rolling cars/trucks into garage

**Sensory Development**

**The Arts**

**Motor Development**

This learning space requires some space for moving and pushing transportation vehicles. It works well near the *Construction Learning Space* or, in some cases, the two learning spaces can be combined for several weeks. Keep wheeled vehicles in the area during the operation of the *Transportation Learning Space*.

## Vocabulary Enrichment

bus
car
fast/slow
garage
move
train
truck
wagon
wheels

## Teacher- and Parent-Collected Props

large pieces of vinyl fabric
low table
miniature cars, trucks, and buses
pieces of linoleum
plastic tub
small boxes
tools for washing vehicles
wagon

**ACTIVITIES**

# Garages for Parking

several shoeboxes or medium-size boxes
various small vehicles with wheels

- Create garages from shoeboxes to store cars, trucks, and buses.
- Cut an opening in the front of the box, large enough for the toys to enter.
- Older toddlers can roll the toys with wheels into the garage and bring them out when they are needed for play.
- This activity also develops an awareness of one-to-one correspondence: one car, one garage.

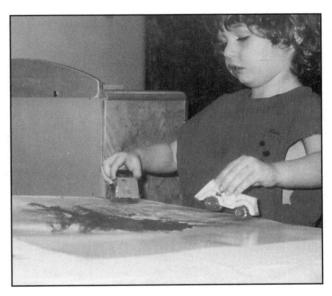

Painting with wheeled toys

# Painting with Wheels

plastic
butcher paper or white roll paper
tape
washable toys
tempera paint mixed with dry laundry detergent
small roller or sponge paintbrush

- Cover the floor with plastic to contain paint and prevent staining.
- Tape a large piece of butcher or white roll paper on the plastic.
- Toddlers can remove their shoes, if desired.
- Select washable toys with wheels with different sizes and designs.
- Allow toddlers to paint the wheels with washable tempera paint using a small roller or sponge brush.
- Once the wheels are painted, toddlers move the vehicles across the paper, producing tracks in the direction of the toddlers' movements.
- This activity provides a visual representation of movement that toddlers can recognize.

## Sounds of Wheeled Vehicles

blank cassette tape
tape recorder

- Make a recording of some sounds from modes of transportation that older toddlers recognize. Include sounds of vehicles the older toddlers have probably experienced or seen, such as a bus, dump truck, garbage truck, fire truck, car, train, motorcycle, or musical ice cream truck.
- Toddlers play the recording in the *Transportation Learning Space* and listen for sounds that they can recognize, which sets the stage for related dramatic play.

Going for a train ride using cardboard boxes and hats

## Road Play

large piece of vinyl or linoleum
black electrical tape
toy cars and trucks

- Select a large piece of vinyl or linoleum to use on the floor of the *Transportation Learning Space*.
- Using black electrical tape, create a long roadway on the vinyl or linoleum. Make sure the road is wide and straight, with only a few curves.
- For toddlers, two highways that are far apart work best.
- Encourage them to use their vehicles to follow the roadway.

## Choo Choo Train

3 or 4 cardboard boxes large enough for an older toddler to sit inside
materials to decorate the boxes

- Make a train out of three or four cardboard boxes. Decorate it as desired.
- Toddlers "ride" in the train, pick it up and move it from place to place, and make tickets to get aboard.

# Incline

1" x 6" lumber or plywood, 4' long
2 pieces of 4' long molding
glue or nails and hammer
blocks to elevate the board 2" to 3"
toy cars and trucks

- Glue or nail molding on each side of the board to hold the cars or trucks on the incline.
- Use blocks to elevate one end of the wood 2"-3" off the floor.
- Toddlers roll toy trucks and cars down the incline.
- The higher the elevation, the faster they will roll. Toddlers will be able to observe the faster motion as they change the incline.

## ADDING SPARK TO THE TRANSPORTATION LEARNING SPACE

*Vehicles can go to a "car wash." Use a tub with warm soapy water to wash the trucks, buses, or cars. Include a dish brush and sponge in the tub to help with the cleanup. Cloths should be available for drying the vehicles.*

## The Essential Literacy Connection
**(* Available as a board book)**

Barton, Byron, (1998). *Trucks*. New York: HarperCollins. *See a variety of trucks in primary colors with simple text.*

Crews, Donald. (1996). *Freight Train*. New York: Morrow, William & Co. *Watch a train travel from fast to slow in this colorful concept book.**

Lewis, Kevin. (2001). *Chugga-Chugga Choo-Choo*. New York: Hyperion Books for Children. *See the day's work of a train ending in the arms of a sleeping child in this rhythmic picture book.**

Morris, Ann. (1994). *On the Go*. Photographs by Ken Heyman. New York: Morrow, William & Company. *A multicultural book about how people get from here to there.*

## Other Printed Materials

The *Transportation Learning Space* should also contain brochures or fliers about different forms of transportation, such as bus trips, train excursions, and air flights.

## Evaluation

1. Is the older toddler moving the wheeled toys around the learning space?
2. Is the older toddler using new vocabulary to identify the vehicles?
3. Can you observe the older toddler examining the wheels and watching the movement?
4. Is the older toddler using dramatic play in the learning space?

# Grocery Store Learning Space

## Overview

Older toddlers are beginning to participate in dramatic play. During this early stage of symbolic play, they use the framework and roles they have experienced and understand. The *Grocery Store Learning Space* is a familiar place for many toddlers; they can use this information in their play. Older toddlers' early dramatic play often imitates behaviors they have observed or happenings they have noticed. For some, it moves into taking on roles using a simple sequence. Props that are "real," or closely resemble the real item, work best during this period. The *Grocery Store Learning Space* provides a meaningful place to talk, play, interact, and work.

## Learning Objectives

Older toddlers will:

1. Relate props and materials to their world.
2. Begin to imitate behaviors, roles, and happenings in their dramatic play.
3. Recognize the symbols or labels of some food items.
4. Use language in their play as they interact in the *Grocery Store Learning Space*.

## Time Frame

This is a high-interest learning space for toddlers. Due to space issues in most toddler classrooms, this learning space should be rotated in and out of the area. Observe the toddlers and determine when they have lost interest in this type of dramatic play. When it is reintroduced later in the year, older toddlers will be interested and involved in the play it encourages.

## Letter to Parents

• • • • • • • • • • • • • • • • • • • • • • • • • •

*Dear Parents,*

*Most of you have taken your toddler to the grocery store. Sometimes, this can be a challenge for you and your curious toddler. However, the grocery store is a place where older toddlers can enjoy learning many things. We are setting up a Grocery Store Learning Space for the next few weeks in our classroom. Many toddlers have experience with the grocery store and some of the food items. They will enjoy participating, selecting, and purchasing their favorite items. Dramatic play in this learning space can be observed as the toddlers roll their carts into the grocery store, select their purchases, and come through the checkout.*

*We are trying to include empty containers of the toddlers' favorite foods in the Grocery Store Learning Space. They will be very excited to see their favorite container of macaroni and cheese or cereal. Many will recognize the food by the label or package design. We are currently collecting empty containers of your toddler's favorites in a box next to the Grocery Store Learning Space. We appreciate your help in stocking our "grocery store."*

# Layout of the Grocery Store Learning Space

# Web of Integrated Learning

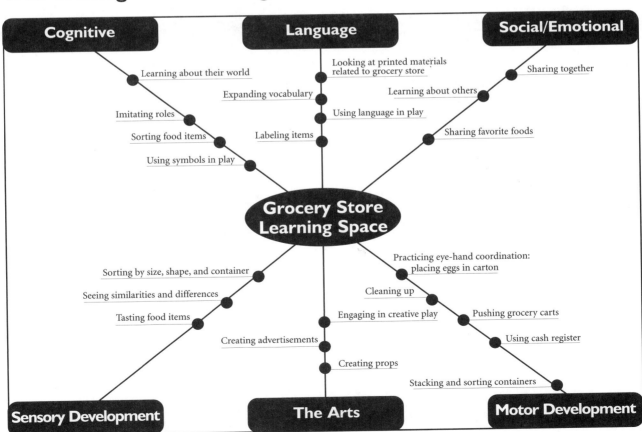

**Cognitive**
- Learning about their world
- Imitating roles
- Sorting food items
- Using symbols in play

**Language**
- Looking at printed materials related to grocery store
- Expanding vocabulary
- Using language in play
- Labeling items

**Social/Emotional**
- Sharing together
- Learning about others
- Sharing favorite foods

**Grocery Store Learning Space**

**Sensory Development**
- Sorting by size, shape, and container
- Seeing similarities and differences
- Tasting food items

**The Arts**
- Creating advertisements
- Engaging in creative play
- Cleaning up
- Creating props

**Motor Development**
- Practicing eye-hand coordination: placing eggs in carton
- Pushing grocery carts
- Using cash register
- Stacking and sorting containers

Include the parts of a grocery store that are the most interesting to toddlers. For example, grocery carts, fruit, vegetables, cereals, drinks, and checkout. These areas should be stocked with "real" containers, plastic fruit/vegetables, and other related items. Include labels and pictures of the items in the grocery store. A cash register, credit card swipe, and play money will inspire additional play.

## Vocabulary Enrichment

bill
buy
canned food
cereal
fruit
grocery cart
grocery store
manager
milk
money
stock
vegetable

A cart for the grocery shopping

## Teacher- and Parent-Collected Props

cardboard boxes that can be transformed into carts
cash register
empty containers of popular items, such as canned food, boxes of pasta or cereal, milk cartons, crackers, cookies, and egg cartons
low shelves
paper and pens for grocery list
paper bags
plastic fruit and vegetables
play paper money
scales
toy plastic shopping carts

**ACTIVITIES**

## Making Play Money

green construction paper
scissors (adult only)
poster board
aluminum foil
money box

- Use green construction paper to make bills to use in the grocery store.
- Cut poster board into round circles. Let older toddlers cover the circles with foil to make coins.
- Use a small box to hold the "money."
- The play money can be used to pay for food purchases and placed in the cash register.

Tasting new foods in the Grocery Store Learning Space.

## Tasting New Things

various new food items

- Many grocery stores provide free samples of food in different parts of the store.

- Each week place a fruit or vegetable on display in the *Grocery Store Learning Space*.
- The toddlers can taste, smell, feel, and see the food in the learning space. Talk with them about the food and determine if they like it.
- This will also provide an opportunity for older toddlers to try a new food.

## Storing the Eggs

several plastic eggs
several egg cartons, cardboard and/or Styrofoam basket

- Collect plastic eggs that are used in the springtime.
- Provide egg cartons for the toddlers to use in storing the eggs.
- Demonstrate how eggs are placed in the cartons and displayed in the grocery store.
- On a low table, place a basket of eggs and a variety of types and sizes of cartons.
- Toddlers place the eggs in the cartons, take them out, and replace them again. They will enjoy the repetition of this activity, as they strengthen their eye-hand coordination.

# Sorting Cans

various empty cans and food
containers
box

- Place a box filled with different sizes of cans and containers in the *Grocery Store Learning Space*.
- Toddlers can explore the cans and food containers.
- Some toddlers may begin to group items together that are similar in some way, by size, color, shape, or food it contains.
- When you observe a toddler sorting using any characteristic, comment on this grouping.

## ADDING SPARK TO THE GROCERY STORE LEARNING SPACE

*Add a new section to the Grocery Store Learning Space, such as a florist area. Include silk or plastic flowers, non-breakable containers, tissue paper, ribbons, note cards, and pens to write messages.*

## The Essential Literacy Connection
(* Available as a board book)

Baggette, Susan K. (1998). *Jonathan Goes to the Grocery Store*. Sterling, VA: Brookfield Reader, Inc. *Grandpa takes Jonathan to the store, where many friendly employees greet them.**

Mayer, Mercer. (1989). *Just Shopping with Mom*. Racine, WI: Western. *Colorful illustrations and simple text tell of Critter's trips to the grocery store, pet shop, and clothing store.*

Miranda, Anne. (2001). *To Market, to Market*. New York: Harcourt. *Enjoy this singsong trip to the market, related to the familiar nursery rhyme.*

## Other Printed Materials

Additional items for the *Grocery Store Learning Space* include newspaper ads for grocery stores, pad and pencil for grocery list, and coupons for food items.

## Evaluation

1. Is the older toddler involved in dramatic play?
2. Is the older toddler using language that relates to the grocery store and food items?
3. Can sorting of items be observed as the older toddler participates in the learning space?
4. Is the older toddler interested in selecting and purchasing items?

# Sand and Water Learning Space

## Overview

Sand and water are two natural materials that older toddlers find fascinating. Each material provides its own opportunities for learning. When sand and water are combined, the possibilities for discovering other unique properties are expanded. In this *Sand and Water Learning Space*, there will be opportunities to use dry sand, wet sand, and water.

Many of the tools that work with one material can be used in combination with others; many will respond to the activity of the toddlers in different ways. Scientific discovery is encouraged in the learning space, as older toddlers engage in exploration using sand and water.

## Learning Objectives

Older toddlers will:

1. Use scientific investigation to learn about sand and water.
2. Expand attention span as they experiment with natural materials.
3. Learn language that relates to sand and water and the tools they use.
4. Develop fine motor coordination as they manipulate materials.

## Time Frame

The *Sand and Water Learning Space* can use sand and water separately or together. The different combination of materials allows this learning space to rotate in and out of the classroom throughout the year.

## Letter to Parents

Dear Parents,

The first three years of life are a critical time for learning. Older toddlers are very interested in natural materials that respond in interesting ways. This week, we are adding a Sand and Water Learning Space to our classroom. In this learning space, toddlers will have many opportunities to experiment and learn about these substances.

It is amazing to observe how long toddlers are interested in exploring sand and water. It provides both an enjoyable and important learning experience for them. Come visit the Sand and Water Learning Space and see our young scientists at work.

# Layout of the Sand and Water Learning Space

# Web of Integrated Learning

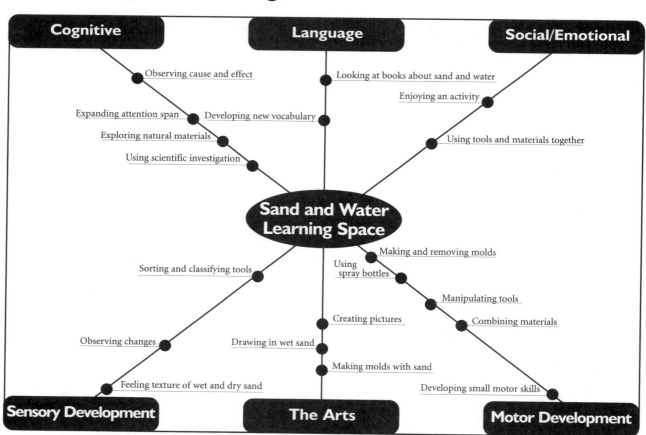

The *Sand and Water Learning Space* encourages manipulation including pouring, filling, and moving the sand and water. To contain the materials, cover the floor and table with plastic. A water table or two plastic tubs can be used to hold the water and sand in separate areas. As play progresses, combine the sand and water to produce varying levels of thickness and responsiveness. Store tools in the *Sand and Water Learning Space* so older toddlers can select the ones they will use during their play.

## Vocabulary Enrichment

fill/empty
funnel
molds
pour
sand
scoop
sift
tools
tube
water
wet/dry

## Teacher- and Parent-Collected Props

bag of white sterilized play sand
clear plastic boxes (to store tools and props)
funnels
kitchen tools, such as large spoons (with and without
    holes), strainer, saltshakers, margarine tubs,
    tongs, and egg beaters
plastic sheeting and/or shower curtains
plastic measuring cups
rocks, shells, and pieces of wood
sand and/or water table (or use two plastic tubs on a
    low table)
small broom and dustpan or small hand-held
    vacuum cleaner
small buckets and shovels
sponges
strainer or sifter
variety of plastic bottles

## ACTIVITIES

# Spray Bottles

4 or 5 easy-to-spray bottles
water
dry sand

- Fill the spray bottles with water.
- Place them in the dry sand area. You may need to demonstrate how the spray bottles work. Allow the older toddlers to practice spraying.
- It may be helpful to place a plastic bowl in the middle of the sand, so they will have a target to aim toward when they are spraying.
- This fine mist will change the color, texture, and responsiveness of the sand.
- Help the toddlers observe these changes and find out for themselves how the wet sand is different from dry sand.
  **CAUTION:** Supervise closely so toddlers don't spray each other!

Spray bottles are used to wet sand, which produces changes in the responsiveness of the material.

# Wet Sand

container of sand
container of water
tools, such as molds, plastic cups,
and cookie cutters
camera and film

- In this learning space, set up a
  table with separate pans of sand
  and water.
- Allow sufficient time for
  toddlers to explore each of
  these materials separately.
- Later, combine sand and some
  water into one tub.
- This "new" substance responds
  differently to the tools that have
  been used with dry sand and
  with water.
- In addition to the previously
  used tools, add molds, plastic cups, cookie
  cutters, and plastic wheeled toys.
- Ask questions related to the toddlers'
  experimentation, such as, "What is happening
  with the wet sand?" and "Can you make tracks?"
- Document some of the toddlers' exploration
  using a camera and display the photographs on a
  panel in the *Sand and Water Learning Space*.

# Drawing in the Wet Sand

sand
water

- Wet the sand.
- Show the older toddlers how you can draw in the
  sand with a finger or stick. Be sure to make a
  simple line or scribble.
- Then, show the toddlers how to erase their lines.
- Encourage them to draw in the sand and watch
  others draw. Older toddlers will also be very
  interested in erasing the artwork, too.

- During this process, toddlers are learning about
  the properties of wet sand and observing the
  work of others.

Wet sand can be used to make prints of objects and animals.

# Making Molds in the Sand

plastic or aluminum items that create an interesting
   shape in the sand, such as Jell-O molds, plastic
   cups and glasses, scoops, small buckets or
   containers, and large shells
sand (dry and/or wet)

- Set up both the dry sand and wet sand in the
  learning space so older toddlers can experiment
  with the molds in both types of sand. They can
  determine that the pattern is produced more
  effectively in the wet sand.
- Encourage the toddlers to explore and talk to
  them about the process.

## ADDING SPARK TO THE SAND AND WATER LEARNING SPACE

*Use a new material in the sand and water table or tubs. Some materials that are interesting to older toddlers include dirt, mud, sawdust, and wood shavings. Many of the tools that were used with sand and water can be included with this new material.*

# The Essential Literacy Connection

Apperley, Dawn. (1996). *In the Sand.* Boston: Little Brown & Company. *This lift-the-flap book illustrates items in the sea and on the shore.*

Jarnow, Jill. (2000). *Splish! Splash!* New York: Penguin Putnam Books for Young Readers. *Simple pictures and text show children playing in the water at various locations including the pool, creek, and beach.*

Knutson, Kimberley. (1992). *Muddigush.* New York: Simon & Schuster Children's. *Creative words describe what it is like to play in mud.*

McMillan. Bruce. (1988). *Dry or Wet?* New York: HarperCollins Children's Books. *Adults can help expand the older toddler's vocabulary by discussing the photographs in this wordless picture book.*

# Evaluation

1. Is the older toddler experimenting with sand, water, and wet sand?
2. Have you observed the older toddler using tools to move or explore the materials?
3. Has the older toddler compared materials and tools?
4. Is the older toddler's interest more sustained in the play with sand and water?

# Doctor's Office Learning Space

## Overview

Most toddlers have visited the doctor's office or clinic many times during their first years of life. Sometimes, they view this as a scary place and have little understanding of the positive things that happen. The *Doctor's Office Learning Space* will provide a place where older toddlers can play out some of their fears and begin to view the doctor visit in a more positive way. This learning space should encourage dramatic play and role-playing, as the older toddler becomes the doctor, nurse, or patient.

## Learning Objectives

Older toddlers will:

1. Have the opportunity to try out different roles in their dramatic play.
2. Alleviate some concerns and fears about visits to the doctor's office.
3. Learn new vocabulary that relates to the *Doctor's Office Learning Space*.

## Time Frame

This learning space will be set up in the classroom for two to three weeks. If older toddlers show real interest in play related to the learning space, it could remain for a longer period. Much of the first week of learning space operation will be spent examining props and materials. After that time, some toddlers will move into play that is more dramatic and involves role-playing.

## Letter to Parents

• • • • • • • • • • • • • • • • • • • •

*Dear Parents,*

*Most toddlers have visited doctor's offices or clinics. Some toddlers have had injuries or illnesses that required a visit to an emergency room or hospital. Sometimes these experiences are scary for the older toddler.*

*This week, we are opening a Doctor's Office Learning Space in our classroom. The learning space will have smocks, stethoscopes, scales, plastic gloves, and other related materials. In the Doctor's Office Learning Space, older toddlers will have the opportunity to play with these items. Some will "pretend" that they are the doctor or nurse. During this play, they will be able to explore some of their experiences and concerns related to the doctor's office.*

# Layout of the Doctor's Office Learning Space

# Web of Integrated Learning

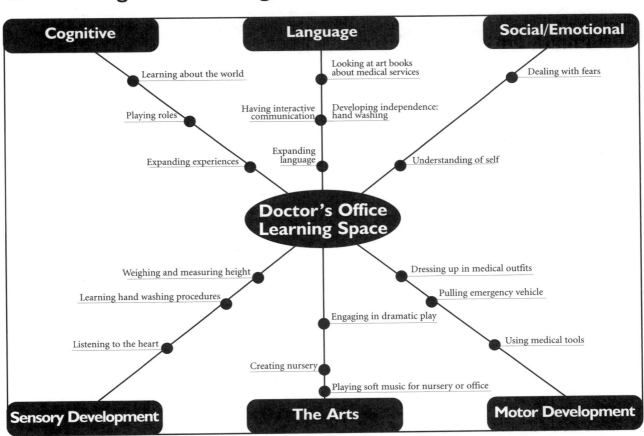

**Cognitive**
- Learning about the world
- Playing roles
- Expanding experiences

**Language**
- Looking at art books about medical services
- Having interactive communication
- Developing independence: hand washing
- Expanding language

**Social/Emotional**
- Dealing with fears
- Understanding of self

**Doctor's Office Learning Space**

**Sensory Development**
- Weighing and measuring height
- Learning hand washing procedures
- Listening to the heart

**The Arts**
- Engaging in dramatic play
- Creating nursery
- Playing soft music for nursery or office

**Motor Development**
- Dressing up in medical outfits
- Pulling emergency vehicle
- Using medical tools

Transform a small part of the classroom into a doctor's office and reception area. Include a desk and chairs for the waiting area. Decorate part of the learning space to resemble an examination room with a bed/table and storage for medical supplies. The wall or divider can have pictures of the human body or x-rays to add to the "realistic" appearance.

## Vocabulary Enrichment

Band-Aid
check-up
doctor
doctor's office
emergency
medicine
nurse
scale
sick
smocks
temperature
well
x-ray

## Teacher- and Parent-Collected Props

bandages
bathroom scale
clipboards
computer/typewriter for office
cotton balls
gloves
lab jackets
mask
old x-rays
rags (to wrap hurt limbs)
sheets for tables
soap
tape
telephone
toy doctor kit with stethoscope

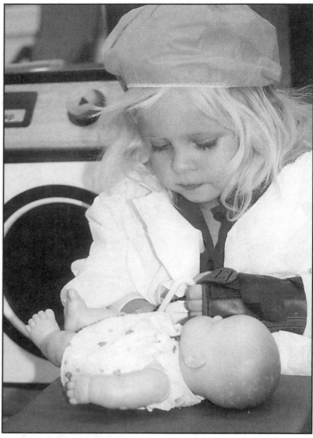

A "doctor" examines a "patient" in the office.

## ACTIVITIES

# A Stethoscope

paper cups
yarn

- Create several stethoscopes because many toddlers will want to use these.
- Punch one hole on each side of the bottom of a paper cup.
- String the yarn through these two holes; be sure it is long enough to be worn around the neck.
- Toddlers use this stethoscope to "pretend" to listen to the heartbeat.
  **NOTE:** Supervise closely because of the potential danger of children wearing something around their necks.

# An Emergency Ambulance

large cardboard box (such as a refrigerator box)
pillow
strong yarn or rope

- Use a cardboard box as the ambulance.
- Place a pillow inside the box to provide comfort for the patient.
- Attach strong yarn or rope to the front of the box for pulling the ambulance.
- While one patient sits in the box, another toddler pulls the box to move the patient to receive medical care.

# Hand Washing

picture chart of hand washing
liquid soap
water
paper towels

- Create a picture chart that shows the steps in washing your hands.
- Provide liquid soap, water, and paper towels for the toddlers to learn the procedure.
- Add this chart to the learning space and to the bathroom area.

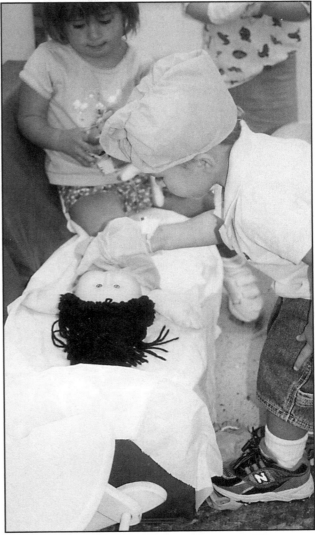

Props assist toddlers in their role playing in the Doctor's Office Learning Space.

# Weight and Height

scale
measuring tool
chart to record growth

- In the doctor's office, weigh the toddlers and measure their height.
- Record the information on a chart and display in the learning space.
- Include the scale and measuring tool for the older toddlers to use in their dramatic play.

# Dress-Up

medical clothing, such as white coats, smocks, masks, and gloves
dolls

- Provide medical clothing for toddlers to use in the *Doctor's Office Learning Space.*
- Include dolls to use as patients, because most toddlers will prefer to play doctor or nurse.

**ADDING SPARK TO THE DOCTOR'S OFFICE
LEARNING SPACE**

*Add a nursery to the Doctor's
Office Learning Space. To set up
the nursery, include baby dolls,
rocking chair, diapers, baby
bottles, cribs, and soft music.
Many toddlers will participate in
this expansion of the Doctor's
Office Learning Space.*

## The Essential Literacy Connection

Allen, Julia. (1987). *My First Doctor Visit.* Provo, UT:
ARO Publishing. *This book introduces the
instruments and procedures of a doctor's office.*

Berenstain, Stan, & Berenstain, Jan. (1999). *The
Berenstain Bears Go to the Doctor.* New York:
Econo-Clad Books. *A father accompanies the cubs
to get their "check-ups" in order to alleviate their
fears.*

Cousins, Lucy. (2001). *Doctor Maisy.* Cambridge:
Candlewick Press. *This bright, simple book portrays
a doctor's visit as being a positive and exciting
experience.*

Oxenbury, Helen. (1994). *The Checkup.* New York:
Penguin Putnam Books for Young Readers.
*Illustrated from a toddler's perspective, this book
conveys one little boy's reaction to the instruments
used in a doctor's office.*

## Evaluation

1. Is the older toddler participating in the play of the
   *Doctor's Office Learning Space?*
2. Does the older toddler seem to be including
   some of her fears and concerns?
3. Is the older toddler manipulating some of the
   tools that are used in the *Doctor's Office Learning
   Space?*

# Photography Studio Learning Space

## Overview

Most toddlers have had their pictures taken during the first years of their lives. This real-life experience provides a record of the changes in their growth and development. The *Photography Studio Learning Space* allows the older toddler to develop a positive self-image while participating in the photography process.

The *Photography Studio Learning Space* will stimulate older toddlers to learn new vocabulary terms such as "picture," "camera," and "photo album." There will be activities that improve toddlers' awareness of their bodies and art projects that encourage fine motor skills. This learning space also provides valuable social interactions through dramatic play.

## Learning Objectives

Older toddlers will:
1. Improve body awareness.
2. Experience the world in new ways.
3. Participate in fine motor activities.
4. Learn new vocabulary.
5. Expand pretend play skills.

## Time Frame

This learning space is most appropriate for a short period of two or three weeks. If the toddlers show a particular interest in this learning space, bring it back later in the year.

## Letter to Parents

Dear Parents,

Most toddlers have had their picture taken with a camera. Some have even been to a professional photography studio. We are going to connect toddlers to this experience by opening up our own Photography Studio Learning Space. In the learning space, toddlers will be able to explore cameras and make their own "pictures." These activities will help toddlers learn about their bodies and promote their fine motor skills by using their hands.

We will be making artwork with pictures in the photography studio. Please bring in as many photographs of your child as you can spare. Keep in mind that these pictures will probably not be returned. Thank you for your help in making our Photography Studio Learning Space a great success.

# Layout of the Photography Studio Learning Space

# Web of Integrated Learning

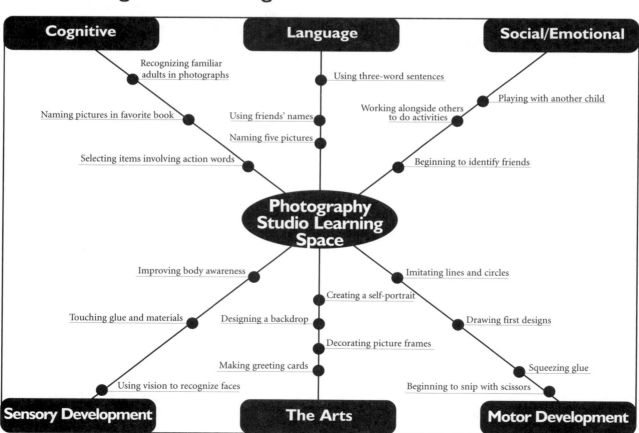

**Cognitive**
- Recognizing familiar adults in photographs
- Naming pictures in favorite book
- Selecting items involving action words

**Language**
- Using three-word sentences
- Using friends' names
- Naming five pictures

**Social/Emotional**
- Playing with another child
- Working alongside others to do activities
- Beginning to identify friends

**Photography Studio Learning Space**

**Sensory Development**
- Improving body awareness
- Touching glue and materials
- Using vision to recognize faces

**The Arts**
- Creating a self-portrait
- Designing a backdrop
- Decorating picture frames
- Making greeting cards

**Motor Development**
- Imitating lines and circles
- Drawing first designs
- Squeezing glue
- Beginning to snip with scissors

Locate the *Photography Studio Learning Space* in a part of the room with a blank wall or where backdrops (sheets) can be hung. Keep props for picture making in a plastic container placed on the floor. Place a cash register, play money, paper, and washable markers on a child-size table to encourage dramatic play experiences.

## Vocabulary Enrichment

camera
cash register
greeting card
photo album
photography
picture
picture frame
portrait
self
shapes
smile

## Teacher- and Parent-Collected Props

35mm film containers with lids
cash register
child-size chairs
different color sheets or fabric for backdrops
flashlights
magnifying glass (to view pictures up close)
old snapshots
paper and washable markers
paper or plastic picture envelopes (collected from
    photo developing site)
photo albums
photographs of friends
picture frames
play money
several small cameras (broken cameras or cameras
    without film work best)
stuffed animals

**ACTIVITIES**

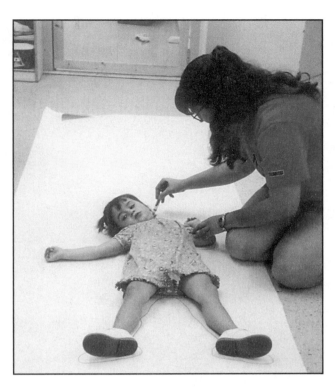

A teacher draws around a toddler to begin a self-portrait.

## Self-Portrait

roll of newsprint
large washable marker
assorted washable markers or crayons
scissors

* Ask each toddler to lie down on a large piece of the paper. Draw an outline around the toddler using a large washable marker. Talk about each body part as you work. For example, "Now I am drawing around your right arm."
* Cut out the portrait.
* Encourage the toddlers to draw simple faces (eyes, nose, mouth, ears, and hair) on their portraits. If desired, they can also color the "self-portrait."
* Also make a self-portrait of each caregiver in the room.
* Label the portraits and tape them onto a blank wall for everyone to see.

- Stimulate the toddlers' thinking about themselves by helping them identify the body parts first on themselves and then on their self-portraits.

# Homemade Greeting Cards

old greeting cards
colorful construction paper
picture of each child
child-safe scissors
glue (glue sticks work great!)
washable markers
stickers

- Show the toddlers a few of the greeting cards.
- Let each toddler choose an old greeting card or piece of construction paper. If they are using construction paper, help them fold it in half.
- Ask the toddlers for whom they would like to make a greeting card.
- Give them a picture to glue inside or on the front of their greeting card.
- Then, they can "write" a poem or note to go inside the card. Ask each toddler what his card says. Write down the toddler's own words next to the drawing, if he would like you to.
- The toddlers can decorate their cards with markers and stickers.
- This is a fun activity to do for special occasions!

# Picture Frames

craft sticks
glue
paper plates
colored tissue paper
seashells, yarn, and dried flowers
pictures

- Glue four craft sticks together to form a square frame.
- Give each child a paper plate and place the square frame on top of the plate.

- Demonstrate how to use glue and colorful tissue paper (or other materials listed) to decorate the picture frame. Encourage them to be creative in decorating their own frames.
- Help toddlers glue pictures to the back of their frames.
- Make a photo gallery to display the toddlers' creations.

# Shape Pictures

various materials, such as wrapping paper, fabric, paper, cardboard, paper plates, and foil
scissors
construction paper
glue

- Cut out different size circles, squares, and triangles from a variety of materials.
- Place all the shapes in the center of the table.
- Give each child a large piece of construction paper and glue.
- Let the toddlers choose the shapes they want to place on the paper.
- Talk about the different "shapes" as the toddlers glue them to the paper.
- Hang the completed shape pictures in or near the *Photography Studio Learning Space* for the children to enjoy.

# Photo Album of My Friends

5" x 7" plain note cards
hole punch
scrap fabric
glue or tape
yarn or string
marker
pictures of all the toddlers and caregivers

- Punch two holes into each note card.
- Glue fabric to one side of two note cards, leaving a ½" space for the holes.

- Place the fabric-covered cards on either side of three or four plain note cards.
- Tie the cards together with yarn or string. (Make one for each child.)
- Let each toddler select a "photo album."
- Write the toddler's name on the front of the album and tell her that this photo album is for pictures of her friends.
- Place pictures on the table. Help the toddlers choose a few pictures to tape or glue into their photo album.
- Ask each toddler, "Who are your friends?" or "Which photo do you want to put in your book?" to help them identify pictures.
- Label the pictures.
- Leave a few blank pages in the album for the child to complete at home.

# Animal Pictures

magazine pictures of animals
scissors
glue or tape
plain index cards
marker

- Cut out pictures of familiar animals from magazines.
- Glue or tape each picture to plain index cards and label the pictures.
- Let the toddlers take turns pulling out one picture from the pile.
- Toddlers pretend to be whatever animal they select. For example, if a toddler pulls out a picture of a dog, she should bark and crawl.

## ADDING SPARK TO THE PHOTOGRAPHY STUDIO LEARNING SPACE

*Invite a guest to take pictures with a digital or instant-print camera. Toddlers can see these types of pictures immediately and enjoy the results. These photographs can be attractively displayed in the* **Photography Studio Learning Space** *at the toddlers' eye-level.*

## The Essential Literacy Connection
(* Available as a board book)

Hoban, Tana. (1997). *Look Book.* New York: Greenwillow Books. *This wordless photography book presents images through a single hole and then a full picture on the next page.*

Intrater, Roberta Grobel. (1997). *Smile!* New York: Scholastic. *Toddlers respond to the photographer's request to pose.**

Marshall, Janet Perry. (1989). *My Camera: At the Zoo.* Boston: Little, Brown & Company. *Close-up and full-frame pictures, accompanied by vocabulary related to photography, describe an older toddler's trip to the zoo with a camera.*

## Evaluation

1. Can the older toddler identify some body parts?
2. Is the older toddler exploring new objects and materials?
3. Is the older toddler using new vocabulary related to photography?
4. Is the older toddler participating in fine motor activities?
5. Is the older toddler demonstrating beginning pretend play skills?

# Shoe Store Learning Space

## Overview

Toddlers are fascinated by their shoes. They take them off and put them on many times during the day. They like to buckle, snap, attach, and attempt to tie them. The *Shoe Store Learning Space* builds on this interest by providing a place where older toddlers can experiment with shoes and accessories. In the learning space, toddlers will be able to participate in dramatic play as they select, buy, and wear shoes and handbags. Some pairing and sorting will also occur as they return the shoes to boxes and clean up the learning space.

## Learning Objectives

Older toddlers will:

1. Investigate the different types of shoes available to wear.
2. Participate in dramatic play as they take on roles in the Shoe Store Learning Space.
3. Develop fine motor coordination as they take shoes off and on.
4. Be more independent as they become able to dress themselves.

## Time Frame

This very specialized learning space adds interest to the classroom. It will probably be set up for two to three weeks, depending on the interest of the toddlers and the unique shoes included. As with most learning spaces, the first visits will involve examining, exploring, and manipulating all of the materials. Later, older toddlers will become more involved in dramatic play related to the *Shoe Store Learning Space.*

## Letter to Parents

• • • • • • • • • • • • • • • • • • • • • • •

*Dear Parents,*

*How many times have you looked for your toddler's shoes? How often do you have to chase your older toddler to get shoes on his or her feet so you can go outside? Do you ever have to wait and wait until your toddler gets tired of trying to secure the buckle or tie his or her shoe?*

*For the next two weeks, we will have a* Shoe Store Learning Space *in our classroom. In this learning space, your toddlers can take off their shoes and try on others as many times as they like. During this repeated process, toddlers will be learning how to remove shoes, how to get them back on, and how to fasten them. As they play with these props, they will be developing coordination and self-help skills.*

*The* Shoe Store Learning Space *will include an area where older toddlers can pretend to purchase shoes using money or credit cards. The learning space will also have storage containers where they can place the shoes when they clean up. Come by our Shoe Store Learning Space and see the interesting collection of shoes and accessories we have available. You may want to try on some shoes, too.*

# Layout of the Shoe Store Learning Space

# Web of Integrated Learning

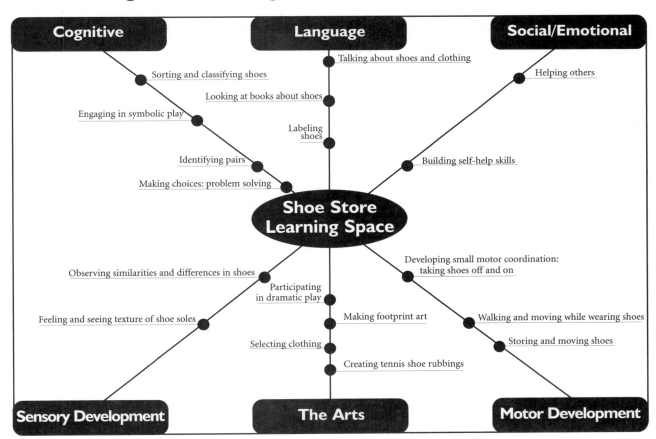

**Cognitive**
- Sorting and classifying shoes
- Engaging in symbolic play
- Identifying pairs
- Making choices: problem solving

**Language**
- Talking about shoes and clothing
- Looking at books about shoes
- Labeling shoes

**Social/Emotional**
- Helping others
- Building self-help skills

**Shoe Store Learning Space**

**Sensory Development**
- Observing similarities and differences in shoes
- Feeling and seeing texture of shoe soles

**The Arts**
- Participating in dramatic play
- Making footprint art
- Selecting clothing
- Creating tennis shoe rubbings

**Motor Development**
- Developing small motor coordination: taking shoes off and on
- Walking and moving while wearing shoes
- Storing and moving shoes

Set up this learning space to resemble a shoe store. Include racks or shelves for displaying the shoes so the options can be seen. Provide several small chairs for sitting and trying on shoes, although the floor is most frequently used for this activity. Include a checkout area, complete with cash register, money, credit card scanner, and pencil. Pictures of shoes on the wall will provide visuals that show the use of the learning space. Hang handbags on pegs or hooks so the toddlers can admire or remove them. A low unbreakable mirror helps older toddlers see the shoes and handbags they have selected.

## Vocabulary Enrichment

boots
buy
cash register
closures for shoes,
    such as buckle,
    tie, Velcro, and
    zipper
dress shoes
handbags/purses
measuring

money
salesperson
shoebox
shoes
socks
storage
tennis shoes

## Teacher- and Parent-Collected Props

advertisements from magazines and/or newspapers
boots
cash register (toy or home-made)
chairs
collection of shoes including dancing shoes (ballet
    and tap), dress shoes, men's and women's shoes,
    tennis shoes with Velcro closing, and baby and
    toddler shoes
measuring tapes
play money and credit cards
posters
purses and handbags
shoeboxes (children's, adults, and boots)

**ACTIVITIES**

# Footprints without Shoes

paper
washable marker
scissors
tape

- Ask each toddler to stand on a piece of paper.
- Draw an outline around each child's feet and cut them out.
- Label each print with the name of the child.
- Tape the prints around the *Shoe Store Learning Space* to make a path to follow.

# Tennis Shoe Rubbings

white paper
large black crayon

- Many toddlers' shoes have interesting textures and designs on the sole.
- Use these designs to produce rubbings of the soles.
- Help the toddlers place white paper over the bottom of their shoes and use a large black crayon to make the rubbing.
- Label the type of shoe and the owner.
- Display these rubbings individually or group them together to make a large mural of interesting tennis shoe rubbings.

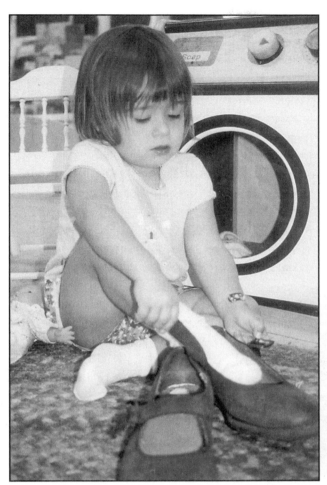

Toddler trying on shoes in the Shoe Store Learning Space

# Choices, Choices, Choices

various pairs of shoes, such as dancing shoes, fancy
    dress-up shoes, camping boots, cowboy boots,
    baby shoes, sandals, house shoes, and colorful
    shiny shoes
low unbreakable mirror

• Collect many different types of shoes. The more
  unique the shoes, the more interesting the play
  will be.
• Make sure all the shoes have been cleaned and
  sprayed with disinfectant.
• Provide a low unbreakable mirror in the learning
  space, so the toddlers can admire the shoes they
  have selected.
• They will enjoy trying on the shoes, pairing the
  shoes, and grouping similar ones together.

# Pairs in a Shoebox

5 or 6 shoeboxes
5 or 6 different pairs of shoes

• Place one shoe of a pair into each of the boxes.
• Make sure the shoes are distinct, so the toddlers
  can easily identify its mate.
• Place the matching shoe in a pile in front of the
  boxes and demonstrate how to store the two
  shoes that look alike together.
• Toddlers develop visual discrimination as they
  determine which shoes to place in shoeboxes.

Practicing shoe buckling develops self-help skills.

# Attachments for Shoes

various child-size shoes with popular closures, such
    as buckle, Velcro, ties, and zippers
basket

- Child-size shoes work well because they are easier for toddlers to maneuver.
- Place the shoes in a basket.
- Toddlers select the shoe and closure they want to learn to use.
- This activity allows older toddlers to work at their own pace and leave the activity when they become tired.

### ADDING SPARK TO THE SHOE LEARNING SPACE

*Add a new collection of shoes that was not included when the learning space opened. These should be very special and unusual shoes. For example, a group of camping shoes or sandals for the beach will spark new interest in trying on the shoes and making purchases.*

## The Essential Literacy Connection

Fung, Karen, & Butterfield, Moira. (2000). *Zippers, Buttons, and Bows.* Hauppauge, NY: Barron's Educational Series, Inc. *This interactive book allows older toddlers to practice their dressing skills while listening to an entertaining story about children getting dressed.*

Morris, Ann. (1998). *Shoes-Shoes-Shoes.* New York: Morrow, William & Company. *This multicultural photography book shows a variety of shoes from around the world.*

Rollins, Susan. (2000). *New Shoes, Red Shoes.* New York: Scholastic, Inc. *Rhythmical, rhyming text shares a young girl's process in finding the perfect new party shoes.*

Winthrop, Elizabeth. (1999). *Shoes.* New York: HarperCollins Children's Books. *Four toddlers share all the lively things one can do in shoes.*

## Evaluation

1. Is the older toddler trying on different types of shoes?
2. Can the older toddler be observed attempting to fasten the shoes?
3. Is dramatic play occurring?
4. Is the older toddler participating in cleanup in the *Shoe Store Learning Space?*

# Big and Little Learning Space

## Overview

Older toddlers are beginning to experiment with some simple math concepts. They continue to be very concrete in their thinking; they learn best by manipulating and exploring "real" objects in their environment. Toddlers can experience quantitative ideas such as big and little, long and short, or high and low through physical activities with real materials. The *Big and Little Learning Space* provides a level of awareness and exposure to these basic concepts.

In the *Big and Little Learning Space*, toddlers will imitate the caregiver's use of measuring tapes, rulers, and scales. They will also begin sorting large objects and small objects. This learning space will provide toddlers with fun and stimulating activities that will introduce them to beginning math ideas and problem-solving activities in a developmentally appropriate way.

## Learning Objectives

Older toddlers will:
1. Be exposed to beginning math concepts: big and little.
2. Expand their language with new vocabulary related to their thinking.
3. Learn about the organization of the world in which they live.

## Time Frame

This learning space will be effective in the classroom for two or three weeks; however, some older toddlers may enjoy it for longer. Observe the toddlers' activities to decide when appropriate play has been completed in the *Big and Little Learning Space*.

## Letter to Parents

• • • • • • • • • • • • • • • • • • • • • •

*Dear Parents,*

*Today we opened a Big and Little Learning Space in our room. In this learning space, toddlers will gain experience with simple math concepts, such as big and little, long and short, and high and low. We are introducing the ideas with real materials and providing opportunities for them to play with the objects. These experiences help toddlers understand how materials are organized in their environment.*

*Older toddlers learn best by using their bodies and hands to explore objects. We will have a variety of different-size objects, rulers, measuring tapes, and a scale to use in play. We will incorporate big and little concepts into fun games such as Hide and Seek, the Limbo, and a Rock Hunt. Our focus is on making older toddlers aware of these concepts as a way to understand their world.*

*The next time you are on a walk with your toddler, name objects and talk about whether that object is "big" or "little." You will be encouraging language and cognitive development.*

# Layout of the Big and Little Learning Space

# Web of Integrated Learning

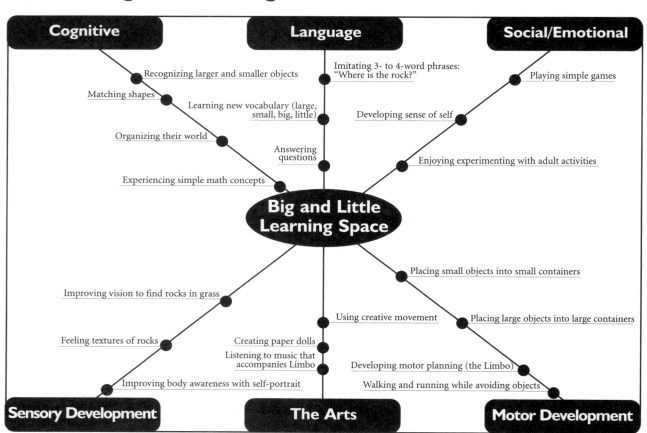

The *Big and Little Learning Space* can easily be transitioned in and out of another learning space such as the *Ball Learning Space* or the *Motor Learning Space*. You can bring materials from other learning spaces not currently in use into the *Big and Little Learning Space,* such as balls, blocks, cars, trucks, and so on. Label objects used in this learning space as "big" or "little."

## Vocabulary Enrichment

big
heavy
hide
high
large
light
little
low
rock
seek
short
small
tall
tiny
treasure

## Teacher- and Parent-Collected Props

boxes and containers of all sizes
large and small balls, blocks, cars/trucks, and stuffed
    animals
large and small measuring tapes and rulers
large, plastic storage container
paper and washable markers (to record information)
scale for weighing objects
unbreakable mirror

## ACTIVITIES

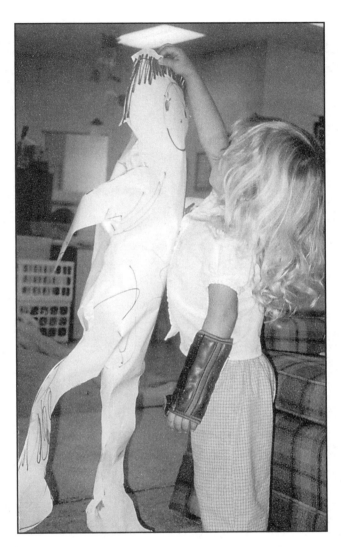

Comparing size in the Big and Little Learning Space

## Big Paper Dolls

large brown wrapping paper
washable markers, crayons, and yarn
glue
scissors
stapler
newspaper

- Stack two pieces of large brown wrapping paper on top of each other on the floor.

- Ask each toddler to lie on the paper. Draw an outline around the child's body.
- Label each paper "doll" with the toddler's name.
- Ask the toddlers to decorate their dolls with washable markers, crayons, and yarn.
- Cut out the outline of each doll, making sure to cut through both pieces of paper.
- Staple around the edges, leaving a large opening at the top and at the bottom of each doll.
- Let the toddlers crumple newspaper and stuff their paper dolls. Staple the remaining openings.
- Make paper dolls for the caregivers in the room.
- Compare the height of the toddlers' real-life dolls to the adult dolls.
- Ask questions such as, "Is Olivia shorter than Ms. April?" "Is Spencer taller than Ms. April?" or "Is Ms. April smaller than Riley?"
- Help the toddlers compare the dolls to themselves by saying, "Look, your doll is the same size as you."

# Big and Little in Action

various poems and songs with big and little concepts

- Select poems or songs that have big and little concepts included in them.
- Make up movements to go along with the words.
- Demonstrate the movements to the toddlers, and encourage them to imitate you as you speak or sing.
- The following is a good poem to use:

### Giants and Elves

*See the giants, great and tall.*
*Hear them bellow, hear them call.*
*Life looks different from up so high,*
*With head and shoulders clear to the sky.*
*And at their feet they can barely see*
*The little people so very tiny*
*Who scurry about with hardly a care,*
*Avoiding enormous feet placed here and there.*
*But together they dwell, the giants and elves*
*In peace and harmony, amongst themselves.*
*(Pica, 1990, p. 23)*

# Rock Hunt

various rocks
several paper bags or plastic grocery bags

- Toddlers love to pick up rocks, so they will be happy to go outside for a rock hunt.
- Give each toddler a paper bag or plastic grocery bag to hold the rocks they collect.
- Talk about the size and weight of rocks the toddlers collect.
- Discuss how some rocks are "too heavy" to put in their bags, while other rocks are very "light." Say, "Let's find a very small rock."
- After completing the rock hunt, help the toddlers sort their rocks into piles.
- Change this activity to fit your environment. For instance, you could look for seashells, leaves, or wildflowers.

# Hide and Seek

toys or stuffed animals
various boxes, such as jewelry boxes, shoeboxes, shirt boxes, cereal boxes, and moving or storage boxes

- Hide a few toys or stuffed animals in different boxes while the toddlers are not watching.
- Place empty boxes and boxes containing items all around the *Big and Little Learning Space*.
- Say, "Treasures are hiding in the boxes. Where are the treasures?"
- After each toddler finds a treasure, ask questions such as, "Is it a big or little treasure?" or "Was it hiding in a big box or a little box?"
- Let the toddlers select treasures and hide them in boxes. Then, you can seek the treasure, asking them questions such as, "Is it a big treasure?" or "Is it in a small box?"

# Teeny Tiny

"Teeny Tiny" story (*Tell It Again!* Raines & Isbell, 1999, pp. 15-16)

props for the story, such as doll clothes, doll bed, stuffed dog, bone, and other appropriate props

- Tell the story of "Teeny Tiny" to the toddlers.
- Pretend to do all the things the teeny tiny woman does.
- Ask the toddlers to imitate your movements, such as getting out of the teeny tiny bed and putting on teeny tiny clothes.
- You may want to use a few props with the story to show the children what "teeny tiny" looks like.
- Toddlers enjoy stories related to "little people" and make a personal connection to the content.

**ADDING SPARK TO THE BIG AND LITTLE LEARNING SPACE**

*Do the Limbo. Take an empty wrapping paper roll (or a broom handle). Hold one end and place the other end against a wall (or ask another person to hold it). Turn on some lively music. Ask the toddlers to stay big and walk under the Limbo pole. Lower the pole and ask toddlers to "be little" and crawl under the pole. Raise and lower the pole. Or, go for a walk outside. Help the older toddlers label things in their environment as "big" or "little."*

## The Essential Literacy Connection
(* Available as a board book)

Haring, Keith. (1998). *Big.* New York: Hyperion Books for Children. *Toddlers' vocabulary will be enhanced with this book that describes oversized clothing on children.**

Hindley, Judy. (1996). *Little and Big.* Cambridge: Candlewick Press. *Toddlers compare the sizes of various items in their neighborhood.*

Wood, Don, & Wood, Audrey. (1998). *The Little Mouse, the Red Ripe Strawberry, and the Big Hungry Bear.* Bridgemead, Swindon: Child's Play International. *Beautiful illustrations and simple text assist the reader/storyteller in becoming an active participant in keeping the strawberry from the bear.**

Yaccarino, Dan. (2001). *So Big!* New York: HarperCollins Children's Books. *This lift-the-flap book asks how big various animals are and encourages toddlers to do the same.*

Toddlers crawling under the limbo broom

## Evaluation

1. Is the older toddler using new vocabulary in the *Big and Little Learning Space?*
2. Is the older toddler exploring material in the *Big and Little Learning Space?*
3. Is the older toddler comparing two objects?

# Gardening Learning Space

## Overview

Toddlers are beginning to be interested in growing things. This learning space will focus on plants that grow quickly and/or produce quick results for the beginning gardener. Older toddlers can be responsible for caring for plants and participating in the growing process. By keeping the gardening simple, toddlers will be able to enjoy the *Gardening Learning Space* and be successful gardeners, as well.

## Learning Objectives

Older toddlers will:

1. Begin to observe plants and growing things in the environment.
2. Understand the basic care of plants that are in the *Gardening Learning Space*.
3. Expand vocabulary that relates to plants and gardening.
4. Develop motor skills by digging, planting, and watering.

## Time Frame

Spring is an ideal time to set up a *Gardening Learning Space* in the older toddler classroom. Because some plants take longer to grow, this learning space can be set up for at least a month. After the *Gardening Learning Space* is closed, the plants can be relocated to a sunny place in the classroom or an outdoor garden area.

## Letter to Parents

• • • • • • • • • • • • • • • • • • • • •

*Dear Parents,*

*As we begin to think about spring and the growing season, we will be adding a Gardening Learning Space to our toddler classroom. This learning space will include plants and activities that encourage your toddler to experience some simple aspects of gardening. They will learn a great deal from participating in this learning space. Toddlers will develop motor skills as they dig and plant. They will learn responsibility as they care for the plants. During the process, they will become more observant of growing things and the changes that occur around them.*

*If you have plants in your home or are thinking about planting a garden, involve your toddler in the planting and caring of these growing things. Choose a small watering can or a small plastic bottle that the toddler can successfully manipulate.*

*If you have houseplants that could come to live in our learning space, we would greatly appreciate your contribution. Enjoy spring and observe the growing plants with your toddler for some wonderful experiences. Learning to appreciate and value the environment can begin early and last a lifetime.*

# Layout of the Gardening Learning Space

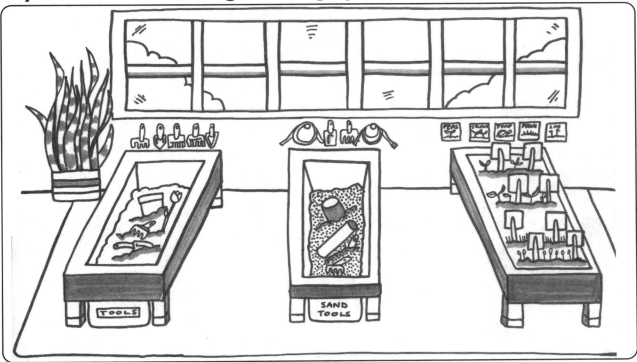

# Web of Integrated Learning

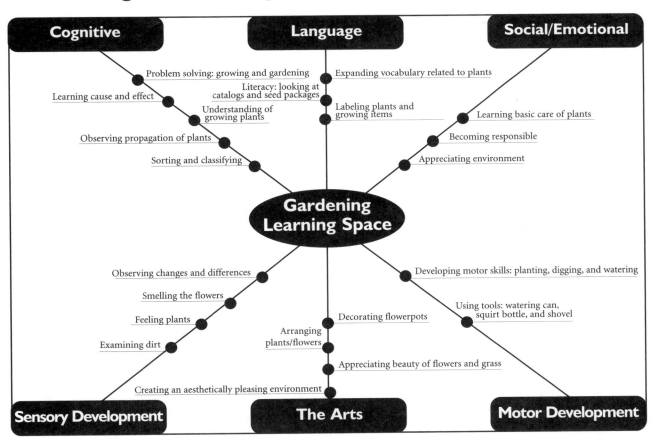

**Cognitive**
- Problem solving: growing and gardening
- Learning cause and effect
- Understanding of growing plants
- Observing propagation of plants
- Sorting and classifying

**Language**
- Expanding vocabulary related to plants
- Literacy: looking at catalogs and seed packages
- Labeling plants and growing items

**Social/Emotional**
- Learning basic care of plants
- Becoming responsible
- Appreciating environment

**Gardening Learning Space**

**Sensory Development**
- Observing changes and differences
- Smelling the flowers
- Feeling plants
- Examining dirt

**The Arts**
- Decorating flowerpots
- Arranging plants/flowers
- Appreciating beauty of flowers and grass
- Creating an aesthetically pleasing environment

**Motor Development**
- Developing motor skills: planting, digging, and watering
- Using tools: watering can, squirt bottle, and shovel

Choose a sunny area of the classroom or a space where there is natural light. If there is none available, use a grow light to encourage plant development. A low table is needed where toddlers can stand and garden. Since dirt and water will be used in the learning space, a tiled area or section covered with plastic works best. Include plastic tubs with different ingredients, such as dirt, sand, packing peanuts, and potting soil. Collect plastic flowerpots of various sizes for filling and emptying. Seed trays also provide other options for starting plants. Hang tools that can be used in planting on a wall or pegboard. Be sure to draw the outline of the tool on the board so the toddlers can begin to learn to return tools to the proper place. Include a broom and/or vacuum to use in the clean-up process.

## Vocabulary Enrichment

| | |
|---|---|
| dig | light |
| dirt | observe |
| fill | planting |
| flowerpots | potting soil |
| flowers | sprout |
| growing | water |

## Teacher- and Parent-Collected Props

collection of plastic flowerpots of
    various sizes
dirt/potting soil
flower seeds, bulbs, and grass
    seed
hand-held gardening tools
houseplants
metal trays and plastic containers (at least 3" deep)
plastic bags
watering cans and misting sprayers that are easy for
    toddlers to use

**ACTIVITIES**

## Growing Area with House Plants

plastic
various hardy houseplants
plastic saucers or trays

- Make a grouping of hardy houseplants in the *Gardening Learning Space*.
- Place plastic or trays under the plants so the toddlers can assist in caring for and watering them.
- Some plants that can survive drought and flood are corn plants, spider plants, and rubber plants.
- These plants grow better when they are grouped together, making it easier for toddlers to care for them.

Plants need water to grow.

## Watering

various items for watering plants

- Collect a variety of items that can be used to water the houseplants and include them in the *Gardening Learning Space*.

- The toddler can successfully use squirt bottles, clear plastic measuring cups, plastic soft drink bottles, plant mister, small watering cans, and small plastic cups.

# Propagation of Plants

small flowerpots
drainage materials
potting soil
various plants to propagate, such as spider plant, piggyback plant, wandering Jew, or fern
watering can
marker
tray

- Some plants are very easy to start from cuttings or runners. These can provide a simple way for toddlers to participate in starting new plants.
- After a demonstration, encourage toddlers to fill small flowerpots with drainage materials and top with potting soil.
- Ask them to make a hole in the dirt with their finger and insert a cutting or runner.
- Next, they can water the plant and carefully pack the dirt around the plant.
- Be sure to label the planting with the toddler's name and the date it was started.
- Place the small plantings, in their individual pots, on a tray in a lighted area.
- During the week, check the plants with the toddlers. "Are they dry?" "Do they need water?" "Can you tell if they are growing?" "Do they need more sunlight?"

# Growing Flowers

plastic window box or plastic flowerpot
potting soil
various flower seeds that germinate quickly, such as marigold and zinnia

- Toddlers can plant and care for flowers that germinate quickly and are easy to grow.
- Use a plastic window box or plastic flowerpot to contain a number of seeds.
- After the seeds are planted, water the soil completely.
- Toddlers fill the pots, plant the seeds, water the plants, and observe the growth.

# Green Green Grass

grass seed (rye is the fastest to grow)
long pan, at least 3" deep
potting soil

- Grass is a great plant to grow with toddlers. Most grass seed can be obtained easily at home and garden shops.
- Many grasses will germinate from seed very quickly; their growth can be easily observed.
- Create a grass "lawn" by planting the seeds in a large metal pan or plastic container.
- Fill the pan with potting soil and sow the grass seed across the top.
- Water the lawn and in six to seven days, you will have green grass.
- Continue to water and grow the grass.
- Toddlers observe and water the grass.

Toddlers discussing and examining bean sprouts that they grew

# Flowering Pots

old flowerpots (clay pots work best)

materials to decorate flowerpots, such as tissue paper, torn magazine pictures, scraps of trim, fabric, contact paper, pictures from seed catalogues, and flower stickers

white glue, thinned with water

paintbrushes

* Collect a variety of sizes of flowerpots for the *Gardening Learning Space*.
* Encourage the toddlers to decorate the flowerpots.
* Show them how to use a brush and thinned white glue to attach decorating materials to the pots.
* After the creations are dry, use the pots to contain seeds, seedlings, or small plants.

# Bean Sprouts

paper towels

several small, zipper-closure plastic bags

dried beans

* Older toddlers can grow bean sprouts in a small plastic bag.
* Dampen a paper towel and place it inside the bag.
* Ask toddlers to place dried beans on the paper towel.
* Close the bag and label it with the toddler's name and date.
* Hang these on a window, wall, or the back of a storage unit close to light.
* Check regularly to see if the beans have sprouted.
* Discuss the growth of the sprouts with the older toddlers.

# Quick Flower Garden

various flowering plants

large plastic pot

potting soil

* In the early spring, go to a local greenhouse.
* Select plants that are growing and already have buds.
* Create a garden in a large plastic pot that can be set in the *Gardening Learning Space*.
* This quick garden can provide immediate gratification for both adults and toddlers.
* Toddlers maintain the flowering garden, once it is established.
* The flower garden will be a beautiful place for the toddlers to enjoy.

**ADDING SPARK TO THE GARDENING LEARNING SPACE**

*Select bulbs that can be grown in water. Use an individual-size, plastic drink bottle to hold the bulb, so the roots can be seen as they begin to grow. Possible bulbs to use are hyacinth and narcissus. Cut off the lid and neck of the plastic bottle. Place the bulb in the top of the bottle and fill with water. Be sure that only ¼" of the bottom of the bulb is in the water, or it will rot. The toddlers can observe root development and sprouting of the bulb. Maintain a consistent water level in the bottle. The project should result in a beautiful fragrant bloom.*

## The Essential Literacy Connection

(• **Available as a board book**)

Anthony, Joseph A. (1997). *The Dandelion Seed.* Nevada City, CA: Dawn Publications. *A magical illustration of the lifecycle of a seed.*

Brown, Ruth. (2001). *Ten Seeds.* New York: Alfred A. Knopf. *Simple text and pictures portray the lifecycle of a sunflower—the last of the ten seeds.*

Cooney, Barbara. (1985). *Miss Rumphius.* New York: Penguin Putnam Books for Young Readers. *Watch as Miss Rumphius plants flowers and continues the cycle of making the world a more beautiful place.*

Ehlert, Lois. (1993). *Growing Vegetable Soup.* New York: Harcourt. *A father and older toddler share the joys of gardening from seed to soup.*

Krauss, Ruth. (1993). *The Carrot Seed.* New York: HarperCollins Children's Books. *Watch a carrot sprout from a tiny seed to a prize-winning vegetable in this simple picture book.*\*

Merberg, Julie, & Bober, Suzanne. (2002). *In the Garden with Van Gogh.* San Francisco, CA: Chronicle Books. *This book describes a garden and introduces toddlers to fine art.*\*

## Other Printed Materials

Additional printed materials for the *Gardening Learning Space* include seed and plant catalogues, garden books with pictures, and seed packages.

## Evaluation

1. Is the older toddler participating in the planting and growing?
2. Have you seen the older toddler observing the changes in plants?
3. Is the older toddler beginning to appreciate plants that are growing in her environment?

# Farm Learning Space

## Overview

Toddlers are very interested in farms and the animals that live in this special place. They enjoy experiencing some of the activities that occur on a farm. The *Farm Learning Space* will work well after a field trip to a farm or sharing a book about farms. The learning space should focus on concrete experiences that older toddlers will understand and relate to personally. This *Farm Learning Space* can work effectively in both the classroom and in the playground area. It is designed to be very simple and portable.

## Learning Objectives

Older toddlers will:

1. Learn about farms and some of the activities that occur on a farm.
2. Recognize animals that might live on farms and the sounds they make.
3. Participate in dramatic play that relates to farms.
4. Develop language that relates to farm life.

## Time Frame

Set up the *Farm Learning Space* in the classroom for about two weeks. As with all learning spaces, observe the interest of the toddlers and determine if the learning space should be dismantled or remain for a longer time. Because outdoor play is often different, the *Farm Learning Space* could be moved outside when it has closed in the classroom.

## Letter to Parents

• • • • • • • • • • • • • • • • • • • • • • • •

*Dear Parents,*

*During the next two weeks, we will have a Farm Learning Space set up in our classroom. Older toddlers are very interested in farms and the animals that live there. We will be visiting a small farm this week, so they will have an understanding of the work that occurs there and see some of the animals.*

*Toddlers enjoy making some of the sounds related to farm animals. Sharing a book that includes some common farm animals will help your toddler connect the sounds with the animal. As toddlers learn language, they will use these sounds to represent the animal—later, they will add the name. While reading a farm book, ask your toddler to touch the picture of a specific animal. If he or she seems hesitant, touch the picture and make the sound of the animal. Ask them, "What sound does the _____ make?" Keep this interactive exchange very relaxed. It should be fun!*

*You know how toddlers like to do things over and over. Sometimes it seems boring to us, but this repetition is very important. Each time they hear about farm animals and participate in the interactions, they will learn more. As in all interactions with toddlers, it is important to follow their lead, continue as long as they are interested, and stop when they become disinterested.*

# Layout of the Farm Learning Space

# Web of Integrated Learning

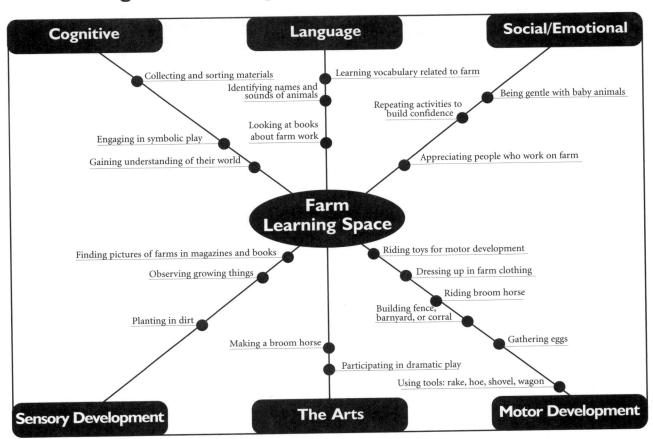

**Cognitive**
- Collecting and sorting materials
- Engaging in symbolic play
- Gaining understanding of their world

**Language**
- Learning vocabulary related to farm
- Identifying names and sounds of animals
- Looking at books about farm work

**Social/Emotional**
- Being gentle with baby animals
- Repeating activities to build confidence
- Appreciating people who work on farm

**Farm Learning Space**

**Sensory Development**
- Finding pictures of farms in magazines and books
- Observing growing things
- Planting in dirt

**The Arts**
- Making a broom horse
- Participating in dramatic play

**Motor Development**
- Riding toys for motor development
- Dressing up in farm clothing
- Riding broom horse
- Building fence, barnyard, or corral
- Gathering eggs
- Using tools: rake, hoe, shovel, wagon

Use a bale of hay to identify the *Farm Learning Space*. Display pictures of farm animals on the wall of the learning space. Create a red barn out of a cardboard box. Cut one side of the box to make a double door, hinge the doors on the right and left to make an entrance, and paint it red. Add a collection of toy farm animals and equipment. Make sure to include a group of child-size farm tools, such as a rake, hoe, shovel, wagon, and hand spade in the learning space. When the learning space is moved outside, add riding toys, such as tractors and trucks.

## Vocabulary Enrichment

| | | |
|---|---|---|
| animals | eggs | pig |
| barn | farm | plants |
| cat | farmer | sheep |
| chicken | fence | tools |
| cow | horse | tractor |
| dog | milking | truck |
| duck | | |

## Teacher- and Parent-Collected Props

books and magazines with farm pictures
broom handles
farm hats (straw, bonnet, and
 cowboy)
old socks
toy farm animals
toy farm tools, such as hoe, rake,
 wagon, shovel, and hand
 trowel
yarn

**ACTIVITIES**

# Introduction to the Farm Learning Space

various books with farm animals

- Sing the toddler favorite, "Old MacDonald Had a Farm," during group time.
- Include animals that are most familiar to older toddlers such as a cow, dog, horse, and pig.
- Share a book that includes pictures of a farm and the animals that live there.
- While reading the book, encourage older toddlers to make the animal sounds.
- Go to the *Farm Learning Space* and model some of the farm play that could occur.
- When play has begun, move out of the learning space so the older toddlers can continue their own activities.

A farm hat and miniature farm animals stimulate play in the Farm Learning Space.

# Farmer Dress-Up

dress-up items, such as straw hats, bonnets, cowboy
  hats, aprons, small-size overalls, boots, and work
  gloves
unbreakable mirror

- In the *Farm Learning Space,* include dress-up items
  that will inspire dramatic play.
- Provide a mirror for the older toddlers to admire
  their farm attire.
- Toddlers try on clothing and pretend to live and
  work on a farm.

# Building a Fence

several 12" to 24" lengths of 1" x 2" wood strips
several 12" high cardboard pieces
stapler
tape
materials to decorate the cardboard
large paintbrushes

- Make fence sections out of the cardboard by
  using 1" x 2" strips of wood for the base of each
  section.
- Staple a piece of cardboard to the wooden base.
- Cover the staples with tape.
- Toddlers move and arrange these sections to
  create a barnyard, a corral, or a pasture.
- They can paint or decorate the fence, if they
  wish.
- Encourage the toddlers to play with toy farm
  animals inside these built areas.

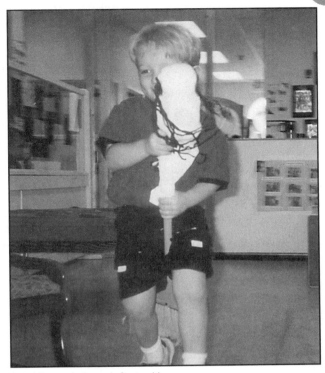
A toddler-made horse is fun to ride.

# A Stick Horse

3 or 4 broom handles or dowel rods, 3' long
3 or 4 white socks
material to stuff the sock, such as paper, fabric, or
  socks
glue
dark yarn
3 or 4 belts or cords

- Use an old broom handle or dowel rod to
  provide the foundation of a horse. Cut it to an
  appropriate length for toddlers to effectively ride
  (approximately 3' long).
- Stuff the sock with paper or old socks to create a
  head shape. Glue dark yarn on it to make a mane.
- Use an old belt or cord for the reins.
- Because toddlers are possessive by nature, it is
  important to create three or four horses to ride
  in the learning space.
- Toddlers enjoy participating in making these stick
  horses and riding them into the "corral" for the
  night.

# Farming Dirt Tray

deep metal pan
potting soil
tools for digging and raking
seed packets

- Create a planting and digging area in the *Farm Learning Space* by providing an aluminum roasting pan or deep metal pan filled with 2" of potting soil.
- Include tools that can be used to dig, make holes, and rake.
- Provide a collection of seed packets to plant in the ground.
- Use some of the toy farm equipment in the tray as well.
- This miniature farm encourages toddlers to be creative, while using their fine motor skills to manipulate tools.

# Milking a Cow

plastic gallon ice cream bucket
scissors
pin or needle (adult only)
rubber dishwashing glove
waterproof tape
water
plastic bucket
child-size chair or stool

- Cut a small hole in the bottom of the bucket (adult only).
- Use a pin or needle to punch a small hole in the tip of each glove finger (adult only).
- Use waterproof tape to attach the glove to the bottom of the bucket with tape. Be sure to cover the hole completely.
- Suspend the bucket so older toddlers can reach the glove "udder."
- Fill the bucket with water and place another bucket underneath to catch the "milk."
- Put a child-size chair or stool beside the udder, so the toddler can "milk" the cow.

## ADDING SPARK TO THE FARM LEARNING SPACE

*Bring a baby animal into the Farm Learning Space for a short visit. Possibilities might include a kitten, puppy, bunny, white mouse, chick, or duck. This is a wonderful time to talk with older toddlers about being gentle and careful with babies.*

## The Essential Literacy Connection
### (* Available as a board book)

Brown, Margaret Wise. (1995). *Big Red Barn*. New York: HarperCollins Children's Books. *A classic story of a day on the farm with familiar animals.**

Fleming, Denise. (2001). *Barnyard Banter*. New York: Henry Holt & Company. *Older toddlers can tour the farm and "hear" the responses of each animal.**

Gibbons, Gail. (1990). *Farming*. New York: Holiday House, Inc. *Through text and illustrations, the older toddler is introduced to various jobs performed on farms throughout the year.*

Rylant, Cynthia, (1999). *This Year's Garden*. New York: Bt Bound. *Details of planting, harvesting, and preserving the harvest from a garden are woven into this warm family story.*

Wood, Jakki. (1996). *Moo Moo, Brown Cow*. New York: Harcourt Brace. *A kitten asks adult farm animals if they have any babies.**

## Evaluation

1. Is the older toddler using the farm tools in the learning space?
2. During play, do you hear the older toddler making animals sounds?
3. Is the older toddler participating in dramatic play?
4. Is the older toddler developing her motor skills as she uses the props?

# Cooking Learning Space

## Overview

The *Cooking Learning Space* provides a focus for play that captures the interest and involvement of older toddlers. This learning space includes many opportunities to expand their understanding of cooking, baking, and eating while involved in meaningful play. Introduce the *Cooking Learning Space* by sharing a collection of cooking utensils found in a home or bakery. After exploring these interesting items, place the utensils in the *Cooking Learning Space* for the older toddlers to use. This learning space encourages toddlers to actively participate, take on roles, and create a sequence to their play. This participation has built-in rewards, as toddlers are able to eat and share the food they prepare.

## Learning Objectives

Older toddlers will:

1. Participate in preparing food that can be eaten.
2. Work together to prepare a product.
3. Develop language as they use utensils, ingredients, and cookbooks.
4. Develop fine motor coordination as they stir, pour, shape, and eat.

## Time Frame

The *Cooking Learning Space* provides interesting activities for approximately two to three weeks. Observe toddlers in the learning space to determine if dramatic play is occurring and if they are continuing to actively participate. If they are still involved, you may want to retain the *Cooking Learning Space* for a longer period and add some new cooking activities.

## Letter to Parents

• • • • • • • • • • • • • • • • • • • • •

*Dear Parents,*

*We are setting up a* Cooking Learning Space *in our classroom next week. We will involve the toddlers in preparing snacks and other foods they enjoy eating. They will learn about recipes, mixing, ingredients, and some utensils used in the kitchen.*

*We are going to create a Toddlers' Favorite Cookbook of our children's favorite recipes. Please help us by sharing one or two recipes of your toddler's favorite foods on a note card. These foods should be simple and easy to prepare. Include your name and your toddler's name, so we can give you credit for the wonderful recipe in our cookbook. We will also include in our cookbook some foods that the toddlers have enjoyed in our* Cooking Learning Space.

# Layout of the Cooking Learning Space

# Web of Integrated Learning

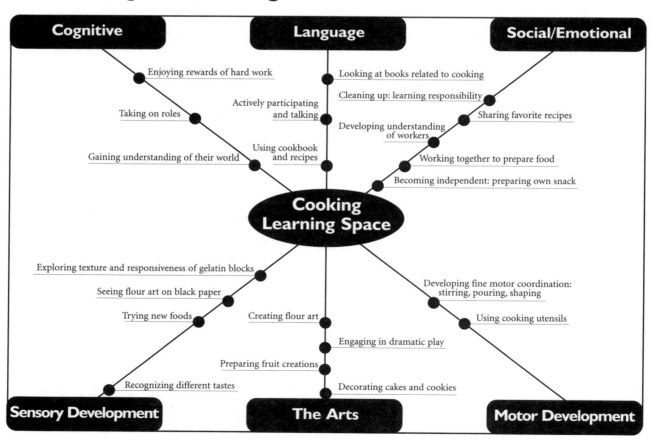

**Cognitive**

- Enjoying rewards of hard work
- Taking on roles
- Gaining understanding of their world

**Language**

- Actively participating and talking
- Using cookbook and recipes

**Social/Emotional**

- Looking at books related to cooking
- Cleaning up: learning responsibility
- Sharing favorite recipes
- Developing understanding of workers
- Working together to prepare food
- Becoming independent: preparing own snack

## Cooking Learning Space

- Exploring texture and responsiveness of gelatin blocks
- Seeing flour art on black paper
- Trying new foods
- Creating flour art
- Developing fine motor coordination: stirring, pouring, shaping
- Using cooking utensils
- Engaging in dramatic play
- Preparing fruit creations
- Recognizing different tastes
- Decorating cakes and cookies

**Sensory Development**

**The Arts**

**Motor Development**

This learning space should resemble a kitchen in a home. Include a stove, sink, refrigerator, low table, and work area. Use shelves to store and display the ingredients that will be needed. Make available a variety of cooking utensils and baking trays. Hang a sign or symbols on the wall with pictures of products that can be made in the *Cooking Learning Space*. Props, such as aprons and chef hats, add to the dramatic play that occurs in the learning space. Put a broom or vacuum cleaner in the area, so the toddlers can clean up. (If space is limited, the *Cooking Learning Space* could be set-up in the *Housekeeping Learning Space*.)

## Vocabulary Enrichment

| | |
|---|---|
| apron | measuring cups |
| bake | mixing |
| bakery | muffins |
| chef hat | oven |
| cook | recipe |
| cooling | sample |
| icing/frosting | sifting |
| ingredients | |

## Teacher- and Parent-Collected Props

| | |
|---|---|
| baking pan | latex gloves |
| cookie sheets | measuring cups and spoons |
| cooking pots | medium-size plastic or |
| crock-pot | aluminum bowl |
| egg beater | muffin pan |
| hand mixer | rolling pin |
| large aluminum or wood spoons | small paper and plastic bags |

## Special Note for the Cooking Learning Space

Be sure to check the medical or parent forms that have identified the toddlers' food allergies. Adjust ingredients included in the *Cooking Learning Space* accordingly. Also, proper hand washing is very important before and after handling food.

## ACTIVITIES

# Juicy Finger Blocks

3 envelopes unflavored gelatin
¾ cup boiling water (adult only)
12-ounce can of frozen apple, orange, grape, or other juice concentrate
medium cooking pot
mixing bowl and spoon
9" x 13" cake pan
oil or grease for pan
refrigerator
cookie cutters

- Dissolve the gelatin in boiling water; add juice and stir until mixed (adult only).
- Pour into a lightly greased 9" x 13" cake pan.
- Chill in the refrigerator approximately two hours, until firm.
- Toddlers use cookie cutters to make shapes or cut squares.
- These shaky blocks are fascinating for toddlers. They can watch the jiggling, feel the smoothness, and then eat the blocks.

# Fruit Creations

various fruits
knife
colorful paper plates
marker

- Prepare fruits that are in season or easily available. Let older toddlers slice the fruit for the creation. **Note:** Carefully supervise, and help as needed.
- Encourage the toddlers to select the fruit or combination they want and arrange it on a colorful paper plate.
- Label each creation with the toddler's name.
- Eat these fruit creations for morning snack.
- Some toddlers in the *Cooking Learning Space* can make snacks for those who did not visit the learning space.

# Trail Mix: Create Your Own Snack

3 or 4 trail mix ingredients, such
    as dry cereal, small
    marshmallows, pretzels, small
    crackers, and raisins
3 or 4 small bowls
3 or 4 spoons
several small plastic bags

- Select three or four trail mix
  ingredients. Pour one ingredient
  into each bowl, and put a
  spoon in each bowl.
- Provide small plastic bags to
  contain the snack.
- Encourage the toddlers to
  choose the ingredients they want and the
  portions of each. (Provide only three or four
  items, so the toddlers will not be overwhelmed
  by too many choices).
- Enjoy these snacks in the *Cooking Learning Space*
  or later in the day.

# Fruit Parfait

small paper cups
spoons
¼ cup Grape Nuts or other crunchy cereal
16-ounce carton vanilla yogurt
¼ cup fruit or several fruits, such as banana,
    strawberry, and blueberry

- Help the toddlers sprinkle cereal in the bottom of
  a paper cup.
- Add a spoonful of yogurt to each cup.
- Let the toddlers choose the fruit they want and
  place it on top of the parfait.
- Toddlers can combine this nutritious snack and
  then eat it.

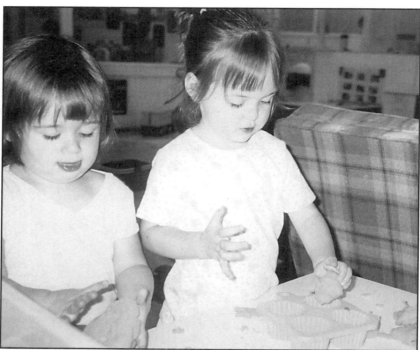

After making "real" cupcakes, toddlers make cupcakes with clay in the Cooking Learning Space.

# Decorating Cupcakes or Cookies

oven and ingredients for making cupcakes or cookies
    OR prepared cupcakes or cookies
variety of toppings, such as frosting, marshmallows,
    sprinkles, cherries, and nuts

- If an oven is available, older toddlers can help
  make cookies or cupcakes.
- If this is not possible, provide cookies or cupcakes
  that are already baked.
- Encourage the toddlers to decorate the cookies
  or cupcakes in their own way.
- Provide various decorating choices, such as
  frosting in plastic bags that can be squeezed out,
  frosting in cans to spread with plastic knives or
  tongue depressors, and so on.
- Toddlers will be creative in their decorating, as
  they use their hands in squeezing and spreading
  frosting and/or toppings.

# Toddlers' Favorite Cookbook

various recipes
paper, construction paper, and
   stapler

- Make copies of recipes that toddlers make in the *Cooking Learning Space* and simple snacks enjoyed in the classroom.
- Ask parents to provide recipes for their toddlers' favorite snack (see Letter to Parents, page 289) and make copies of these as well.
- Compile all the recipes and put them between two pieces of construction paper (the front and back covers).
- Staple the pages together and label the book, "Toddlers' Favorite Cookbook."
- Make copies of the cookbook to give to families of the toddlers.

# Flour Art

vinyl or plastic to cover the floor
large sheet of black paper
glue
large paintbrushes
flour
sifters or large saltshakers

- Cover the floor of the *Cooking Learning Space* with a sheet of vinyl or plastic.
- Place a big sheet of black paper on the covered floor.
- Use a large brush to paint the black paper with a thin coat of commercial or homemade glue.
- Older toddlers use sifters or large saltshakers to sprinkle flour on the paper.
- When the glue is dry, hang the flour art on the wall.

In the Cooking Learning Space, toddlers are "reading" the recipe and turning the beater.

## ADDING SPARK TO THE COOKING LEARNING SPACE

*Ask a parent who enjoys cooking or cake decorating to come to the Cooking Learning Space and make something with the older toddlers. Be sure to talk with parents about making a simple recipe so the toddlers can assist with preparation. This experience should focus on the older toddlers helping, not on creating a "perfect" product.*

## The Essential Literacy Connection

Dooley, Norah. (1997). *Everybody Bakes Bread.* Illustrated by Peter J. Thornton. Minneapolis, MN: Lerner Publishing Group. *During Carrie's errand through her multicultural neighborhood to find a "three-handled rolling pin," she gets to taste a variety of different breads.*

Lass, Bonnie, & Sturges, Philemon. (2000). *Who Took the Cookies from the Cookie Jar?* Boston: Little, Brown & Company. *The repetition, rhythm, and rhyme of this chant will entice older toddlers to play along.*

Morris, Ann. (1993). *Bread, Bread, Bread.* Illustrated by Ken Heyman. New York: Morrow, William & Company. *Colorful photographs illustrate the kinds of bread eaten by people around the world.*

Numeroff, Laura Joffe. (1996). *If You Give a Mouse a Cookie.* Illustrated by Felicia Bond. New York: HarperCollins Children's Books. *Bright illustrations and repetitive language convey a sequence of events that result from giving an energetic mouse a cookie.*

Wells, Rosemary, (2000). *Bunny Cakes.* New York: Penguin Putnam Books for Young Readers. *Watch the hilarious adventures of Max and Ruby, as they make a cake for their grandmother's birthday.*

## Other Printed Materials

Additional materials for the *Cooking Learning Space* include cookbooks and the Toddlers' Favorite Cookbook.

## Evaluation

1. Is the older toddler participating in the preparation of food and snacks?
2. Is dramatic play occurring, as the older toddler works in the *Cooking Learning Space?*
3. Is the older toddler using cookbooks and charts during the cooking?
4. Is the older toddler using new language as she works with others?

# Beach Learning Space

## Overview

Going to the beach can be a very special activity for older toddlers. However, many toddlers have never been to the beach, so the *Beach Learning Space* will be a new experience for them. In the *Beach Learning Space*, older toddlers gain more knowledge of the environment. They can explore water, sand, and seashells in their play, using tools such as buckets, shovels, rakes, sand wheels, and sifters.

This learning space will encourage language development, cognitive skills, and motor skills. Older toddlers will learn new words, such as "ocean," "sandcastle," and "shovel." They will begin experimenting with conservation of liquids and solids. Finally, older toddlers will practice motor skills, such as pouring, stirring, and scooping, as they build sandcastles.

## Learning Objectives

Older toddlers will:

1. Expand knowledge of the environment.
2. Participate in parallel play.
3. Develop simple problem-solving skills using tools.
4. Improve motor skills as they pour, stir, and move sand.

## Time Frame

This learning space should be interesting to toddlers for several weeks. If the children have visited a beach frequently, their play in the learning space may last longer.

## Letter to Parents

• • • • • • • • • • • • • • • • • • • • • • • •

*Dear Parents,*

*We have just opened our Beach Learning Space. Toddlers love to play in sand and water, and our Beach Learning Space will encourage many areas of their development. They can improve their motor skills by pouring, stirring, and splashing in the water; develop social skills by working together to build a sandcastle; and learn simple problem-solving skills by observing how much sand it takes to fill a cup or bucket. Finally, toddlers can expand their understanding of the environment in our Beach Learning Space.*

*We are collecting pictures of the beach or magazines with beach scenes for the children to use in projects. Please come by and visit your toddler enjoying the fun in the Beach Learning Space.*

## Layout of the Beach Learning Space

## Web of Integrated Learning

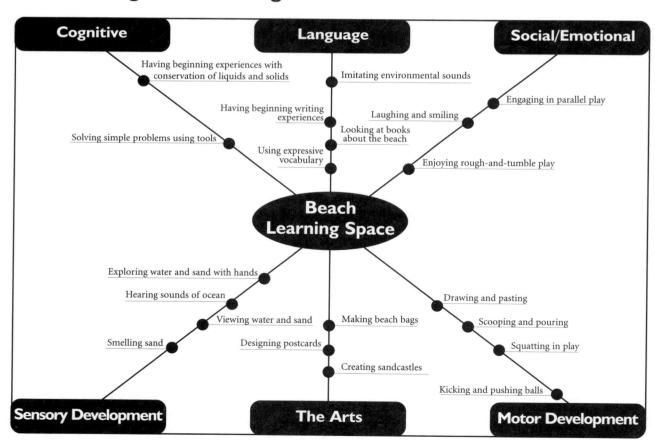

**Cognitive**
- Having beginning experiences with conservation of liquids and solids
- Solving simple problems using tools

**Language**
- Imitating environmental sounds
- Having beginning writing experiences
- Laughing and smiling
- Looking at books about the beach
- Using expressive vocabulary

**Social/Emotional**
- Engaging in parallel play
- Enjoying rough-and-tumble play

**Beach Learning Space**

**Sensory Development**
- Exploring water and sand with hands
- Hearing sounds of ocean
- Viewing water and sand
- Smelling sand

**The Arts**
- Making beach bags
- Designing postcards
- Creating sandcastles

**Motor Development**
- Drawing and pasting
- Scooping and pouring
- Squatting in play
- Kicking and pushing balls

Beach chairs and a small baby pool full of sand help older toddlers identify the *Beach Learning Space*. Place the baby pool on top of a large sheet or shower curtain to help with cleanup. Include a collection of plastic beach toys such as buckets, shovels, and scoops for the sand. Toddlers also enjoy dressing up in beach attire such as swimsuits, hats, and sunglasses.

## Vocabulary Enrichment

beach
bucket
ocean
postcard
pour
sand

sandcastle
scoop
shovel
water
waves

## Teacher- and Parent-Collected Props

beach balls
beach chairs
beach hats
beach towels
buckets
cassette tape or CD of beach music
clean sunscreen bottles
flip-flops and/or sandals
picnic basket
plastic and/or paper tableware
pretend food
radio, tape player, or CD player
rakes
sand toys
sandcastle molds
seashells
shovels
sifters
small baby pool (fill with sand or water)
Styrofoam swim noodles (cut into fourths or halves)
sunglasses
swim suits
toy boats

## ACTIVITIES

# Bucket Play

variety of buckets
water
small plastic toys
funnels
plastic shovels
handled strainers

- Fill buckets ¼ full of water. Add plastic toys to each bucket.
- Show the toddlers how to "fish" for the toys with shovels or their hands.
- Some toddlers may put toys from one bucket into another; some may sort the toys by a characteristic, such as color, size, or shape.
  **Note:** Carefully supervise the toddlers while they play with buckets of water.

# Sandcastles

sand
water
baby pool
beach tools, such as shovels, spoons, and rakes
sandcastle molds
plastic cups or containers
large shells and small sticks
camera and film

- Add water to the sand in the baby pool.
- Show the older toddlers how to use their hands and tools to make sandcastles.
- Then, stand back and observe their work.
- Take pictures of the sandcastles to document the toddlers' work.

A beach ball is light and easy to carry.

# Beach Balls

several beach balls of different colors and designs
several beach towels

- Beach balls provide a fun and different way to promote gross motor development. They are especially good for toddlers to use because of their softness and size.
- Demonstrate how to roll, kick, push, bounce, and throw the beach balls.
- Place a beach ball on a beach towel.
- Show older toddlers how to hold the edges and shake the towel to make the ball bounce and dance in the air.
- This encourages toddlers to move as they participate in making the balls move.

# Postcards from the Beach

travel magazines or pamphlets
scissors
3 ½" x 5" note cards
glue
washable markers and pencils
beach postcards, optional

- Cut out pictures of beaches from travel magazines or pamphlets.
- Place beach pictures, note cards, glue, washable markers, and pencils on a table.
- Talk to the older toddlers about writing a "postcard" to their families, telling them about their "trip to the beach."
- Show the toddlers the materials they can use to make and decorate their postcards.
- Demonstrate how to write a letter, reading it aloud as you go.
- Give the toddlers time to create their own postcards.
- All marks and scribbles are viewed as "writing" for toddlers, so appreciate their beginning efforts.

# Beach Bags

several paper grocery bags
washable markers
glue
colored paper
child-safe scissors
string
sand

- Collect paper bags from the grocery store.
- Encourage the older toddlers to decorate their own beach bag.
- They can use the bags to carry treasures found in the *Beach Learning Space*.

**ADDING SPARK TO THE BEACH LEARNING SPACE**

*Play recordings of ocean sounds. Help the toddlers identify what they are hearing (waves, wind, seagulls, and other noises heard at the beach).*

A toddler makes waves with an ocean in a bottle.

# Ocean in a Bottle

clear, plastic drink bottles with lids
water
blue food coloring
oil
hot glue gun (adult only)
tape

- Clean the drink bottles and remove the labels.
- Fill bottles ½ full with water. Add a few drops of blue food coloring and mix. Add a few drops of oil to the bottle.
- Hot glue the lid onto the bottle (adult only) and tape it securely closed.
- Encourage the older toddlers to make ocean waves by turning, shaking, or moving the bottles.

## The Essential Literacy Connection

Frasier, Debra. (2002). *Out of the Ocean.* New York: Harcourt. *See what kinds of treasures can be found while walking along the seashore.*

Hayles, Marsha. (1998). *Beach Play.* Illustrated by Hideko Takahashi. New York: Henry Holt & Company, Inc. *Older toddlers will enjoy reading about a lazy, hot day at the beach with bright illustrations and bouncy text.*

Rockwell, Anne, & Rockwell, Harlow. (1991). *At the Beach.* New York: Simon & Schuster Children's. *Brief text and simple pictures tell of a trip to the beach through the eyes of an older toddler.*

Ward, Helen. (2002). *Old Shell, New Shell: A Coral Reef Tale.* Grand Ledge: MI: Millbrook Press. *Full of illustrations of marine life, this story tells of a hermit crab's search for a bigger shell.*

## Evaluation

1. Is the older toddler participating in parallel play?
2. Is the older toddler exploring the water and sand?
3. Is the older toddler using tools to pour and scoop the sand or water?
4. Is the older toddler using language to describe her experiences in the *Beach Learning Space?*

# Shadow Learning Space

## Overview

Young children are curious about the world around them. Sometime during the second year of life, an older toddler will recognize a shadow for the first time. These shadows can provide new and valuable experiences for older toddlers. Shadows help them realize that every object has meaning. Young children instinctively want to explore and find the explanation for shadows. This process of exploration will develop problem solving, language, social, emotional, and motor skills.

The *Shadow Learning Space* will be new and exciting for the older toddlers. There will be both indoor and outdoor activities for toddlers to observe how a variety of objects make shadows. Older toddlers will also make their own shadows with their bodies.

## Learning Objectives

Older toddlers will:

1. Demonstrate emotions.
2. Recognize their own shadows and movement.
3. Improve eye-hand coordination.
4. Have experiences with size and shape concepts.

## Time Frame

The *Shadow Learning Space* is most effective as a two- or three-week learning space. It is best to use this learning space in the fall, spring, or summer of the year, because observing shadows outside is such an important activity. You can always revisit this learning space at another time of the year.

## Letter to Parents

• • • • • • • • • • • • • • • • • • • • • • • • • • •

*Dear Parents,*

*We are very excited to announce that we have opened our Shadow Learning Space. Shadows are amusing and educational for older toddlers. By experiencing shadows, toddlers can develop an understanding of concepts such as large, small, short, tall, and upside down. We will be taking the toddlers outside to see everyday shadows. We will also set up a light and screen for the toddlers to make their own shadows inside. They will use objects such as toys and furniture or their own bodies to make shadows.*

*Talk about the shadows you see outside with your toddler. Exploring shadows is a simple scientific experience for both you and your toddler to enjoy.*

## Layout of the Shadow Learning Space

## Web of Integrated Learning

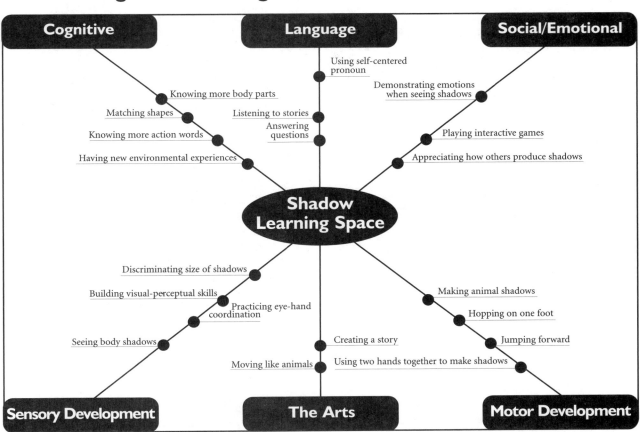

Set up the *Shadow Learning Space* in an area of the room that can be made dark. Turn off overhead lighting, if possible. Cover windows with dark sheets. A blank wall or a white sheet taped to a wall makes a perfect backdrop for indoor shadow making.

## Vocabulary Enrichment

| | |
|---|---|
| backward | me |
| behind | outside |
| forward | shadow |
| in front | short |
| inside | small |
| large | tall |
| light | upside down |

## Teacher- and Parent-Collected Props

1 or 2 large flashlights and several small flashlights
batteries
colored cellophane
hats
home objects, such as umbrella, broom, and plastic cooking and eating utensils
lid of shape sorter
netting
other options for making shadows, such as overhead projector, portable screen, and a light table (see page 310 for directions)
paper
plastic animals
scissors
sheer scarves
small toys
stuffed animals
washable markers
white sheet taped to the wall or light-colored blank wall to use as a screen
wooden or plastic shapes

## ACTIVITIES

# Shadows Outside

- Go for a walk outside on a sunny day to observe and identify the common objects that make shadows.
- Examples of shadows you might see include:
  - birds
  - buildings
  - cars
  - cats
  - dogs
  - flowers
  - plants
  - stairs
  - strollers
  - trees

Toddlers creating shadows on the wall

# Me and My Shadow

large flashlight
screen, sheet, or blank lightly colored wall

- Turn off or dim the lights in the *Shadow Learning Space*.
- Place a large flashlight on a table or chair facing the wall or screen.
- Ask a toddler to stand in front of the light source.
- Ask the other toddlers questions such as, "Who is that shadow?" or "What is that shadow's name?"
- Encourage the toddlers to do certain tasks while they are making shadows, such as:
  - stand, sit, jump, or dance
  - walk forward and backward
  - bend over
  - put their arms in the air
  - make a straight line, circle, and triangle with their body
  - hop on one foot
- After this experimentation, toddlers can create their own shadow play.

Using a flashlight to create finger shadows

## Making Animal Shadows

large flashlight or light source
screen, sheet, or blank lightly colored wall
books about making shadows (see page 304)

- Older toddlers can begin to make very simple animal shadows with their hands.
- There are books available that show how to make shadows with your fingers.
- Choose finger shadows that do not require separate finger movements.
- Read a book or sing a song about animal shadows. Then, demonstrate how to make that finger shadow.
- If needed, help the toddlers form their fingers. With practice, they will be able to make simple shadows themselves. Shadows to make include:
  - alligator (place two palms together, and open and close hands)
  - bird (put two hands together and spread fingers apart)
  - dog (stand thumb, pointer, and pinky fingers up and bend down middle and tall fingers)
  - fish (put two palms together and move arms and wrists to simulate a fish swimming)
  - rabbit (keep pointer and middle fingers up, and thumb, ring, and pinky fingers down—like a victory sign)

## What Size Is It?

large flashlight or light source
screen, sheet, or blank lightly colored wall

- Toddlers experience how shadows change when objects move closer and farther away from the light source.
- Use vocabulary such as "big," "little," "tall," or "short," while the older toddlers change the size of their shadows.
- As toddlers become more skilled with shadow making, ask them to make their shadows "smaller" or "larger" and see if they can move themselves into the right position in front of the light source.

**ADDING SPARK TO THE SHADOW LEARNING SPACE**

*Watch the shadows the older toddlers are creating. Make up a story to go along with the shadows. You may want to write down the stories to read with the toddlers at a later time.*

## The Essential Literacy Connection

Hoban, Tana. (1991). *Shadows and Reflections.* New York: Greenwillow Books. *Older toddlers will realize that there are shadows all around them after viewing these photographs.*

Raines, Shirley, & Isbell, Rebecca. (1999). *Tell it Again!: Easy-to-Tell Stories with Activities for Young Children.* Beltsville, MD: Gryphon House. *Storytelling tips are shared with the retelling of 18 traditional children's stories.*

Robson, D. & Bailey, V. (1990). *Rainy Days Shadow Theater: Games and Projects.* New York: Aladdin. *This book allows older toddlers and teachers to see how both hand and prop shadow puppets can be made against a screen or wall.*

Sayre, April Pulley. (2002). *Shadows.* New York: St. Martin's Press. *Chalk drawings of older toddlers in different settings that show shadows.*

Swinburne, Stephen R. (2002). *Guess Whose Shadow?* Honedale, PA: Boyds Mills Press. *This book of photographs will help older toddlers learn how shadows are created, while allowing them to guess what creates the shadows on each page.*

## Evaluation

1. Does the older toddler show an emotional response to the shadow, such as worry, excitement, wonder, surprise, and curiosity?
2. Does the older toddler recognize herself in her own shadow?
3. Can the older toddler use her body to make shadows?
4. Is the older toddler able to recognize the difference in large and small shadows?

# CHAPTER SIX

# Building and Creating Items for the Infant and Toddler Areas

The ideas included in this section can be made by teachers and included in their infant or toddler areas. Parent volunteers can also collect materials and assist in the building process. Many parents will enjoy participating in the construction and watching their child using the items in the classroom.

305

# Canopy Area

Infants and toddlers are small people in a big world. They need places where they feel secure and cozy. A canopy provides a special feeling for the very young child. Canopies can be created at a low cost with everyday materials. Use an old sheet or piece of beautiful fabric to lower the ceiling in the area. In the authors' area of the country, the canopy must be at least 18" from the ceiling and lighting. A canopy hung low to the floor will also work effectively for infants and toddlers. This design makes the large space feel smaller and cozier to infants and toddlers. **Note:** The distance from the ceiling that you are required to hang items may be influenced by fire or environmental regulations in your area.

## Materials

colorful sheet or fabric
heavy-duty rubber band
strong fishing line or macramé rope

- Gather the center of the sheet or fabric and hold it with a heavy rubber band.
- Hang the gathered fabric from the ceiling with fishing line or macramé rope.
- Drape the corners of the fabric and attach them to the ceiling, so the sheet resembles a canopy.

# Community Drum

The drum is a very popular musical instrument for toddlers. When toddlers hit the drum, it produces a sound: It is responsive to their actions.

## Materials

3-gallon galvanized steel bucket
spray paint
tape, such as duct, electrical, and packing
large piece of rubber roofing (often scraps can be obtained from a roofing company)
6 to 8 grommets or eyelets
polyester rope, nylon rope, or clothesline

- Use the galvanized bucket for the base. Remove the handle from the bucket.
- Spray paint the bucket in a well-ventilated area, away from children.
- Put tape around the top edge of the bucket to cover any rough edges.
- Cut the rubber roofing scrap 2" larger than the top of the bucket.
- Make 6 to 8 evenly spaced holes around the edge of the rubber for grommets or eyelets.

Community drum

- Thread the rope or clothesline through the grommets and make the rubber tight.
- Tie the rope together on the bottom of the bucket.
- This community drum can be played with the hands or a mallet.

- Sew the opening of the "crash pad" closed.
- Sew three sides of the larger pair of sheets together, leaving one end completely open, to make a washable cover for the crash pad.
- Stuff the crash pad inside the cover, which may be removed and washed as needed.

# Crash Pads

The crash pad acts as a safe indoor spot for toddlers to jump, roll, and crash into, as they work on new motor skills.

# Cylinder

Use large carpeted cylinders with the bottom and top cut out in the obstacle course in the *Motor Learning Space* (for children to crawl through). Turn a cylinder on its side and place pillows inside for a private place for young toddlers. Large cylinders also make great storage for balls or other hard-to-shelve items.

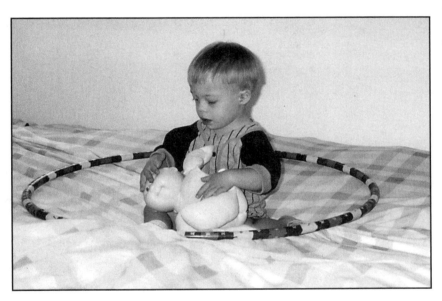

Crash pad

## Materials

heavy cardboard cylinders
material to cover the cylinders
glue

- Find heavy cardboard cylinders that have been used for shipping china or building supplies.

**Note:** The cylinder must be big enough and sturdy enough for a toddler to climb inside.
- Select a material to cover the cylinder—carpeting will cushion the cylinder, while vinyl protects and supports the surface for long-term use.
- Glue the material to the inside of the cylinder; fabric on the outside is optional.

## Materials

2 full- or queen-size flat sheets (size selected will be determined by the size of space available)
2 twin- or full-size flat sheets (one size smaller than the other two sheets)
scrap foam or old pillows
thread and needle or sewing machine

- Sew the edges of the smaller pair of sheets together, leaving a large opening on one side.
- Stuff the sack with large pieces of scrap foam or old pillows. Fill the sack as full as possible, as some settling will occur.

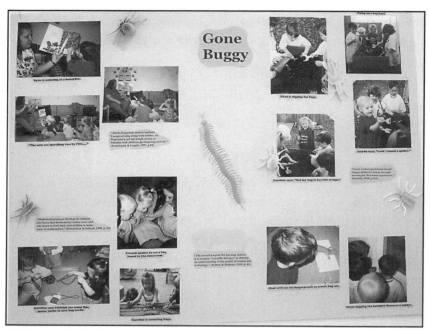

Toddlers investigating bugs

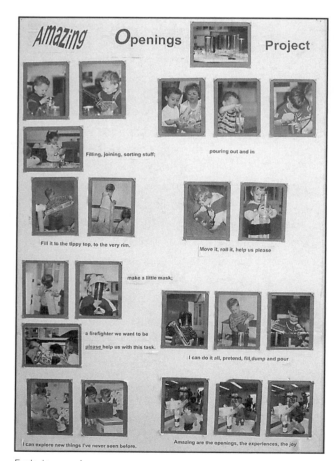

Exploring openings

# Documentation Panel

This is a visual representation showing what children are learning while working on a project. It includes photographs from the beginning of the activity until the completion. Educators in the Reggio Emilia Schools first demonstrated this type of panel, and it is now widely used in early childhood programs.

## Materials
poster board or art board
photographs of the infants and/or toddlers
camera and film or memory stick glue

- Assemble the photographs attractively on the board and glue them in place. Reading the panel will help adults understand what the infants and toddlers are learning.

# Foam Wedges

Older toddlers need a variety of new experiences to expand their motor skills. Foam wedges may be used in the *Motor Learning Space* as a ramp to roll down, climb up, or jump off.

Foam wedges

## Materials

large piece of dense foam (thick enough for toddlers to walk on)
sturdy fabric to cover the wedge, such as denim or corduroy

- Collect a large piece of dense foam that is thick enough for a toddler to walk on.
- Cut the foam into a wedge at least 2' long and 1' high (on the tall end).
- Cover the wedge with thick, sturdy material.

# Knob Hanger

## Materials

8 wooden knobs (may be purchased from a home supply store)

1 piece of lumber, 24" long
10 screws and screwdriver

- Use wooden knobs that are found on furniture.
- Attach the knobs to the lumber, spacing them 3" apart, starting 1½" from the edge.
- Screw the hanger to the wall in the *Housekeeping Learning Space*. Be sure to place the knob hanger at a height that is easy for the toddlers to use.
- The knobs work well for toddlers because clothes do not fall off after they are placed on the pegs.
- This hanger helps toddlers be more independent as they select and return clothing.

# Light Table

A low, light table can be constructed for toddlers to use in their activities. This low and inexpensive light table works well for toddlers.

Light table

## Materials

2 - 4' long 1" x 10" boards
2 - 2' long 1" x 10" boards
hammer and nails or screwdriver and screws
saw
1 - ⅜" thick piece of 2' x 4' plywood
4 - 10" long 2" x 2" wood pieces
silver spray paint
fluorescent shop light with on/off switch and cord
glue
1 - ¼" thick piece of 2' x 4' translucent Plexiglas
non-toxic paint and paintbrush

- Assemble the four 1" x 10" boards into a 2' x 4' frame.
- Cut a notch in one of the 10" sides of plywood, large enough for the shop light plug and switch to pass through.
- Nail or screw the plywood to the bottom of the box.
- Glue a 2" x 2" support into each corner of the box.

- Spray paint the interior of the box with silver paint, which increases the reflection of the light.
- Fasten the shop light to the inside bottom of the box. Pass the off/on switch to the exterior of the box.
- Attach the Plexiglas to the open top of the box.
- Place molding strips around the edges to hold the Plexiglas in place.
- Paint the entire unit in any color you choose.

# Milk Carton Blocks

These lightweight blocks are easy for toddlers to move and use in their constructions.

## Materials

10 to 15 cardboard milk cartons
duct or electrical tape
materials to decorate the milk cartons, such as
    contact paper, paint, washable markers, and
    crayons

- Wash the milk cartons to remove all milk deposits.
- When dry, fold the tops down flat.
- Tape the tops down.
- The toddlers can decorate the milk carton blocks as desired.

# Nest

This nest, suggested on page 33, is designed to help infants feel safe and secure in a small, cozy environment. Three- to eight-month-old infants can rest in this nest or enjoy looking around from this location. Mobile infants can move into the nest when they want to slow down, and move out of the nest when they are ready to reenter an activity. Teachers who have used these nests say they allow infants to follow their own timetable. The nest allows the infants to rest when tired and leave when rested. It begins to give the infants some control of their environment.

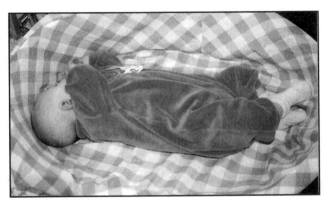

Young infant resting in nest

## Materials

heavy foam or small pet bed
soft washable fabric

- Use heavy foam that is formed into an oval shape, resembling a small pet bed. It is also possible to purchase a small pet bed that will work as the foundation for the nest.
- Provide an opening on one side that allows the mobile infant to move in and out of the nest.
- Make two or three nest covers from soft washable fabric. These can be removed and replaced, as needed.

# Plexiglas Picture Frame

It is very important to display pictures so infants and toddlers can see and enjoy them. Of course, they want to touch the pictures and manipulate the paper. An effective approach is to build Plexiglas picture frames to mount on the wall at the infants' and toddlers' level. The infants and toddlers can touch and pat these pictures in the frames without harming them.

## Materials

2 - 1" x 2" wood molding pieces, 12" to 24" long
4 to 6 screws and a screwdriver
clear Plexiglas

- Use two pieces of wood molding to make the top and bottom of a simple frame. Cut these pieces of molding to the width of one or two pictures.
- Cut a piece of Plexiglas to fit between the two pieces of molding.
- Screw the molding frame into the wall at the eye level of the infants or toddlers in the classroom.

Framed pictures of infants at their eye level

Framed pictures of infants at their eye level

- Be sure to leave a ½" space between the Plexiglas and the wall.
- Leave both sides of the frame open with no wood molding. With the sides of the frame open, pictures can be changed simply by sliding them in and out of either side. However, infants and toddlers will not be able to remove the pictures.

# Riser

The riser provides a safe and interesting place for infants to pull up, hold on, or cruise. Toddlers can place toys on the riser and view the objects from their eye level. They can crawl or sit on the riser when they complete an activity. Good dimensions for the moveable riser are 2' wide, 4' long, and 10" high. This size allows for the thrifty use of a 4' x 8' piece of plywood; a single sheet of plywood will make the tops for four risers.

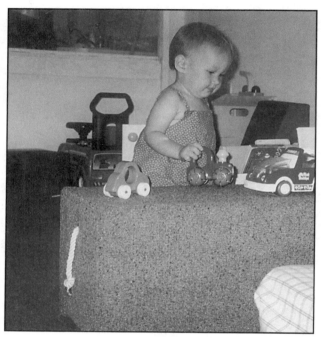

Carpeted riser

## Materials

1 - ⅜" thick, 4' x 8' plywood piece
2 - 4' long boards, 1" x 10"
2 - 2' long boards, 1" x 10"
hammer and nails or screwdriver and screws
durable carpet or vinyl
heavy-duty staples and stapler
4 - 12" pieces of strong rope

- Cut the 4' x 8' plywood into four pieces: 2' wide and 4' long.
- Make the two sides of each riser from the 4' long boards.

- Make the two ends of each riser from the 2' long boards.
- Cover the risers with durable carpet or vinyl so the surface is soft and washable.
- Staple carpet or vinyl to the underside of the riser and cover the staples with duct tape.
- Attach a short rope handle to each side to help move the riser from place to place.

# Sand Pillows

Toddlers like to snuggle with pillows and stuffed animals. Sand pillows can be used in the *Private Place Learning Space* for toddlers to lie on and under. The "heavy weight" of a sand pillow can help toddlers develop a sense of body awareness and can have a calming effect on them.

## Materials
2 pillowcases
2 pounds of white sand
thread and needle or sewing machine

- Place the sand inside one pillowcase.
- Sew the open end of the pillowcase closed.
- Use the other pillowcase to cover this Sand Pillow, so it can be easily removed and washed.

# Terrarium
## Materials
large plastic 2-liter drink bottle with lid
scissors
1 piece of charcoal (without additives)
gravel
potting soil
collection of small plants (collected from outdoors or purchased from a greenhouse)
water mister

- Cut off the top from the drink bottle (keep the top to reapply).
  **Note:** Toddlers can help assemble the terrarium.

- The teacher should break the charcoal into several smaller pieces and place a few pieces of charcoal in the bottom of the bottle.
- Pour a layer of gravel in the bottom of the bottle, on top of the charcoal pieces.
- Add a layer of potting soil, about 2" deep.
- Place small plants in the soil.
- Water the plants and mist the foliage.
- Replace the top of the bottle (with the lid) on the container.
- Place the terrarium in a lighted area of the room.
- If the terrarium seems to be getting too moist, remove the top. If the system is working, the terrarium will not need watering.
- Toddlers can enjoy their creation and watch the plants grow.

# Wall Bookrack

Library bookracks that sit on the floor are often hazardous for toddlers. They also take up valuable space in the area. This wall-mounted rack provides a solution for both of these issues. This simple building project is a low-cost and effective library rack for toddlers. It allows the teacher to place the books low and with the covers displayed so toddlers can select and retrieve the one they want.

## Materials
2 - 2" x 4" lumber pieces, 3' long (shelves)
2 - 1" x 4" lumber pieces, 3' long (sides)
2 - ⅜" dowel rods, 38" long
hammer and nails
drill with ⅜" bit
non-toxic paint and paintbrush

- Attach the 2" x 4" shelves onto the 1" x 4" sides with one at the bottom and the other 18" above the first.
- Drill holes for the dowel rods 3" above each shelf.
- Paint the entire unit with non-toxic paint.
- Mount the bookrack to the wall at a height toddlers can reach comfortably.